# THE LEGENDS AND THEORIES OF THE BUDDHISTS COMPARED WITH HISTORY AND SCIENCE

# THE LEGENDS AND THEORIES OF THE BUDDHISTS COMPARED WITH HISTORY AND SCIENCE

WITH INTRODUCTORY NOTICES OF THE LIFE AND SYSTEM OF GOTAMA BUDDHA

R. SPENCE HARDY

GYAN

*Published by*

Gyan Publishing House
5, Ansari Road
Daryaganj, New Delhi-110002
Phone: 011-47034999, 9811692060
E-mail: books@gyanbooks.com

*Distribution Network*
gyanbooks.com
India, USA, Canada, UK, Australia, France



ISBN : 978-81-212-3695-9 (PB)
First Published, London, 1866

2nd Impression 2020

*Printed at:* Gyan Press, Delhi.



**The Legends and Theories of the Buddhists**
Author: R. Spence Hardy

# PREFACE.

THE system attributed to Gótama Buddha is one of the oldest beliefs in the world. It demands, therefore, a place among the records of religious opinion, if for its antiquity alone. But it has other claims upon our attention. There is in it the germ of many of the speculations that are the most prominent in the shifting philosophies of the present day; and it is now professed, at the lowest computation, by three hundred millions of the human race. The information presented in these pages has a further importance, as the Dharmma is comparatively unknown in England. Of this we have evidence in the singular fact, that the name of Gótama Buddha is not found in any work in our language that is exclusively biographical,* although no uninspired man has exercised a greater influence than he upon the social and religious interests of the world.

* In the last edition of the Encyclopædia Britannica there is an article under the head of "Gótama Buddha," derived from the same sources as the present work.

The first edition of this work was published in the island of Ceylon. Its principal aim w , to reveal to the adherents of the system the errors it contains; but the original form is retained, as the doctrines here attributed to Buddha have not been controverted, so far as I can learn, by any of the priests; though, of course, they repudiate the inferences I have drawn from them. We are thus warranted in concluding, that they may be received as a faithful and trustworthy exposition of this wide-spread creed; and it is the more necessary to notice this fact, as there are many things in them that are contrary to the teachings on this subject of several authors of great name in western literature. The supporters of Protestant missions will also learn in what manner and spirit their agents are conducting the great controversy, that must increase in magnitude and moment, until the truth has universally prevailed throughout the realm of India; and a lesson may be learnt, of no small significance, as to the acquirements, the mental furnishing, requisite in the men who are chosen to do battle, in this onslaught upon the most formidable of all the superstitions that oppose the spread of the Gospel of the Son of God.

There are some things here inserted that would justly be regarded as puerile or unnecessary, if I were writing exclusively for European readers; and in the sections on native geography and astronomy many things appear that would have assumed an entirely different form, if the appeal were made to persons acquainted with the higher departments of science. I was only a visitor in Ceylon when the work was written, and laboured under some disadvantages, as my library was in England. But the pages for which I have to make this apology are few, as a great part of the volume consists of statements taken from the original Pali, that have not previously appeared in any European language. I have since published a similar work in Singhalese,* more adapted to the comprehension of the priests and others who know no tongue but their own, and whose information is confined to the limited circle of their own books.

I have to return thanks to the Rev. John Scott, my successor as the General Superintendent of the Wesleyan Mission in South Ceylon, for many valuable suggestions. I am also under a debt of obligation, that I can never repay, to the Rev. David de Silva, a native minister of the same mission. His attainments in general knowledge are of a high order, he is well acquainted with Pali, and he is the foremost and most able among the controversialists of the island who have come forward in the defence of Christianity. It was at one time my intention, with his aid, to make an abridgment, or complete index, of the whole of the sacred Pitakas. For this purpose I employed a learned ex-priest, Don Johannes Panditatilaka, of Kóggala, who began to read with us the section containing the Sutras,

* Suddharmma-nikashaya.

which he orally translated into Singhalese, sentence by sentence; but he was unwilling to proceed further than the third or fourth Nikáya, probably deterred by the supporters of Buddhism; and as no one of competent information could be induced to continue the task, even for high reward, I was reluctantly obliged to abandon my design. I had, however, previously secured his aid, in culling from the Pitakas the extracts I required in preparing the present work.

A controversy, of great interest, has recently commenced in Ceylon, between the Christians and the Buddhists. The priests have purchased presses and type, and possess printing establishments of their own. They now refuse to render any assistance to the missionaries, as before, in explaining the native books, or lending those that are in their libraries for transcription. Happily, there is a copy of nearly all the sections of the canonical text and commentaries in the Wesleyan mission library at Colombo, bequeathed to it by the late Rev. D. J. Gogerly. Tracts, pamphlets, and serials issue in large numbers from the Buddhist presses. The king of Siam, and one of the native chiefs in Kandy, have contributed largely towards their publication. They present some arguments that are new and ingenious; but the defiant and blasphemous expressions they contain, against the sacred name of "Jehovah," are probably the most awful ever framed in human language. I left Ceylon on my return to England, for the third time, in June last, with thankfulness for the evidences I had been permitted to witness, on the part of many of the more intelligent of the Singhalese, of a sincere desire to attain to the possession of the light and truth. I have formed bright anticipations as to the future. There can be no doubt as to the result of the contest now carried on; for although it may be prolonged and severe, it must end in the total discomfiture of those who have arisen against the Lord and his Christ, and in the renunciation of the atheist creed that now mars the happiness, and stays the enlightenment, of so many of the dwellers in Lanká; beautiful, from the waters that lave its shores to the storm-tried trees that crown the summits of its highest mountains, and rich in historic associations, throughout more than two thousand years.

HEADINGLEY, LEEDS,
*January* 1, 1866.

# INTRODUCTION.

THERE are few names among the men of the west, that stand forth as saliently as that of Gótama Buddha, in the annals of the east. In little more than two centuries from his decease the system he established had spread throughout the whole of India, overcoming opposition the most formidable, and binding together the most discordant elements; and at the present moment Buddhism is the prevailing religion, under various modifications, in Tibet, Nepal, Siam, Burma, Japan, and South Ceylon; and in China it has a position of at least equal prominence with its two great rivals, Confucianism and Tauism. At one time its influence extended throughout nearly three-fourths of Asia; from the steppes of Tartary to the palm-groves of Ceylon, and from the vale of Cashmere to the isles of Japan.

In the following pages I have endeavoured to expose some of its most notable defects and errors: but although it was for this purpose that they were originally written, there is a further lesson that its history loudly teaches, of wider range and still greater consequence. With all earnestness and sincerity, the prince Gótama set himself to search out the truth; and if he failed in his attempt to discover it, those who may follow him in the same path, and use only the same means, will have much to accomplish, if they intend to be more successful in its pursuit. In those who would surpass, or even equal, the so-called Tathágato, if we accept as true the records of his life, there must be the exercise of a severe penance; and their search for the inner illumination must be continued, with firm resolve and singleness of purpose, throughout many weary years. They who set themselves to this task, must possess an insight into the vanities of the world equally clear, from a lengthened residence amidst the splendours of the palace; they must at once forsake all that men regard as pleasant, for a life of extreme self-denial amidst the solitudes of the wilderness; they must struggle with the powers of evil until demon spirits seem to become visiblé, with foul gibe and fearful menace; they must add to this an intense hatred of all that is low and mean, in those with whom they come in contact, and a life-long passion to resolve the great problems of existence; they must possess a calmness of thought, "like a waveless sea," that no opposition can ruffle, the result of a discipline that has the acquirement of this serene state as its principal object; they must scrutinize all the powers and possessions of man, with an exactness like that with which the skilful anatomist seeks to learn the manner and use of every nerve and articulation of the bodily frame; and when they have suffered, thought out, and accomplished, in this high service, as much as the old man of Mágadha, before he expired under the sal-tree near Kusinára, they will be entitled to speak of the majesty of intuition, and we will listen heedfully to their words. The system elaborated with so much travail of spirit, and under circumstances so impressive, is one of the most wonderful emanations that ever proceeded from man's intellect, unaided by the outward revelation of God: but, as we look at it as it is, calmly and without prejudice, we see, that although it presents so many evidences of deep thought, and possesses so many claims to our regard, it manifests throughout the most palpable ignorance, not only as to the facts of science, but also as to the great and essential principles of morality; and that after all its promise, it tends only to increase man's perplexity as to the present, and his uncertainty as to the future, leaving him at last in hopelessness and desolation.

But before some of my readers can see the force and verity of this conclusion, it will be necessary that they become better acquainted with the sage of whom I thus write; and it is to furnish those who may be uninformed of the history of Buddhism, with a rapid sketch of the doings and doctrines of its founder, that this Introduction has been penned.

Neither the age, nor even the individual existence, of Buddha, is established beyond all controversy; but the system is a reality, and stands before us in imposing magnitude; forcing itself upon our attention, by its own inner power, as well as by the consequences it has produced, widely and in so many ages. We must try, if we would know rightly the circumstances under which Gótama is said to have lived, to transport ourselves to the time of the prophet Daniel; but to forget all about Babylon and its stately monarchs, and imagine ourselves in an appanage of Rajagaha, the capital of Mágadha, where the lord paramount of the Aryan race holds his court. We have before us a state of intellectual culture resembling that of Athens, in the age of its earlier philosophers; a splendour and magnificence like that of Bagdad, in the days of its most famous caliphs; a commercial activity like that presented along the course of the Tyrian caravan, when Tadmor appeared in the desert, beautiful as its mirage, but no mockery, as its majestic temples rose in view before the merchant from some distant land; and a freedom of manners and constancy of intercourse between the different grades of society, like that seen now among the nations of Europe. The story of a people migrating from beyond the snow-clad hills, where the gods are thought to hold their seat, has long since been forgotten; numerous sectaries live together, in ceaseless antagonism, but without any overt acts of persecution; and a general opinion seems to prevail, that some great personage is about to appear, who will make all one, from being gifted with unerring intelligence and unbounded power. It is an era of great importance in the history of the east; and men are waiting for some event that will decide whether future ages are to be ruled by a Chakrawartti, a universal monarch, or guided by a Buddha, an all-wise sage.

The most successful candidate for supremacy who then arose was a prince of the race of Sákya, said to have been born at Kapilawastu, a city supposed to be on the borders of Nepal; on Tuesday, the day of the full moon, the lunar mansion being Wisa, in the month of May, in the year answering to B.C. 623; thus exact are the chroniclers of this auspicious event. Five days afterwards he received the name of Siddhártta. He was also called Gótama, Sákya Singha, and Sákya Muni; and for all these names fanciful reasons are given. On the following day his mother Máya died. At an early age his preceptors foretold that he would become a recluse, which led his father, Suddhódana, to take means by which he hoped that the prince would be induced to pursue a different course; and in the pursuit of pleasure, or the excitement of war, seek glory in a manner more consistent with his position and prospects, as the scion of a house so illustrious that it could trace its descent through the race of the sun, to Sammata, the first monarch of the world. The anxiety of his father increased as he grew older; and even when he was married, at the age of sixteen, to the princess Yasodhará, peerless in excellence as in grace, there were reasons why former precautions should be continued. The sight of a decrepit old man, supported by a staff, his form bending in weakness toward the ground, taught Siddhártta a memorable lesson on the infirmities to which man is subject. Not long afterwards he accidentally met a loathsome leper, with attenuated limbs, and sores covering his entire body, which added to the impressiveness of his former reflections. And when he saw, after the lapse of another period, a dead body, green with putridity, offensive, and the prey of creeping worms, he learnt, with a force that the witchery of music and the wiles of woman could not overcome, the vanity of all that is existent, at its best estate. Here was the discovery of the evil, the danger; but where was the remedy, the way of escape? This was presented to him, after months of further thought and anxiety. He saw a recluse, gravely clad, gentle in manner, and of placid countenance, walking quietly along the road. His determination to follow the example he had seen was formed at once, and it was a sturdy and indomitable resolve. To increase our estimate of his self-denial, it is said of him that on the very day when he heard of the birth of his firstborn. whilst the festivities of the palace were conducted with unusual splendour, he determined to carry his resolution into effect; and that though he saw the sleeping mother and his new-born babe, lovely as a lotus flower, from the threshold of the room in which they lay, he forsook them, without any expression of regret, and rushed into the forest, far away from all that could bind by affection or attract by smile, accompanied by only one attendant, whom he soon afterwards dismissed. The vigilance of his father was on this day relaxed, as it was a thing not to be thought of, that at such a time, when the whole city was as one great festive-hall, he could cast away the royal diadem, with all its attendant attractions, for the alms-bowl of the mendicant and its privations.

The garment of the recluse was adopted, but it was impossible to conceal the superiority of his birth; and when he went to the city of Rajagaha, to seek alms from door to door, as was then the custom of those who had abandoned the world, the beauty of his person, and the gracefulness of his manner, attracted general attention, and made many suppose that some celestial personage had visited their land. The food he received was different in kind from that to which he had been accustomed in the palace; but he retired to the shade of a tree, and thoughtfully ate it, the sight of its uncleanness reminding him of the vileness and impurity of man's body, though tended with so much care, and pampered by so many indulgences. Five other persons, brahmans, were partakers in his exercises of asceticism, and remained with him in the wilderness, until, by his excessive austerities, life itself appeared to be extinct. From this state of extreme weakness he recovered; but when, after six years of penance, and the endurance of a mental agony intense beyond utterance, in his attempts to acquire a mastery over all attachment, and a clear understanding of all truth, he returned to the carrying of the alms-bowl, without having succeeded in his aim, the patience of his five companions was exhausted, and they left him to pursue his painful course alone. But the time of deliverance, the hour of triumph, was at hand. Taking with him as much food as would support him during forty-nine days of additional trial, he retired to the spot that was afterwards to become of world-wide renown. There, under a bo-tree, he was assaulted by innumerable demons, and the contest was fierce and prolonged; but he resisted, with like success, the menaces of frightful fiends, and the allurements of beauty, under all the forms that licentiousness could devise, until, before the setting of the sun, he was the acknowledged victor; and before the light had again dawned, the great end of his toils was accomplished, and he stood forth before all worlds a supreme Buddha, "wiser than the wisest, and higher than the highest."

As he was twenty-nine years of age when he left the palace, and remained six years in the wilderness, this event must have occurred about his thirty-fifth year. From this time the monastery was his residence, and he was soon surrounded by numerous disciples, as he claimed to be the only teacher of men free from all error. At first, from seeing the difficulty attending the establishment of a new and stringent system, he resolved that he would confine to his own breast the discovery he had made; but at the intercession of others he was induced to change his resolution, and commence the preaching of the Dharmma. It was to his old friends, the five brahmans, that he first unfolded the principles of his religion. They were at that time resident near the city of Benares. The discourse he then delivered is called the Dhamma-chakkappawattana-suttan. In it he declares that there is sorrow connected with every mode of existence; that the cause of sorrow is desire, or attachment (to sensuous objects); that the destruction of sorrow is to be effected by being set free from attachment to existing objects (which secures the possession of nirwána); and that to be set free from this attachment there must be right conduct, mental tranquillity, and other similar virtues. These truths were previously unknown; they were revealed by former Buddhas, but had long been entirely forgotten. Gótama now received them by intuition, and he proclaimed them once more to the world, authoritatively, from having attained to the most perfect wisdom.

The king of Mágadha, Bimsara, was converted to the faith of his former friend, now become Buddha. His two principal disciples were Seriyut and Mugalan. The first was convinced of the truth of the Dharmma by hearing the stanza so often found upon monuments now existing in India:—

"Yé dhamma hétuppabhawá
Yésan hétun Tathágato,
Aha yésan chayo niródho
Ewan wadi Maha Samano."

"All things proceed from some cause; this cause has been declared by the Tathágato; all things will cease to exist; this is that which is declared by the great Sramana (Buddha).

On a visit to his native city, his father, Suddhodana, embraced his faith, and his half-brother, Nanda, and his son Ráhula, entered the order of the priesthood that he established. The same course was followed by Anurudha his cousin, Ananda his nephew, who became his personal attendant, and Déwadatta, his wife's brother. The second wife of his father, who was also his own foster-mother, Maha Prajápati, was the first female admitted to profession.

The authority of Buddha was not undisputed, nor his high position maintained without opposition and trial. At one time a low female was suborned by his enemies to accuse him with breaking the law of continence, but her artifice ended only in her own confusion. The son of Bimsara, Ajásat, supported the cause of the brahmans, and was joined in his enmity to Buddha by Déwadatta, at whose instance he caused the death of his royal father. These sectarists attempted to take the life of Buddha on three several occasions; first, by means of 500 archers, then by a stone hurled from a machine, which struck his foot, and caused it slightly to bleed, and lastly by the attack of a wild and infuriated elephant; but on all these occasions their wicked designs were frustrated. The king afterwards repented of his crimes, and embraced the faith of the Dharmma; and Déwadatta was also led to see the folly of the course he had pursued; but though he sought forgiveness, his offences were too great to go unpunished, and he died a hopeless death. The same reckless course was followed by his father-in-law, Supra Buddha, whose end was equally sad. The days of Buddha were spent in carrying the alms-bowl, and in other acts required by the disciplinary code of his order, to all of which he was as submissive as any member of the novitiate; in conversing with his friends and opponents on the principles of his religion; in visiting distant places, even the heavens, that he might preach the bana to men and gods; and in performing more astounding miracles than were ever even thought of by any wonder-worker among the western nations. His death, when eighty years of age, was caused by partaking of pork given to him in alms by the smith Chunda, which produced diarrhœa. In great pain he travelled from Páwa, a distance of twelve miles, during which time he had frequently to rest; and as he had been born under a tree, and under a tree attained to the wisdom of a Buddha, it was under a tree that he died, near the city of Kusinára.

In these legends there may be a portion of truth, but

they have been intermixed with so many events of impossible occurrence, that we are necessitated to regard the whole with distrust. The easterns are great adepts at dovetailing a number of stories, taken from widely different sources, into one even and unbroken narrative. We can sometimes detect the traces of this method of manipulation, in Buddhist authors, and discover in what way it has been brought about; but there are other instances in which the keenest critic must confess himself at fault. There are some events, such as his extreme asceticism in the wilderness, his hesitation about declaring to others the truths he had learnt, the opposition of certain of his relatives, the attempts upon his life, the circumstances attendant on the admission of women into his community, the powers he acknowledged in his adversaries, and, above all, the cause to which his death is attributed, for the invention of which we can see no reason, and so conclude that they may have been real occurrences. Of the exaggerations and myths contained in the Buddhist records, I have spoken elsewhere. It may suffice, therefore, to state here, that the sage is regarded by his followers as having unlimited knowledge and power, though a man, and subject to all the passions and infirmities of humanity, previous to his reception of the Buddhaship. In his youth he married and had a son; his inferior wives were numbered by thousands; he had to eat and drink like other men, and seek relief from pain and sickness by the use of medicine; and it was from an ordinary disease that he died. But all the principal events of his life are represented as being attended by incredible prodigies. He could overturn the earth in an instant, pass through the air at will, and know the thoughts of all beings, in whatever world. The legends in which these powers are assumed, and the incidents connected with their exercise detailed, may be learnt from the three Pitakas.

These works constitute the sacred canon of the Buddhists, and if it can be proved that they were formed under the circumstances in which they claim to have been originally revealed and rehearsed, at three general convocations, the system they contain must be entitled to more regard than we should infer from their foolish legends; but the arguments in favour of their trustworthiness fail in one most important and essential particular. We cannot trace them to the time in which Buddha is said to have lived. In this respect they are in a similar position with the greater part of Zend and Vedic lore, about the origin of which we know little more than the name of the author, and this not always with certainty. It is said by Dr. Murray Mitchell, that it is not possible that Zoroaster, the supposed great founder of the Zend system, promulgated it in the shape it now possesses; at all events, that it cannot be demonstrated. The system of Zoroaster, the system of the Zend books, the system of the Pahlvi books, the system of the Persian books written by modern Parsis, and the system of the Parsis of our own day, are on no account to be assumed to be identical.* We might make a similar statement in relation to Buddhism. There can be little doubt, however, that the system known by this name originated in some part of India between the

* Transactions of the Bombay Asiatic Society.

Ganges and the borders of Nepal, though we may have no proof of this beyond the traditions of its adherents. The reign of Asóka is the starting point of Buddhist chronologists; and we know from other sources that they are here not far from the truth. Nor do I see any reason to doubt that the system originated about the time of Bimsara. The internal evidence presented by the Pitakas of the age in which they were written will be more definite when they have been more thoroughly studied. The insight we receive therefrom into the social and religious position of the people of India, would lead us to conclude that the time in which Buddha lived was strictly neither Vedantic nor Brahmanical, but a transition state between the establishment of the two systems, with a greater tendency towards the latter. This opinion we found upon the following circumstances. There is no reference in them, so far as I can learn, to the question that was afterwards the moot-point in all Hindu speculation, the relation of man to the Supreme Spirit. Few of the gods at present worshipped were then known, or if known by the same names, they had offices given to them differing from those now assigned to them in Indian mythology. In the accusation brought by Gótama against the Brahmans of corrupting the Vedas, there may be evidence of the commencement of the changes that were afterwards so extensively effected, as seen in the Puránas and other legendary works. We do not find that he rebuked them for their grossness or licentiousness, which he would have done, if these evils had been as prominent in their religion then as they are now. Neither is there any allusion to human sacrifices, which may be regarded as a proof that Buddhism commenced before they were practised in India. The tenets afterwards professed by the Brahmans were not yet fully developed, nor had they begun to influence popular opinion to any great extent, or to produce that change in the manners and customs of the Hindus that has since been effected. The Brahman held an important position in the king's court, but it was a subordinate one, and the royal caste was placed by Buddha in the highest rank. Though caste had for some time exerted an evil influence, it still had to contend for universal acknowledgment and reception. The Vedas were not regarded with the same reverence by the other castes as by the Brahmans, nor were they looked upon generally as a standard of appeal. When men refused to receive their revelations as an infallible guide, it was not accounted as a crime against the state, or as an innovation upon the polity of the social order then established. The claims of Brahmanism were argued in the same manner as those of other religious systems. The position of woman was much in accordance with her place in the western world. We read of females in the higher ranks who never stepped upon the ground for delicateness; but when individuals are brought before us, as Maha Máya, the mother of Gótama, or Wisákhá, the wife of Púrnna-wardhana, we see them moving freely in general society, and speaking to men without restraint. It was the custom for certain classes of women to wander about from place to place, and challenge even men to enter into controversy with them, apparently without any sense of impropriety on their part, or of condemnation in the minds of others. These criteria are confessedly indefinite; but yet, in the absence of more authoritative demonstration, they are of some value, as they seem to fix the era of the commencement of Buddhism in some age previous to the oldest of the philosophies now received on the continent of India.

But the period in which Buddhism originated, and that in which the Pitakas were written, are widely different questions. By no authority is it said that the sacred books, as we have them now, were *written* in the time of Buddha. In speaking of these books historically, we shall pay no attention to their claim to be the record of unmixed truth, as there is scarcely one of their pages that does not contradict this pretension. But placing them on a par with the works of other men, there may be, as we have seen, a vein of truth running through their confused and abnormal strata, though the opinions of the Buddhists are disregarded as to their having been framed in a given period, or by hands divine. The value of the record as an historic authority depends almost entirely upon its age, and upon the position and circumstances of the men by whom it was originally made. It is here that its claim to our confidence is set aside; and though my reasons for coming to this conclusion are stated in another place,* the subject is of so much importance, that I may be forgiven for referring to it here. About the year 432 A.D., the commentaries were translated from Singhalese into Pali, by Buddhaghóso. The Singhalese version has disappeared from the island, and cannot now be recovered. The Pali

* Page 66.

version was lost for a time to the Singhalese, but it has been renewed from Burma or Siam. I will concede that the present recension may be the same, in all essential particulars, as it was fourteen hundred years ago. The works forming it profess to be a transcript of others written for the first time in the reign of Waṭṭagamini, about 90 B.C. That they cannot be exactly and identically the *ipsissima verba* of the older canon, we have internal evidence; but how far the difference may extend cannot now be determined. The works committed to writing by the Singhalese priests are said to have been the same as those brought over in the memory of Mahindo, who introduced Buddhism into the island in 307 B.C. There was thus an interval of more than 200 years, during which the sacred canon, according to the Buddhists themselves, was preserved in the memory alone. It was transmitted at this early stage from one generation of the priesthood to another, by oral tradition. But, upon historical grounds, we can neither accept the oral transmission nor the subsequent committal to writing. The former is not possible, and the other is opposed by facts of which we have present evidence. No one acquainted with modern research on eastern subjects will contend that the annals of the Buddhists were now committed to writing for the first time. We know that writing was in use by the Aryan race before this period, and that it was employed for religious purposes by the Buddhist monarch Asóka, the father of Mahindo, by which means he sought to extend its doctrines among all classes of his subjects, and in all parts of his dominions. We cannot suppose that he who is said to have erected 84,000 shrines in honour of Buddha, with Pali inscriptions upon them, some of which still exist, would neglect the more important matter of the preservation of the words of the sage, so far as they could then be recovered. In his reign the canon of the Dharmma is said to have been rehearsed for the third time; and as this was professedly on account of the number of heresies that then abounded, the necessity must have been seen of committing it to some more certain medium than that of memory. The great legacy that Buddha left to his disciples was the Dharmma. This, with its exponents, the priests, was, by his own appointment, to represent him when he was no more visible, or had become extinct; and we may conclude, from the exact knowledge of human nature he exhibited on so many occasions, that he would see the futility of naming it as his representative, unless its chief principles and requirements were written, and thus placed beyond the reach of mistake. And we can further suppose that among the numerous innovations made by Buddha upon established custom, one would be, the writing down of the principia of his religion, in the vernacular of his country, as it was intended that his system should be of general acceptance, and not confined to any particular class. The rehearsal of the Pitakas in the time of Asóka professes to be a repetition of two former rehearsals, on each occasion the same words being repeated, syllable by syllable, and word by word. The canon as we have it now (with a few necessary additions in relation to events that took place afterwards), is declared to be the same as that rehearsed in the year of Buddha's death. Upon the circumstances of this first rehearsal, most important consequences depend. If the miracles ascribed to Buddha can be proved to have been recorded of him at the time of his death, this would go far towards proving that the authority to which he laid claim was his rightful prerogative. They were of too public a character to have been ascribed to him *then*, if they had not taken place; so that if it was openly declared by his contemporaries, by those who had lived with him in the same monastery, that he had been repeatedly visited by Sekra and other déwas; and that he had walked through the air, and visited the heavenly worlds, in the presence of many thousands, and those the very persons whom they addressed, we ought all to render him the homage awarded to him by even his most devoted followers. But the legend of the early rehearsal has nothing to support it, beyond the assertion of authors who lived at a period long subsequent. The testimony of contemporaneous history presents no record of any event that quadrates with the wonderful powers attributed to the rahats, which would undoubtedly not have been wanting, if these events had really taken place. The text of the Pitakas is considerably more ancient than the commentary, as we learn from internal evidence; and, from the style in which it is written, we may conclude that the two could not have been simultaneously repeated, at the period assigned to the first convocation. The text is the composition of men who were well acquainted with the localities of India, and probably resident upon the continent; but many of the mistakes made in the commentaries are of a kind that could not have been fallen into by persons familiar with the places of which they write. The statement that the sun passes annually from Maha Meru to the Sakwala rock, and back again, and therefore appears in the zenith of all places in Jambudípa, must have been made by some one resident in a region where the sun is annually vertical; but the cities in which the Pitakas are said to have been recited are all to the north of the tropic of Cancer, where the falsity of the account would at once be seen. The age that succeeded that of Buddhaghóso is represented by Colonel Sykes as a period strikingly marked by the invention of legends; and it may have been from the publication of the commentaries that many of them originated, or were more extensively diffused. In an extract from the Wibhanga Atuwáwa the case is supposed of a person speaking Damila and Ardha, which would scarcely have occurred to one then living north of the Ganges. There are incidents, more especially in the Játakas, that have their parallel in the lore of the western side of the Indus; which would seem to bring them within some period later than the establishment the Indo-Macedonian kingdom. Whether the similarity is accidental, or the origin identical, is not yet certain; but the framework of the greater number of the tales with which nearly all Buddhist works are so plentifully interlarded, is so eminently Hindu in its character that there can be no mistake about the place of their birth.

There are other things that tend to throw suspicion on the authority of the Pitakas. Among these I may reckon as one of the most prominent, the number of the heresics that are said to have prevailed at an early period of

Buddhism. If there were any proof that the several sectaries all acknowledged the validity of the Pitakas, and only differed as to the interpretation of certain parts of them, these very differences would be an argument in favour of the purity of the canon. But from the dignity of the persons connected with some of these schisms, or the importance of the subjects upon which they treat, as we learn from their names, we may conclude that some of the heresies were of such a character as necessarily to involve the rejection of the Pitakas as the rule of faith. We are told that, in the first century after Buddha there were no sects formed; but this statement is disproved by the names of some of the schisms, one of which, it would appear, proceeded from Rahula, the son of Sákya, as we learn from the works of the Tibetans; and the other from Déwadatta, his brother-in-law, as we learn from Fa Hian. From these premises we conclude, that though there might be Buddhist works in existence at an early period, neither the text nor the commentary of the Pitakas was compiled or completed, in its present form, until long after the death of Buddha.

We shall have a better insight into the circumstances of the world in the time of Buddha, if we remember that Lycurgus had flourished, and the Messenian wars had been fought, in the century preceding his death. If the reckoning of Carpzov is correct, making Ezekiel to have received his commission as a prophet in the year 594 B.C., when he was nearly thirty years of age, he and Gótama must have been born within a few months of each other, 623-4 B.C. At this time Josiah reigned in Jerusalem, and that city was destroyed by Nebuchadnezzar in the year in which Gótama obtained the Buddhaship. Crœsus in Lydia, and Cyrus in Persia, lived about the same period; in Greece, Anacreon, Sappho, Simonides, Epimenides, Draco, Solon, Æsop, Pythagoras, Anaximander, Anaximenes, and Pisistratus; in Egypt, Psammeticus; and in Rome, Servius Tullius. About thirty years after his death, Ahashuerus reigned from "India even unto Ethiopia." This was a stirring era in the history of the world, when nations were agitated, and men were seeking out new channels of thought and action. The idea of man now flying through the air at will is unfounded and absurd. It so happens, that the intercourse of the west with the east commenced in this age; and we can deny, on historical grounds, the possibility of the appearance of any sage in India with powers like those fabled of Buddha, with greater certainty than if he had lived at any previous period.

We may now leave all questions relative to the origin of Buddhism and its sacred code, and proceed to an examination of its more important principles. Throughout our investigation it will be necessary to bear in mind that there is a great and essential difference between Buddhism and Brahmanism; and this caution is required the more, because in many instances, the same terms are used in both systems, but in senses widely different. The antagonism of the one to the other is decided, continually presented, and extending to nearly all their more prominent speculations. The religion of the earlier portions of the Vedas is that of the countryman, the peasant: not of men living in the city, nor always in the encampment or the rude village; but often abroad, by the rock, near the river, or in the broad plain. Here the lightning gleams, and the heavy clouds pour down fatness, and the bright sun seems to bring into existence all that breathes in the air or waves in the wind; and at another time the soft moonlight sleeps upon the bank, and the lotus lies still as it is outspread upon the waters, and the leaves of the tall sal tree are unstirred, as they stand out against the pale sapphire of the sky. Surrounded by these influences, the Aryans were led to worship the elements; first, the gods who direct them, and then the material powers themselves. When the son of Suddhódana passed at once from the walls of the palace to the open wilderness, the physical changes by which he was met must have appeared to him, in great measure, as they had done to the first Aryan settlers, and their poets, the rishis, when they descended from the rugged mountain, and entered the vast plains of Hindusthan. But the effect produced upon the mind was widely different in the two instances. The prince retired to the forest to search for truth; not to lurk as a robber or watch for prey. He saw what others had not seen, and what others had seen he disregarded. His attention was fixed upon himself; and when the thunder shook the earth around him, its roll came not to him as a voice telling of the presence of God, but as a monition to remind him that nothing whatever is permanent. In the brightest sunlight, as in the darkest storm-cloud, everywhere and always, there appeared to him unquiet, disappointment, and sorrow.

There were other lessons of the wilderness to which he was not unheedful. He had seen that all things outward are vanity. He now set himself to discover a well-spring of happiness in other sources. But in his search he was continually met by opposing influences of mighty power, that thwarted all his designs; and the more profound his thoughts to learn the way in which these antagonisms were to be overcome, the more distant and difficult appeared to be the result at which he aimed. What am I? What have I been? What shall I be? These important themes were the subject of his meditation, and constantly agitated his mind. Had there been some one near to tell him of God, he might have been led to rejoice in the outgoings of divine power, and sought rest in the presence of the Eternal. But he was alone. The teachings he had received from the preceptors of his earlier days, were seen to be without power or profit; and the end of his searching was, to declare the emptiness of all that is earthly, and the unreality of everything that appears to be existent.

In the privations of the forest he further learnt the effect of temperance upon the mind, fitting it for quiet contemplation. In his efforts to put away the thoughts arising from the memory of scenes connected with the revelry in which he had formerly joined, he acquired the power to fix his attention continuously on one single object. From all outward and visible things he turned away; and as he concentrated all his powers on the contemplation of his own being, he learnt, by this process, to look upon man as a mere rúpa, an organised body, attached to which are certain qualities or attributes.* He also saw that neither raging element nor prowling wild beast had any respect for him as a king's son; that there is no mystic power surrounding royalty; and the futility of all caste pretension was thereby discovered. He learnt, again, that man requires not, for his preservation and support, costly array, a substantial dwelling, or a luxurious couch on which to repose; and these were accordingly rejected. In the woods he was away from all kinds of domestic or social entanglement; and as he saw that home associations are a hindrance when seeking the perfection of tranquillity, these were sternly set aside. When in the world he had felt only disappointment and dissatisfaction; and as he now discovered that even the shade of the tree, and the most secret recesses of the cave, are not free from the thoughts that bring uneasiness and apprehension, he concluded that perfect peace is not to be found with the living in any world. Over these conclusions he long brooded, sometimes battling with them as with real existences, until he had satisfied himself that the cessation of man's restlessness can only be brought about by the cessation of his existence. He then sought out the means by which this is to be accomplished; and when he had discovered four paths to this desired end, he proclaimed that through the power of intuition he had seen, by the divine eyes with which he had become gifted, the foundation of all knowledge, the most important of all the truths that can possibly be presented to the intellect.

* As in the case of D'Holbach, "nature becomes in his scheme a machine, man an organism, morality self-interest, deity a fiction."—*Farrar's Bampton Lectures*, p. 256.

In this arrangement I have followed the guidance of Buddhist authors. It is probable, however, that the conclusions I have described were not the product of one individual mind. Long periods may have elapsed between one discovery and another, and many different persons may have been engaged in the adjustment of the whole into one uniform and connected system. Under the influence of the impressions said to have been thus produced, Gótama is represented as again seeking intercourse with the world. But whilst in it, he was not of it. He sought only to expose its follies, and to reveal to others the wisdom of the Dharmma, which he had himself acquired with so much difficulty. After a slight hesitation as to the propriety of the course he was about to pursue, he was at first, in the greatness of his pity for mankind, ready to receive into his community any one who presented himself for acceptance; but as he found that many evils were attendant upon this indiscriminate admission, he rejected, for obvious reasons, the leper, the being not human (amanusya), the slave, the debtor, the king's servant, the minor, and the youth who had not received the consent of his parents. The form of admission was simple, being little more than the utterance of the words "Come hither;" and even at a subsequent period, though greater formality was used, certain obligations were implied, and the consequences of their non-observance stated, no vows were taken, and no promise was made. The professed Bhikkhu was to shun all sexual intercourse, "of whatever kind or in whatever form," and to avoid all conversation or familiarity that might lead his mind toward evil. The recollections of home were to be put away; all relationship that was not within the monastery was to be unheeded; and he was to live as one who had nothing to do with the world, but to repudiate alike its frown and its favour. Except certain specified garments, an alms-bowl, a razor, a needle, and a water-strainer, he was not to possess anything of his own. He was to be a mendicant, in his appointed round to seek for food, passing by no house on account of the poverty or low caste of its inmates. He was not to make any sign that he was present as he stood before the door, but to wait in silence; and after a certain time, if he received nothing, he was to pass onward to some other habitation. He was meditatively to eat what he had received, in the reverse order of that in which it had been put into the bowl, taking the last first, however inferior it might be to other portions lower down in the vessel. No food that he had not received in alms was to pass the door of his mouth, nor was he to eat anything solid after the noon of the day. He was not to touch gold or silver; indolence was to be avoided; sleep indulged in sparingly; and all luxuries were to be rejected.

As to the outward person, the priest was to regard his body as a loathsome wound, of which his garments are the bandage. The robe was to be made of a prescribed form, divided into patches, and sewn together; and if he took for this purpose a piece of cloth that had been trampled upon in the street, blown away by the wind, cast on shore by the waves, or that had covered a dead body, so much the better, as it would be the greater mortification to his pride. No ringlets were to cluster around his head, as it was to be close shaven; and no kind of ornament or perfume was to be used. He was not to live in a permanent or substantial house; his residence was to be made of leaves; and he who sought the higher attainments of his profession was never to lie down, but to live at the root of a tree, in a cave, or in a cemetery.

It is evident that so stringent a code of discipline would require, for its right enforcement, a vigilant mode of supervision. The Prátimóksha, which contains the precepts and prohibitions, 227 in number,* to be attended to, is, therefore, to be read bi-monthly in an assembly of the priests, at which at least four must be present. No more painful penance is exacted for transgression than the sweeping of the court-yard of the temple, or some act equally easy of performance; but there are certain crimes that are followed by permanent exclusion. If all the priests present at a chapter are found, on examination, to be guilty of the same offence, they cannot absolve each other; but if one has broken one precept, and some one else a different precept, they can give each other absolution.

It has been supposed that one method by which Buddhism gained so great an ascendency over its rivals, and one reason why it spread so rapidly, was, that it adopted the custom of preaching to the people in the vernacular tongue. But I have not learnt, from the records I have read, that there was any difference in this respect, between Gótama and the other teachers who in his day professed to

* These laws, translated from Pali by the late Rev. D. J. Gogerly, and from Chinese by the Rev. S. Beale, appear at length in the Journal of the Royal Asiatic Society, vol. xix., 407.

proclaim the truth. The formulas they adopted, the doctrines they taught, and the controversies they maintained, were all in the same tongue as the teachings of Buddha. Even the Vedas were in a dialect generally understood at the time in which they were composed. Nor can I see that there was anything like preaching, as practised in our own day, or as was once heard from the great word-master of Constantinople. Whoever wished might have access to Buddha, at all proper hours, and he was willing to answer any question that was asked of him by any one who was not impertinent, or who evidenced a desire to know the truth. The rude opponent he caught in the meshes of his own net, and silenced his objections, quietly, but with withering effect, as he was a most accomplished dialectician. Nearly all his recorded discourses arose out of conversations he held with persons whom he sought out with the intention of teaching and converting to his faith, or with persons who came to his residence to dispute his propositions or listen to his words. There does not appear to have been any particular hour of the day, or day of the week, when he regularly preached to a promiscuous company, as was the practice of Mahomet. He is said to have kept "was," in which the public reading of the bana is now essential, and, when he visited the heavenly worlds, he is represented as delivering a long discourse; but the first is a custom of later times, which arose when the canon of the Dharmma was completed, and the last is away from the province of history, and we must pitch our tents in dreamland before we can receive it as true. As Mahindo is said to have translated the Pitakas into the vernacular Singhalese, we may suppose that something similar was done in other countries when Buddhism was introduced. They are now usually read in Pali, in the month when "was" is celebrated. It is believed that the mere hearing of the words, without the understanding of them, is an opus operatum; but they are sometimes read by one priest and interpreted by another. The power arising from the use of the vernacular is now overlooked by the priests; but there are lay devotees who read and interpret the sacred canon in families, after the manner of Scripture-readers. The images of Buddha sometimes represent him as in the attitude of preaching, as if this were one of his common practices; but image-worship is altogether an innovation upon primitive Buddhism; and it is possible that the posture we take to indicate preaching may rather refer to the act of blessing.

When the Aryan race became a settled people, and were no longer nomads, it would be seen by the more thoughtful that the spirit of the Vedas was not in unison with their present circumstances; and that the most important questions they were now anxious to understand, received no solution from this source. The same defects would be noticed by Gótama, amidst his meditations in the forest, and he there learnt to disregard the Vedas as a revelation of truth. He must have had some acquaintance with these ancient records, though, perhaps, not to any great extent, as they were in a language that differed from his own; and when a youth he would not be permitted by his anxious father, to spend much time in study. We have no reference to them in his discourses, until the controversies are recorded that he held with the Brahmans; and then the allusions are inexact, and not unfrequently intended only to convince his opponents that the recension then in use had been surreptitiously interpolated, in order to promote the interests of the Brahmans.

The principal precepts are ten in number, the first five of which may be taken* by the laity. They are all negative; they set before man no God to "love" and "obey," and no one to "honour." They are observances rather than obligations. The ethical works of the Buddhists, however, give a more favourable insight into the morality of the system than its ten precepts, as will be seen by reference to the Dhammapadan, or "Footsteps of Buddha." This work, though forming part of the last section of the discourses of Buddha, is evidently of more recent origin, from its deference to the authority of "the ancients," and its statements as to the happiness of "the next world."

By the earlier Buddhists there is much said about certain rites, connected with meditation, abstraction, and the acquirement of supernatural powers. In the subduing of the passions, some of the rules laid down may be found of benefit. The meditation of kindness, maitrí, is to be thus conducted. The priest must think that if the words of any one with whom he is at enmity are bad, his actions may be good; that if his words and actions are bad, his mind may be still free from evil; and that if his mind and actions are bad, his words may be good. Again, if he

* This expression, though not idiomatic, is a literal rendering of the word used by the Buddhists.

has only a few things about him that are good, the priest must think about these alone, and forget the bad entirely. That sympathy may be produced, the priest must think of what his enemy must afterwards suffer, and of what he himself must suffer if the enmity is not overcome. Again, he must think that the person in question may have been his own father or mother, or some other relative, in a former birth. And if all these thoughts are of no avail, he must ask himself, What am I at enmity with? With a lot of bones, a skin covered with hair, vessels filled with blood, or what? Thus his enmity will have nothing upon which it can lay hold, and will disappear. But, as to all overt acts of self-denying charity, the meditation is of no avail, and is inoperative as the dead faith spoken of by the apostle James.*

We have seen that although Buddha was so long resident in the forest of Uruwela, there is no evidence of his mind having been impressed, to any great extent, by the mysterious forces that are there seen alternately to smile in the sunbeam, or threaten in the thunder. When he came forth from their presence, it was to speak to man of subjects more important in themselves, and more influential upon his destiny. He disregarded all mere forms. On one occasion, when he saw the householder, Singhalóka, with wet hair and streaming garments, making obeisance in the six cardinal directions, he pointed out

* "The whole of the precepts (which are comprised in 250 articles) display a negative character; thus, charity is inculcated, not by the command 'to give,' but by the prohibition 'to take,' save when the gift be offered as alms."—*Schlagintweit's Buddhism in Tibet.*

the folly of what he was doing, and recommended him rather to honour his relatives, rulers, friends, and teachers.

The tradition of God's existence, dimly seen in the earlier Sanhitas of the Rig Veda, had now passed away; and it is possible that this great truth may never once have been presented to his mind.* This is not an axiom that the physical elements teach us, with all their wondrous revelations. They may tell us of power, and wisdom, and prevailing goodness; but their own untaught and unaided voice cannot lead man up to God; nor is the the thought of the fanciful Renan correct, that the desert is monotheistic.† With the furtive propensities of the rishis, Buddha could have no sympathy, and to the gods who were said to aid them in the chase, the raid, or the battle, he could pay no reverence or respect. In his meditations, intense and long continued, he thought that he had discovered all that belongs to man, all the essentialities of existence. Under the influence of former disappointment the search was conducted. He was prepared to find man an empty, unreal, and disconsolate being. When he had seen man's body, feeble, decaying, and

* The nearest approach to it that I have met with is found in page 171.

† The following thoughts are more in accordance with fact. "If the eye of sense be the sole guide in looking around on nature, we discover only a universe of brute matter, phenomena linked together in a uniform succession of antecedents and consequents. Mind becomes only a higher form of matter, Sin loses its poignancy. Immortality disappears. God exists not, except as a personification of the Cosmos. Materialism, atheism, fatalism, are the ultimate results which are proved by logic and history to follow from this extreme view. The idea of spirit cannot be reached by it."—(*Farrar's Bampton Lectures*, 35.) These sentences might have been written expressly to illustrate the origin and character of Buddhism, so true are they to its principles and teachings.

loathsome; when he had marked well the way in which he feels and thinks; and when he had traced the entire circle of his hopes and fears—he supposed that he had seen all of man; and then it was he inferred that he is a mere collection of atoms, organizations, and mental powers, which at death are broken up and dissipated, and all their, mutuality lost for ever. There is nothing, he concluded connected with man like a spirit or soul; all that is regarded as the self being an unreality, a delusion, a mere name.

But though Buddha could discover no connexion between the individual man, now and in other states of existence, there were around him constantly-recurring events that might have something parallel in the story of intelligent existence. The changes of the seasons, the appearance of the same wonderfully-formed insects and many-tinted flowers at one period of every year, the coming of the monsoon and its destructive storms, and the cycles of the stars, could not fail to make some impression on his mind; and may have awoke the thought that something in man may come and go, appear and disappear, and then re-appear, in a similar manner. The sight of the seeds that germinated around his retreat, and of the fruits that grew everywhere in the verdant wilderness, producing other seed-bearing and fruit-bearing trees, taught him that there is some nexus of communication betwen life and life: the life that now is, and the life presented in lineal succession. He saw, too, that the virtue of the seed or fruit is imparted to the grain or tree that springs from it, and to all its products; that like produces like; and that this process may go on for ever, unless the principle of life be extinguished. There was a plain analogy to all this in the appearance of the successive generations of men; but he strangely applied the process to man as a moral agent. He thought that another being was, in some mysterious way, produced from the being that was "broken up;" and that to this new existence the virtue of the former existence, not only its mental idiosyncrasies, but its moral responsibilities, was communicated intact. But as he saw that there are anomalies which were not by this means explained, he concluded that not only the virtue of the individual seed is communicated to the seed next produced, but that the separate virtue of all the preceding seeds from which it had been produced for thousands of generations, was communicated also, though in the seed itself that virtue might not be apparent; or, to pass away from the analogy to the actuality, he inferred that all living beings are under the influence of all that they have ever done, in all the myriad states of existence through which they have passed in by-gone ages. But here his analogy becomes a fallacy and a delusion; and the moment he passes away from the visible to the invisible, he is lost in a devious maze. The productive power of the seed or the fruit may illustrate man's origin, as possessed of an organized body, but we may not carry it further. The passing on of an apparent moral and mental identity may be witnessed in some families, and a strong and healthy parentage will probably produce an offspring with similar characteristics. That offspring will not only be of the same species as the parent, and similar in appearance, but may have the same dispositions, endowments, and propensities. But Buddhism teaches that the new being may be of an entirely different species to that from whence it proceeded; and we have no trace of an invisible transference of the virtue of the grape to the haw, or of the fish of the sea proceeding from the fowl of the air, which ought to take place for the analogy of its founder to hold good. There is something belonging to man which no unaided mind can discover, and which no eye can see, unless the darkening film that rests thereon be taken away by the hand of God; but as this was too subtle an object to be found out by Buddha, it entirely eluded his search, and he was unable to trace its pathway into the other world. He knew not that man had received within himself, in the beginning, the breath of life; and that in creation he is alone, with an essential difference, and an impassable distance, between himself and the highest of the other creatures in his own world.

By the Hindus man is considered to be an emanation from God, and an almost imperceptibly small part of a vast whole; his very existence being an illusion, without permanence or reality. The relationships of life are of importance, as influencing his position in another state of existence; but there will be no cessation to his wanderings until he is re-absorbed in God. By Buddha, however, all thoughts of dependence on any other power outward to man, either as to present or future existence, was discarded. He concluded that each congeries we call a man is the maker of his own fortune, the establisher of his own position; it is he who shapes out his own destiny, whether of partial blessedness or of mingled woe; inasmuch as he inherits the karmma, the moral power, of all his actions, in all former states of existence, whether it be good or evil. So long as he is under the influence of upádána, or attachment to sensuous objects, that attachment will necessitate the repetition of existence. On the overcoming, or excision, of attachment, and not till then, he attains nirwána; after which he will never again be re-born, but will cease to exist. There is no appeal by the Buddhist to any exterior power to assist him in the attainment of this grand consummation; if he is faithful to his position and privileges, he himself may become a better and nobler being than any of the gods. He is isolated and independent; he joins no one else in seeking assistance by prayer, though from the teachings of another he may receive aid, to do in a better manner what, after all, must be his own work. When he enters upon the most exalted of all the exercises it is possible for him to have recourse to, that of dhyána, he retires to some secret place for the purpose, where, shutting out all the world, he seeks to overcome the motion of his own breath, and then enters upon a course of meditation so abstract and profound, that if a blast from the war-trumpet were to be blown close to his ear, he would no more perceive it than if he were dead.

It will have been noticed that the thoughts of Buddha on the subject of transmigration are peculiar, and I know of no approach to them in any other system. He teaches that it is not a spirit that passes from one state of existence to another, nor any material vehicle, but the moral principle of the man, as formed and moulded by the acts of the present and all preceding generations. This doctrine was repudiated by the priests of Ceylon when it was first presented to them by the late Mr. Gogerly; but, on further examination, they acknowledged that it was in accordance with the teaching of Buddha; more especially if Nágásena, who had many conversations with king Milinda on this and kindred subjects, is to be regarded as an authority. The earliest reference to transmigration, a tenet now universally received among the Hindus, appears to be in the Dharmma, as it is not alluded to in the earlier Vedic hymns, nor is it received now by "the un-brahmanized denominations of India."* The absurdity of Buddha's teachings about the reproductive power of attachment to sensuous objects, and the transference of the karmma, was soon seen, and was never imitated; but the doctrine of transmigration was retained, as it appeared to explain many of the difficulties presented in the moral universe. We trace the origin of this tenet to the same period both in the eastern and western world.

In contrast to the worldly spirit of the Vedas, were the speculations of Buddha as to the chief end of man. In these old records there are few confessions of sin, and still fewer supplications for its pardon, or for the reception of power to put it away. But all the forthputting of the utmost energy of the sage of Mágadha, in the whole of

* "Professor Weber remarks that owing to the fragmentary nature of the surviving documents of Indian literature, we are not yet in a position to trace with any distinctness the rise and growth of the doctrine of transmigration, though he considers it to admit of no doubt that the tenet in question was gradually developed in India itself, and not introduced from any foreign country."—*Dr. J. Muir, Journal R.A.S.*, vol. i. 307.

his teachings and communications, had for its main object to convince man that the plague-spot of his being is attachment to sensuous objects. All the imagery is invoked that it is possible to summon to his assistance, that he may impress upon his followers, with the greater power, the earthliness and sensuousness of their nature, and the necessity of getting entirely free from all worldly attractions and entanglements, if they would enter "the city of peace," and be for ever at rest. Of sin, in the sense in which the Scriptures speak of it, he knows nothing. There is no authoritative lawgiver, according to the Dharmma, nor can there possibly be one; so that the transgression of the precepts is not an iniquity, and brings no guilt. It is right that we should try to get free from its consequences, in the same way in which it is right for us to appease hunger or overcome disease; but no repentance is required; and if we are taught the necessity of being tranquil, subdued, and humble, it is that our minds may go out with the less eagerness after those things that unsettle its tranquillity. If we injure no one by our acts, no wrong has been done; and if they are an inconvenience to ourselves only, no one else has any right to regard us as transgressors. The Dharmma has some resemblance to the modern utilitarianism; it is not, however, the production of the greatest possible happiness at which it aims, but the removal of all possible evil and inconvenience—from ourselves.

Notwithstanding the materialism of his system, it must not be forgotten that Buddha acknowledges the existence of an ethical power, both in relation to the individual and the economy of the world at large, which exercises an all-pervading influence. It is not allied to any intelligence, but it is productive of benefit to those who seek merit in the right way; and acts with as much regularity and certainty as any other law of nature. The dewdrop is formed, and the heart is tranquillised, and the practice of virtue is rewarded, through the instrumentality of causes that are alike in the manner of their operation.

In consistence with the thought that man, by his own unaided power, can work out his own redemption, is the rejection of sacrifice. When the design of the offering of blood, as being vicarious or propitiatory, or as shewing forth the death of some purer and nobler victim, is forgotten, the rite loses all its significance and power. We can see something meet and congruous in the offering of the first-fruits of the harvest, as an acknowledgment that it is God who has "crowned the year with his goodness," and filled our storehouses with the rich fruit or nutritious grain. But when the fat of lambs is brought, under the idea that the deity to whom it is offered will in some sense partake of its sweetness, or receive from it strength; when the intoxicating juice is poured out with the thought that the divine being to whom it is given as a libation will be thereby cheered; when blood is offered under the supposition that the rage of the power who receives it will be appeased thereby, as thirst by the water of the brook—sacrifice becomes a derogatory act, and lessens the dignity of the man who can imagine his gods to be thus low and creature-like. This was seen by Buddha, who was sensibly alive to whatever is of evil tendency, however high the authority for its practice. In his conversations with the brahmans he continually dwelt upon the inutility and harm of sacrifice. In his mind there was connected with every rite of blood the greater iniquity, as he regarded all life as homogeneous, and to offer sacrifice was a transgression of the first of the precepts. In Buddhism, therefore, all manner of sacrifice is rejected, and it now knows no further rite or ceremony than the repetition of the precepts in the presence of the priest, the placing of flowers before the image of the sage, and the occasional reading of the bana on sacred days. But the system becomes thereby too cold and abstract for the popular mind. Its mode of help is too shadowy to impart confidence to man in the hour of his trial. In Ceylon the people look to Buddhism for deliverance as to the future world. By its instrumentality they suppose that they can gain merit; but for present assistance, when the burden of affliction is heavy upon them, their resort is to the demon priest, with his incantations and sacrifices.

There are one or two other characteristics of the system that we may briefly notice, before concluding these remarks. Buddha demanded an implicit submission to the doctrines he enunciated. He said, "I know, and therefore you must believe." But to convince those who were not his followers that they were wrong, he argued with them in the usual manner, generally by asking a series of questions, by means of which he gradually brought them into an unexpected dilemma, and made them stultify their own propositions. The charge of novelty that might have been brought against the doctrines he taught, was set aside by his asserting that he knew, from the power of intuition, that they were the identical doctrines taught by all former Buddhas, though entirely lost to the world after the lapse of certain ages.

On the supposition that the system of Gótama, as we have it now, was commenced in the period to which it is generally attributed, it is an interesting subject of enquiry how much of it was original, and how much taken from others, and what were the sources whence its borrowed portions were derived. The principal works then in existence were the Vedas; and in them, so far as they are accessible to a general reader like myself, it would be difficult to discover even the semblance of his more distinctive principles. Yet at this period there was an intense desire manifested to investigate and understand all subjects connected with mental philosophy, ethics, and religion. These enquiries were not, as in Greece, confined to the schools, but seem to have pervaded all classes of the community. There was less that was æsthetic in the genius of the Aryan race than in that of the Hellenes, but there was greater intensity of feeling on all subjects connected with man's duty and destiny. In the fact that Buddha encountered many rivals, whose power he confessed, we have evidence that he was not alone in the search after truth, or in the supposition that he had discovered it. Upwards of five hundred years had passed over since the appearance of the earlier rishis. Of that interval, who shall tell the story? It appears, at present, to be an impenetrable mystery. The dispersion of the Jews in the reign of Nebuchadnezzar could have little to do with the intellectual position of India at this period. The Aryan nations were too proud and stern to have been stirred to activity in so short a period. The destruction of the polity of the ten tribes, which took place one hundred and thirty years previously, may, however, have originated the undulation that now swept over the land with so much power; but the contrast between the teachings of the prophets of God and the Tathágato is still greater than that between the Pitakas and the Vedas.

The venerable leaves consulted by the magicians, the astrologers, and the sorcerers, in the doomed palace of Belshazzar, might have thrown greater light upon this enquiry than they did in relation to the hand-writing upon the wall; but they are lost, and their secrets are gone with them. The influence of the monarchs of Persia, who reigned from India to Ethiopia, must not be disregarded in our estimate of the causes that originated, or the influences that directed, the philosophical speculations of the Hindus in the earlier ages of Buddhism. The sages of Greece may seem to have been too far away to have made any impression upon the Sramanas or Brahmans of India, though some of them are said to have visited the far east; but they have thoughts in common, that appear to have been derived from one and the same source. We have a more extended insight into the system of Pythagoras than of any other of the contemporaries of Buddha. We see it through the mists thrown around it by the writers of a later age; but there is a striking similarity between the thoughts and doings of the two sages. They both itinerated. They both taught the alternate destruction and renovation of the universe; that true knowledge is to be obtained, not by the medium of the ears or the eyes, but by abstract thought; they both instituted communities, and imposed upon their followers a strict discipline, insisted strongly on the necessity of temperance to preserve the mind in unbroken serenity, forbade the use of sumptuous garments, regarded purity of heart as of greater value than offerings or sacrifices, taught a oneness of nature between gods, men, and animals, and made a distinction between living above nature and according to nature. This identity of sentiment extended not merely to the outward life, but to the deeper questions of philosophy. In teaching the doctrine of transmigration, the Greek spoke of a triad, and of three worlds; he gave information to his disciples as to what bodies he had previously inhabited, and under what circumstances he had then lived; his memory was perfect as to past states of existence; he told others what sort of persons they had been in former births; and he made known that there had been a gradual deterioration of the human race, from a state of original purity and peacefulness. The source of the great philosophies of the ancient world seems to have been some region near the birth-place of the nations; and if we could summon from the past, and make audible, the primitive language, and reveal the thoughts and imaginations then eliminated, we should have a key by which we could lay open and explain many an enigma now clouded by misunderstanding or hid in utter darkness.

We have referred to the difficulty of comparing one

system of philosophy with another, from the difference of meaning in the terms that are used; and this becomes the greater, when we set ourselves to the study of Hinduism without a special training for the purpose; because the meaning we attach to many important terms is at variance with that in which they are regarded by the native mind. Hence the numerous mistakes that have been made by men of name; first, as to the terms themselves, and then as to the arguments they have founded on them. In not a few instances, things that appear absurd to the western student are no longer so when viewed through the medium of the mind by which they are received, and from the same premises. The Hindu does not clearly separate matter from spirit; but confounds the properties and powers connected with each. Even thought is supposed to be a material operation. The whole of the outer world is within us by the impression it produces. It is, therefore, not a reality, and is not something separate from us, except in appearance. In like manner, we ourselves appear to be without the universal Paramátma, though in reality within; we are one with God, and not distinct existences.

The aim of nearly all the philosophies of India is the same, to free existent beings from the power of evil, and its consequences; but this is almost the only subject upon which they agree. They nearly all, either in truth or semblance, acknowledge the existence of a Supreme Soul, though differing as to the attributes they give to it; but as Buddha ignores the existence of any such Universality, there can be no agreement between him and the other Hindu sages upon this most fundamental of all truths;

and this one divergence includes and necessitates innumerable variances. The Hindus do not believe in creation, in the Semitic sense of the term. They say that something may come from something; and though they do not seek for any proportionateness between cause and effect, they insist that something cannot come from nothing; all changes are but the revolutions of one original existence. These, however, are not the axioms of Buddha. He teaches that at the dissolution of any given world, the destruction of the elementary materials composing it is complete, no more of anything being left than can be found in the void inside the drum; and that another world is produced *de novo*. On another subject of primary importance, the existence of the soul, Buddha is equally heterodox, as regards the general standard of Hindu philosophies. They nearly all acknowledge the existence of some kind of soul, though differing widely as to its nature. One tells us that each person has a separate soul, pointing out where it resides in the body. Another tells us that all souls are one, and can have no corporeal locality. Now we are informed that the soul is a monad, an atom, an imperceptibly minute substance; and then that it has existed from eternity and is infinitely extended, having the same qualities as space and time. But there were some of these old thinkers, who had right ideas of the office of the soul, and described it as like a charioteer who has the guidance of the horses attached to a car.

As to the evils to which man is subject, there is more unison of thought between the two great systems of India.

It may be possible to set aside the great facts of the existence of God and of a soul; but no one can deny that the state of man is one that calls for some remedy, if a cure for his miseries can be found. Yet the schools differ as to the cause of evil. Whilst one says that it arises from the separation of the individual soul from the soul of the universe, another affirms that it proceeds from the union of the soul and matter, and a third teaches that it comes from the restless activity that is natural to the soul; whilst Buddha proclaims, with wearisome prolixity, that it is the consequence of attachment to the objects that are apparent to the senses. The remedy is the same verbally in nearly all the systems: receive the truth, and it will make you free; but whilst each system declares its own creed to be the truth, the bewildered Hindu has to ask, amidst this conflict of opinions and pretensions, What is truth?

But the subject is interminable in its ramifications; vast and complicated, as is all that proceeds from the Aryan mind; and of ever-increasing interest in connexion with the speculations of other thinkers on man and his coming and going, his present and past existence, and his immortality. These introductory remarks, though imperfect, may at least throw some light upon the system, and enable the reader to understand more readily the chapters upon which he will now enter. Further notices must be left to other expositors, or to a more favourable period for research.

COLOMBO, CEYLON,
*June 18th*, 1865.

# LEGENDS AND THEORIES

OF THE

# BUDDHISTS.

## CHAPTER I.

## THE LEGENDS AND LITERATURE OF INDIA.

### 1. TESTS OF THE TRUTH OF HISTORY.

It is the maxim of the age in which we live, not to take any assertion for granted, merely because it is so said by some one else; but, to ask for the ground on which we are called upon to believe it. Formerly, a statement was made, and if it had authority for its repetition, and was confirmed by antiquity, it was received, and believed in, without further search; arguments arose from it, theories were founded on it, and conclusions were drawn from it, that no one disputed. But it was seen, when the world had become more enlightened, and was about to leave the deep ruts of other ages, that this was not the right way in which the search for truth is to be conducted; for if the statement itself is wrong, all the results supposed to flow from it are thereby vitiated. We are now told to act in this way: "Begin at the beginning; be sure that you city." But the whole has been proved by the unsparing critic to be a mere legend, without any real authority; and it has now to be set aside as "unhistorical." The story can be traced back, in this form, only to a certain distance in the ancient chronicles of the city. It is then told in ways that contradict each other in important particulars; and it has also to struggle with other legends, almost equally rich in poetry, but equally destitute of foundation in truth. And at an earlier period still, there is the burning of the city, in which its archives are lost, and beyond that time all is uncertainty and confusion. "The claims of reason," we are told by Niebuhr, in reference to the subject before us, must be asserted, and we are "to take nothing as historical which cannot be historical."

## 3. THE SINGHALESE LEGEND OF KALYANI.

To show more clearly still the manner in which these conclusions are arrived at, I will apply the same process to one of the earliest of the Singhalese legends, in itself not without interest, and in some respects resembling the story I have just repeated from the traditions of Rome. About the middle of the third century after the death of Buddha, Ceylon was divided into several petty states, and among the rest was that of Kalyáni (Calány), of which Tissa, was king. His wife was beautiful; his brother, Uttiya, was a libertine; and there was evil committed in the royal household. But the king having heard of the wrong that was done, sent secretly for a Rodiyá, and spoke to him thus: "I will call together my retinue, including my younger brother, and I will say to thee, in their presence, Is there any one of lower caste than thou art? and the reply thou must make is, The king's younger brother is a meaner man than I am." This was accordingly done; and the prince, thus put to shame, fled to Udagampala; but he contrived to send a letter to the queen, by a messenger disguised as a priest, who was to enter the palace with the rest of the priests when they went to receive the usual alms. The letter was filled with the common topics of a guilty lover; but it had no name, nor was the place mentioned whence it came. The queen was accustomed to assist at the giving of alms; and as she was looking towards the messenger, he took the opportunity to let the epistle fall on the ground. Its fall, however, caused a rustling noise, which attracting the notice of the king, he took it up; and on reading it he saw that his queen was unfaithful to her exalted position. Uttiya had been the pupil of the high priest of Kalyáni, and their hand-writing was alike. The king charged the high priest with having written the letter; listened to no protestations of his innocence; and commanded him to be put to death by being cast into a caldron of boiling oil. For seven days the attempt was made to heat the oil, but it still remained cold; but the priest, when a herdsman in a former age, had acted contrary to the precept, by drowning a fly that fell into some milk he was boiling, and for this offence, though he escaped the death appointed by the king, he was turned into a heap of ashes. The queen was thrown into the river, and the messenger was cut in pieces. But to punish the king for this act of impiety towards an innocent priest, the déwas who protect Ceylon caused the sea to encroach on the land, and much damage was done to the country. To appease their wrath, as it was supposed that the country could be saved in no other way, the king resolved to sacrifice his virgin daughter. Placing her in a golden vessel, on which was inscribed the word "rájadhítáti," which signified that she was a royal maiden, the vessel was committed to the waves of the sea. But the flood still raged, until 100,000 towns, 970 fisher villages, and 470 villages inhabited by divers for pearls, had been submerged.* As the king, from the back of his elephant, was watching the progress of the devastation, the earth opened, flame burst forth from beneath, and he was no more seen by his people. By this time twenty miles of the coast, extending inland, had been washed away, and the distance from Kalyáni to the sea was reduced to four miles. The royal virgin drifted towards the dominions of the king of Mágam, when the vessel was seen by some fishermen, who brought it to land. The monarch Káwantissa, having heard of the wonderful capture made by the fishermen, went to examine it; and when he had read the inscription upon it, he released the princess from her confinement, and she became his queen.

* The same legend informs us that, in a former age, the citadel of Ráwaná, 25 palaces, and 400,000 streets, were swallowed up by the sea. This was on account of the impiety of the giant king. The submerged land was between Tuticoreen and Manaar, and the island of Manaar is all that is now left of what was once a large territory. This legend, notwithstanding its manifest exaggeration as to the extent of the injury, may be founded on fact, as the Hindu and other nations have a similar tradition, and suppose that Ceylon was then much larger than it is at present.

As the vessel was brought to shore near a wihára, she was called Wihára-déwi; and she afterwards became the mother of Dutugemunu, famous as the expeller of the Malabars from Ceylon. On the day on which the child was named, the king invited 10,000 priests to the palace, who were presented with an alms-offering of rice-milk.

This story, taken from the Rájawaliya and the Mahawánso, cannot be received as true; for the following reasons, among others that might be named: 1. We are certain that at this time there could not be one hundred thousand villages in a province so far distant from the seat of the principal government, or that 470 of these could have been inhabited by pearl divers. There are no ancient ruins here found that would indicate the existence of a large population at this early period, though such remains are abundantly presented in other parts of the island. 2. It is equally improbable that the use of letters should in this age (as we shall afterwards more distinctly notice) and in those lawless times, have been so general an accomplishment as it is here taken to be; as, according to the story, the two kings, the prince, the priest, and the queen, must all have been able to read; and it must have been the supposition of the king that those who might find the golden vessel would possess the same advantage. 3. The monarch Dutugemunu, who bound on the royal diadem in 161 B.C. is represented, in the record where these events are found, as being the great grandson of Panduwása, who became king in 504 B.C. For 343 years we have only four generations. 4. It is said that 10,000 priests were present at the naming of Dutugemunu.* How could so small a province as that of Mágam support by alms so great a number of persons; and how could the king provide milk for the rice of all, in a country where the traveller finds it difficult now to procure a single measure? 5. The motive for the origin of the legend is too apparent—the exaltation of the priesthood. An innocent priest is put to death, upon presumptive evidence of his guilt. For this unintentional crime, a king loses his life, his virgin daughter is sacrificed, and more than one hundred thousand villages are destroyed. How sacred then, how divine, must be the character of the priesthood, if no inferior expiation could take away the consequences of the sin. 6. We have no record of these events that we can trace to the time when they are said to have occurred. The date of the Rájawaliya we do not know; that of the Maháwanso is about A.D. 460. These are the only sources whence our information is derived; and they are too distant, or too uncertain, in their date, to allow of our placing confidence in their statements about the reign of Tissa. These objections, independently of those arising from the supposed interposition of the déwas, the awkward introduction of the outcaste Rodiyá, and the improbability that the king would in this way proclaim his own dishonour, are fatal to the credibility of the story. We can only receive it as legend, in which there may be some truth; but to what extent no one can tell. It is in a similar manner that all the events recorded of the past are sifted and examined by the modern historian, in order

* Turnour's Maháwanso, cap. xxii.

that he may discover to what extent they are entitled to reception as real occurrences. I have chosen the story of the princess of Kalyáni as a tentative example, because it is one that Christians and Buddhists can alike examine dispassionately. It is not referred to in any of the sacred books; it belongs to secular history, and not to religion; and whether it be true or false makes no difference to Buddhism as a system of belief.

## 4. THE CASTE OF THE BRAHMANS.

Oriental students, whose attention has hitherto been directed almost exclusively to Brahmanism, have been as unsparing in their attacks on systems hoar with age, as the professors of western lore. I shall notice their innovations at some length; as we shall thereby be aided in bringing the same agency to bear upon the system that claims as its author "the all-wise Buddha."

The most prominent institution on the continent of India is that of caste; which, under whatever aspect we may view it, is an unmitigated evil. It seeks to unman the whole race of human beings; for it would make us believe that a portion is composed of those who are more than men—they are gods: and the rest, including the immense majority, are less than men—they are things made to be huffed, oppressed, and degraded, every moment and every where, to an extent that the people of other lands have never known; not even the African, in his lowest humiliation. Yet in the command that bids the binding of the mighty fetter, there are words that ought to shame every one who repeats it as a plea for oppression; for, though the Sudra proceeds from the foot, he is equally with the twice-born an emanation from Brahma; still "his offspring." The pretensions of the Brahmans are founded on a legend contained in the Jatimálá, of which the following is a translation:—"In the first creation by Brahma, Brahmanas proceeded, with the Veda, from the mouth of Brahma. From his arms Kshatriyas sprung; so, from his thigh, Vaisyas; from his foot Sudras were produced: all with their females. The Lord of creation viewing them, said, 'What shall be your occupation?' These replied, 'We are not our own masters, O god, command us what to undertake!' Viewing and comparing their labours, he made the first tribe superior over the rest. As the first had great inclination for the Divine sciences (brahmaveda), therefore he was called Brahmana. The protector from ill (kshayate) was Kshatriya. Him whose profession (vesa) consists in commerce (which promotes the success of wars, for the protection of himself and mankind) and in husbandry, and attendance on cattle, he called Vaisya. The other should voluntarily serve the three tribes, and therefore he became a Sudra: he should humble himself at their feet."* This legend has been made to minister to an arrogance that has no equal in the whole story of man's usurpations. "The Chandála," says Manu, "can never be relieved from bondage or emancipated by a master. How can he, whom the supreme God has destined to be the slave of Brahmans, ever be released from his destiny by man? .... Whatever exists in the

* Colebrooke, Miscellaneous Essays.

universe is all, in effect, though not in form, the wealth of the Brahman; since the Brahman is entitled to all by his primogeniture and eminence of birth. The Brahman eats but his own food, wears but his own apparel, and bestows but his own alms. Through the (permissive) benevolence of the Brahmans, indeed, other mortals enjoy life."

The Jaṭimálá is a comparatively recent work; and before we bow down, whether as Sudras or as Nishádas, to the haughty Brahman, we require to have made known to us, in order to secure our submission, some more ancient authority; something that comes to us from times nearer the era of the supposed emanation. But it is a fact of modern discovery, that the further we go back in the history of the Hindus, the fewer allusions we find to the subject of caste, until, in the oldest of the Vedas it is a thing unknown. One of the noblest among the many friends of India, Dr. Muir, now of Edinburgh, and late of the Bengal Civil Service, has set himself to the task of collecting, from every available source, the principal Sanskrit texts that bear upon the social and religious interests of India.*

* Three parts of this work, entitled "Original Sanskrit Texts, on the Origin and History of the People of India, their Religion and Institutions," have been published. 1. On the Mythical and Legendary Accounts of Caste. 2. The Trans-Himalayan Origin of the Hindus, and their Affinity with the Western Branches of the Aryan Race. 3. The Vedas: Opinions of their Authors, and of later Indian Writers, in regard to their Origin, Inspiration, and Authority. I regret that I have, at present, access to only the third of these parts; but I have made free use of a series of papers I wrote, at the time of the publication of the Texts, in the Wesleyan Methodist Magazine, for 1861. I have made extracts from Dr. Muir's priceless volumes to a greater extent than might have been right under other circumstances; as I know that gain is not his object, but the spreading of information that will advance the interests of India. [Since the above was written, a fourth part has been published, which I have not seen.]

This important work he is executing with an industry and erudition that demand the gratitude of all who are seeking to place man in his proper position, as the free, noble, and happy creature of a loving and most merciful God. There is only one power that can bring about this grand consummation; but before we can expect that power to be rightly effective a previous work will have to be done: many an error will have to be exposed, and broken many a tyrant's gyve.

The results of Dr. Muir's investigations on "The Theory of the Origin of Caste," are summed up in a section of so much value, that I insert it without abridgment:—

"The contents of this chapter [On the General Theory of the Origin of Castes] have made it abundantly evident that the sacred books of the Hindus contain no uniform and uncontroverted account of the origin of castes; but, on the contrary, present the greatest varieties of opinion on the subject. Explanations, mystical, mythical, etymological, and critical are attempted: and the freest scope is given by the writers to fanciful and arbitrary conjecture.

"First of all, we have the mystical statement of the Purusha Sukta, that the forefathers of the three superior castes *formed* three of the members of Purusha's body, while the servile issued from the feet. This, the oldest extant passage in which the castes are connected with the different parts of the creator's body, seems to have given rise to all the subsequent representations to the same effect in later works. The idea which it contains is repeated, with little substantial alteration, in two texts of the Bhagavata Purana: while, on the other hand, in passages cited from Manu, from the Vishnu Purana, and the Vayu Purana, and in one extracted from the Mahabharata, the mystical character of the original Vedic text disappears, and the castes are represented as if literally *produced from* the several members of Brahma's body. This theory is not, however, carried out consistently, even in those works where it is most distinctly proposed; and the original division of castes, after being lost sight of during the first age of perfection, is again introduced at a later period in such way as to necessitate a fresh explanation to account for its re-appearance.

"By two other authorities, the Harivansa and the Mahabharata, the origin of castes is etymologically connected with colours: (*varna*, the Sanskrit word for caste, meaning originally colour:) an explanation which, however fancifully carried out in these passages, is really founded on fact: as there can be no doubt that the Aryan immigrants into India, coming from northern countries, were of fair complexion, while the aboriginal tribes, with whom they came into contact, were dark. This circumstance seems to be alluded to in the Vedic text. 'He destroyed the Dasyus, and protected the Aryan colour.' Again, attempts are made to explain the assumed characteristics of the several castes by fanciful etymologies of their respective names; the word Kshatriya being connected with *protection*, the name Vaisya with *agriculture* and *cattle*, and the denomination Sudra with *service*. In the case of the Brahman, indeed, the derivation is reasonable; as his appellation is probably connected with *brahma*, prayer, or sacred learning, or the Veda.

"Finally, we have passages of a different tenor, as in a quotation from the Mahabharata, in which the distinction of castes is derived from the different characters and pursuits of the several sections of the community; or such as that other text from another part of the same work, in which men of all castes are said to be descended from Manu."

In these discoveries, we have a powerful auxiliary in the preparatory work that has to be undertaken for the evangelizing of India, coming to us from an unexpected source. It will now be a pleasant undertaking, to trouble the Brahman with the same mantra spell wherewith he has disquieted millions of men during more than two thousand years; and to proclaim to the Sudra the novel intelligence, that the rishis, whom his oppressors so much venerate, are his own friends, and never gave the Brahman any particle of the power he has wrongfully exercised during so many ages.

I need not say to any one resident in this island, that Buddha was uniformly the opponent of caste.* He proclaimed the original equality of all men. He ordained his priests equally from all classes of the people, and gave them precedence according to the order of their initiation,

* "The hope of Ceylon arises from various causes, and we shall here notice the influence of caste on religion. It is a fact that the Singhalese are not so much attached to the system of castes, as are their neighbours on the continent of India. Caste exists in Ceylon, but with greater force in India. Here it is a mere custom—there a part of the national Hindu institutes. Here it is more political than religious—there more religious than political. Here no man loses his caste by the adoption of a new faith—there the Brahman becomes an utter outcast by changing his creed. Though demurred to in this very place (the Hall of the Legislative Council) by the higher

without regarding the circumstances of their birth or their previous position. It was his doctrine, that it is the greater or less development of the moral principle, that makes the essential difference in the status of men. Though it is too much to say that "no hostile feeling against the Brahmans finds utterance in the Buddhist canon,"* the opposition of Buddha to the principle of caste was at first seen in the maintenance of an opinion contrary to that of the Brahmans, rather than in direct attack upon their system or express exposure of their errors. The third Sutra records a conversation between Buddha and the Brahman Ambatta, in which the sage asserts the superiority of the Kshatriya caste. Another Brahman is referred to who was called "the white lotus," from the colour of his skin. In the fourth Sutra, Sónadandha, Buddha asks a Brahman of that name what it is that constitutes a Brahman. Is it descent, learning, fairness of complexion, good conduct, or an acquaintance with the rules of sacrifice? He then asks of these things separately, whether, if the one he named were wanting, the man would still be a Brahman. Sónadandha answered, that if a man had learning and good conduct, he would still be a Brahman, though he had not any other of the

classes of the Singhalese, we, nevertheless, find all castes and classes meeting together in the jury box with the greatest harmony. All sit on the same form in the Christian churches; all partake of the same cup when the wine is distributed at the Lord's Supper. The Wellálas (the highest caste among the Singhalese) now follow different trades, which were anciently restricted to the lower orders, and occasionally marriages take place between persons of different castes. Caste is thus losing its iron grasp on the affections of the Singhalese."—Alwis's Lectures on Buddhism, p. 30.

* Max Müller, Ancient Sanskrit Literature.

five advantages. This was the answer that Buddha wanted to bring out, but it was not assented to by the other Brahmans who were present. There is evident a growing antagonism upon the part of the Brahmans, from the time it became apparent that Gótama intended to set aside their pretensions; and we learn from more than one of the Buddhist Sutras, that the theory of caste was the subject of anxious investigation upon the part of those who resorted for instruction to the hierarchs of the system after his death.

Here Buddha is on the side of truth; as to principle, but not as to fact. It is the teaching of Buddhism, that when our earth was first inhabited, the beings who appeared in it were produced by the apparitional birth; that their bodies still retained many of the attributes of the world from whence they had come—the Abhassara brahma-loka; that there was no difference between night and day, and no difference of sex; that they lived together in all happiness and in mutual peace; and that they could soar through the air at will, the glory proceeding from their persons being so great that there was no necessity for a sun or moon. The dogma of the Brahmans can be traced back, in their own books, until it becomes extremely attenuated, and then altogether invisible. That of Buddha is confessedly, as are all his other doctrines, the result of his own intuition; and as there is no known fact to support it, coming to us from any other source, it is to be regarded as "unhistorical," and to be rejected.

## 5. THE SANSKRIT AND PALI LANGUAGES.

The Brahmans have been deprived, by a similar process, of another immunity that has long been ceded to them by the inferior castes. They not only supposed themselves to be above the rest of men because of their origin; but they maintained as another proof of this great fact, that their language is divine; that it is not, and never has been, spoken by any other race upon earth; that it is the language of the gods, and that its majestic rhythm is heard in the crystal palaces of heaven. So sacred is it, that if the Sudra, even by accident, hear its words as enunciated in the reading of the Vedas, bitter oil, and boiling, is to be poured into his ear, that the orifice may be closed for ever against a similar act of desecration. But when Jones, Colebrooke, and other learned men, began to study Sanskrit, they soon found that there are striking affinities between languages that had previously been supposed to have no resemblance to each other. The Zend, spoken formerly in Persia, the Greek, and the Latin, it is now evident, have all had the same origin as the language of the Brahmans. The present vernaculars of India can be traced back two thousand years, through inscriptions on rocks, works in Pali, poems, dramas, and other compositions; and the further we go back the more nearly does the language we meet with resemble the Sanskrit. It is thought by many philologists that there must have been a time, when Sanskrit was the common language of the people of India. In the style of the Sanskrit compositions which have come down to us, there are changes and varieties that can only be accounted for on the supposition that it was once a spoken language; since it is only when a language ceases to be spoken that it becomes set and unchangeable. The Brahmanas, for instance, equally differ from the ancient Vedic hymns and from the more modern Sutras. These hymns present various forms of inflection and conjugation not seen in the works of later authors, and are to be regarded as by far the most ancient specimens of Sanskrit literature now extant. By some disruption of the Sanskrit-speaking population the country became divided into separate provinces, each of which, in process of time, had its own distinct dialect, from which has been formed the present vernacular, whether it be Bengali, Hindi, Mahratni, or Guzarati. The Tamul, Malayalim, and other languages of the Dravidian family, are not included in this arrangement, for reasons that would require, for their development, too long a digression from our main object. The process we have referred to closely resembles the formation of the French, Portuguese, Spanish, Italian, and other languages of modern Europe, from the parent Latin. There is also a remarkable resemblance in the manner in which the phonetic changes are made. In Pali all harsh sounds are avoided; the letter *r* is frequently omitted; and one word is made to flow into another with wonderful ease and rhythm. The style of the language and the character of the religion taught in it assimilate; and few languages would have been equally adapted for uttering the soft tones and gentle sayings of the Tathágato. Parwata, a rock, becomes pabbata in Pali;

aswa, a horse, in a similar manner becomes asso; rakta, red, ratta; dharmma, truth, dhamma; vriksha, a tree, rukha; sisya, a disciple, sissan; sarpa, a serpent, sappa; singha, a lion, sího; and chaura, a thief, chóra. In composition, as we learn from Clough's Bálawatára, lóka aggo, the chief of the world, becomes lokaggo; and tatra ayan, there is, becomes tatráyan.

The following positions have been established by Dr. Muir:—

"1. That these forms of speech have all one common origin:—*i.e.*, that Sanskrit, Zend, Greek, and Latin are all, as it were, sisters,—the daughters (some perhaps elder and some younger, but still all daughters) of one mother who died in giving them birth: or, to speak without a figure, that they are derivations from, and the surviving representatives of, one older language, which now no longer exists. And, 2. That the races of men who spoke these several languages are also all descended from one stock; and that their ancestors at a very early period lived together in some country (situated out of Hindustan), speaking one language; but afterwards separated, to travel away from their primeval abodes, at different times, and in different directions,—the forefathers of the Hindus, south-ward, or south-eastward, to India; the ancestors of the Persians, to the south; and those of the Greeks and the Romans, to the west. The languages of those branches of this great Indo-European stock which remained longest together in their earliest home,—namely, the Persians and the Indians,—continued to bear the closest resemblance to each other; while the tongues of those offshoots which separated earliest from the parent stock exhibit in later times the least amount of resemblance, the divergencies of dialect becoming wider and wider in proportion to the length of time which had elapsed since the separation."

It is thus evident that the ancestors of the dark and dreamy Brahman, and of the pale and practical European, once chased each other under the shade of the same tree, and lived in the same home, and had the same father, and spoke to that father in the same language: and though the difference is now great, both in outward appearance and mental constitution, not more certainly do the answering crevices in the cleft rock tell that they were once united, than the accordant sounds in the speech of the two races tell that they were formerly one people; and this unity is proclaimed every time that they address father or mother, or call for the axe, or name the tree, or point out the star, or utter numbers. The Singhalese being allied to the Sanskrit to an extent not surpassed by any other vernacular now in use, there must have been a time when the two races, the Ceylonese and the British, were far more nearly related to each other than as being residents in the same beautiful land, or subjects of the same gracious queen. The resemblance in the languages that have been named will be more clearly seen from the following list of words, taken from Bopp's Comparative Grammar.

| SANSKRIT. | ZEND. | GREEK. | LATIN. | ENGLISH. |
|---|---|---|---|---|
| *pitri* | *paitar* | πατήρ | *pater* | *father* |
| *bhrátri* | *bartar* | φρατρία * | *frater* | *brother* |

* Band or brotherhood.

| SANSKRIT. | ZEND. | GREEK. | LATIN. | ENGLISH. |
|---|---|---|---|---|
| *duhitri* | *dughdhar* | θυγάτηρ | —— | *daughter* |
| *aswa* | *aspa* | ἵππος | *equus* | *horse* |
| *náman* | *náman* | ὄνομα | *nomen* | *name* |
| *tára* | *stáre* | ἀστήρ | *astrum* | *star* |
| *upari* | *upairi* | ὑπέρ | *super* | *above(upper)* |
| *dwi* | *dwa* | δύο | *duo* | *two* |
| *tris* | *thris* | τρίς | *ter* | *thrice* |
| *shat* | *khscas* | ἕξ | *sex* | *six* |
| *tishtámi* | *histami* | ἵστημι | *sto* | *stand* |

Here an interesting enquiry presents itself, By what people was the Sanskrit originally spoken, and what was their origin or character? The authors of the Sanskrit books regard themselves, and the heroes of whom they speak, as Aryans, and their country is called Arya-bhumi or Arya-désa. The word *arya,* as may be learnt from the Singhalese Lexicon, means "noble, excellent, of respectable lineage." It was the national name of the ancient inhabitants of India who worshipped the gods of the Brahmans, in contradistinction to the Dásyas, who are regarded as barbarians or demons. The word is still preserved in Iran, the modern name for Persia, and even the green isle, Erin, may have derived its name from the still more luxuriant east. In the earliest traditions we see the Aryans forcing their way across the snows of the Himálawana; and then, as they rush onward toward the sun-lit region that lay at their feet, like the Paradise of which their fathers had told them, they take possession of it as their permanent home. In their old songs there are allusions that prove the fact of their migration from a colder country; they are a fair race; and in one of the Brahmanas there is a tradition that the first man, Manu, descended from "the northern mountain," after a deluge. The Aryans advanced along the borders of the great desert of Marvar, from the Sutlej to the Saraswati; and here they halted for so considerable a period, that this region has since been regarded as sacred ground. They must afterwards have spread themselves far and wide, as in their more modern writings there are numerous references to ships and maritime commerce; and it is evident that a language similar to Sanskrit was in use on the sea-coast in the time of Solomon, as his ships are said to have brought from the distant land they visited, apes, ivory, peacocks, and algum trees; the names of which, as they appear in the Scriptures, are Sanskrit rather than Hebrew.*

It must be a source of extreme mortification to the lordly Brahman, when he finds, upon evidence provided by himself, and which he cannot controvert, that the language he uses, under the supposition that it is known only to himself and the gods, is derived from the same source as the language spoken by the races he regards with such utter contempt, and from which he turns away with disgust as from a pollution and a curse.

The Buddhists have put forth the same pretensiens in reference to Pali, that the Brahmans have done as to Sanskrit. It is the language in which their sacred books, the Pitakas, are written, and is sometimes called Mágadhi. The word Pali is unknown on the continent of India. It was the vernacular of the country in which Buddha lived;

* Max Müller, Lectures on the Science of Language.

and is thus spoken of by the grammarian Kachcháyano: "There is a language which is the root (of all languages); men and brahmans spoke it at the commencement of the kalpa, who never before uttered a human accent, and even the supreme Buddhas spoke it: it is Mágadhi."* The same statement is made in the Patisambhidá Atuwáwa, and the following extract is taken from the Wibhanga Atuwáwa: "Parents place their children when young either on a cot or a chair and speak different things, or perform different actions. Their words are thus distinctly fixed by their children (on their minds), thinking that such was said by him, and such by the other; and in process of time they learn the entire language. If a child born of a Damila mother and an Andhaka father should hear his mother speak first, he would speak the Damila language; but if he should hear his father first, he would speak the Andhaka. If however he should not hear either of them, he would speak the Mágadhi. If, again, a person in an uninhabited forest in which no speech (is heard) should intuitively attempt to articulate words, he would speak the very Mágadhi. It predominates in all regions, such as hell, the animal kingdom, the petta sphere, the human world; and the world of the devas. The remaining eighteen languages, Kiratha, Andhaka, Yonaka, Damila, etc., undergo changes, but not the Mágadhi, which alone is stationary, as it is said to be the language of Brahman and Aryas. Even Buddha who rendered his tepitaka words into doctrines, did so by means of the very Mágadhi; and why? Because by doing so it was easy to acquire their

* Appendix, Note A.

true significations. Moreover, the sense of the words of Buddha which are rendered into doctrines by means of the Mágadhi language, is conceived in hundreds and thousands of ways by those who have attained the Patisambhidá, so soon as they reach the ear, or the instant the ear comes in contact with them: but discourses rendered into other languages are acquired with difficulty."*

It is said, moreover, that all the birds of the air and the beasts of the forest speak the same language; but as they cannot learn letters, they speak it indistinctly, and in a manner unintelligible to men. A similar thought to the first has been entertained by many nations in behalf of their own tongue, and even in modern times experiments have been tried to find out the primitive language, but without any satisfactory result; for if it were possible to isolate children entirely, they would not speak at all, or use a single articulate sound; as may be seen in the case of deaf mutes, many of whom have all the organs of speech perfectly developed, but as they never heard a sound, they are not able, except in cases where they are specially instructed, and with great labour, to make one, unless it be a murmur or a scream. There are tales among all nations about persons who could understand the language of bird and beast, that are popular in the nursery, but are not repeated by men. The statement is not correct that the Mágadhi language has been "stationary," as there is a wide difference between the style of the text of the Pitakas and that of the Commentary. The Buddhist must, therefore, submit to

* Alwis's Lectures on Buddhism, p. 55.

the same humiliation as the Brahman, and confess that the language of his sacred books is derived, and not original; and that it comes to us from the same source as the dialects spoken by the nations of Europe. This conclusion derives additional confirmation from the statements on page 19. There is thus another reason why the Buddhist should distrust the Atuwáwas, which he has been taught to revere as the word of the unerring; inasmuch as they are proved to contain statements that are not true.

## 6. THE VEDAS.

As a solace in the midst of his trouble, "the twice-born" Brahman may resolve to turn toward the volume of the holy Veda, and comfort himself with the thought that here he still remains supreme. Of this divine emanation he is the sole guardian. Of the eternal word he is the one authorized keeper. At intervals in the great ages of the past, its existence has been hid in the mind of the deity; but it is now revealed to him, that he may live as a god among men, and then return to be absorbed in the infinite Paramátma, of which he now forms a part. But even here the Brahman is followed by his stern and unrelenting antagonist—Research. The orientalist can now stand on the highest step of his temple, regardless of both idol and priest, and proclaim to the millions of India, with an energy of voice that the clang of the cymbal, the blast of the chanque, the roll of the tomtom, the shouts of the people, and all the other appliances brought to his rescue by his numerous retainers, cannot overpower, that the older Vedas pay no respect whatever to the Brahman; that they know nothing, even by name, of the gods he teaches men to worship; and that the rishis who composed their most sacred portions, acknowledge themselves to have been the same as other men in their ignorance and weakness. As the Brahman and the Buddhist are alike in their veneration for the rishis, the removal of the errors so long prevalent, respecting these ancient sages, will not be without some importance and significance in this island, as well as upon the continent.

The Vedas, when referred to in Pali works, are the same, in name and number, as those of Sanskrit authors: Rich, Yajush, Sáman, and Atharvána; but Buddha, when he referred to them, spoke of the Ti-weda. The Buddhists regard the Atharvána as of less authority than the other Vedas. They believe that they originally contained pure and unmixed truth, when uttered by Maha Brahma, but that they have been corrupted by the Brahmans to suit their own purposes, and are not now to be relied upon as a divine revelation. This thought would be worthy of further notice, were it possible to test its value; but the memories of dead men cannot be called as witnesses, and we have no written documents as our guide. Each Veda consists of two parts: 1. The Mantras, or Hymns, in which the gods are praised, and their assistance is invoked. 2. The Brahmanas, illustrative and explanatory of the Mantras, with the Upanishads, in which expression is given to ideas of a more spiritual and mystical character. The Mantras constitute the original and most essential part of the Veda. The Hymns are collected together in portions called Sanhitas, which from the archaic style in which they are written, are supposed to be the oldest part of the Veda. There are copies of the Vedas in several of the libraries of Europe, and portions of them have been translated into English, French, German, and Russian. By Max Müller the Vedic literature is divided into four periods: 1. The Chhandas period, in which the first, the oldest hymns of the Rig Veda were written, extending from 1200 to 1000 B.C. 2. The Mantra period, in which the more recent Vedic hymns were composed; lasting from 1000 to 800 B.C. 3. Then came the Brahmana period, during which the chief theological and liturgical tracts bearing this title were composed; from 800 to 600 B.C. It was at the end of this interval that Gótama Buddha appeared, according to the chronology of the Singhalese. The authors of this period appeal to various preceding unwritten authorities; and present the clearest proof that "the spirit of the ancient Vedic poetry, and the purport of the original Vedic sacrifices, were both beyond their comprehension." 4. The Sutra, or most modern period, extended from 600 to 200 B.C., in which the ceremonial precepts were reduced to a systematic form. There can be no absolute certainty as to these dates; but they are not adopted without reason, or from mere conjecture. There are no mile-stones in Vedic literature; but by the change in the character of the scenery that presents itself, we can have some idea of the distance we have travelled. Not unfrequently, an author refers to a previous author. There are differences in construction and metre. The gradual development of a great system can be traced, from the figurative expression, through the literal interpretation, to the accomplished fact and the established custom. There is a perceptible change in manners and usages, and the introduction of new modes of thought, new restrictions, new laws, new ceremonies, and new gods. The influence of the ascetic principle, at first scarcely seen, secures to itself from age to age, a position of greater prominence. The further we go from the present, the fewer are the personages introduced, whether divine or human, and there is a greater simplicity and unity, both in liturgy and rite. By thus sounding the stream of the past, and examining the sand and shells that the plummet brings up from the depths of other ages, the learned have criteria to guide them in the judgment they form of the age in which the Vedic books were composed.

The worship prescribed in the earlier Vedas comprehends prayers, praises, and offerings; the latter consisting principally of clarified butter poured on fire, and the intoxicating juice of the Soma fruit. There is no reference in them to the Trimúrtti, Brahma, Vishnu, and Siva; to Durga, Káli, or Ráma; or to any other of the gods that are at present the most popular in India.* The principal deities are Agni and Indra: Agni, at once fire and the god of fire, is now regarded with indifference, and seldom worshipped. Indra is a personification of the firmament as sending rain, and is now ridiculed by the Brahman, although under the name of Sekra, he is still honoured by the Buddhists.

* Wilson, Rig-Veda Sanhita.

In the most ancient hymns the unity of God is acknowledged; just as we should infer it would be from the still unshaken Pentateuch. We there find that up to the time of the Exodus, there were men who, apart from the teachings of Israel, worshipped the one true God, or believed in his existence and might.* The path by which man wandered away from primitive truth to polytheism and idolatry can be seen most clearly in the literature of the Hindus. In the earliest of their forms of invocation, germs of error may be traced. The elements, in these regions seen in their most sublime and terrific modes of working, are personified. There is no mention of the image of any god, nor is there any allusion to any form of idol worship, and there is no formal temple; but heaven is regarded as the father of the universe, and earth the mother. The stars are the radiant flock, held in captivity by the god of storms, until set free by the swift arrows of the god of lightning. The god of thunder has the wind as his watch-dog, chasing the clouds as they career along the sky, or acting as a faithful guide to lead the spirits of the good to the realms above, beyond the broad river, or the atmosphere, that separates the two worlds. All the great changes that take place around us are described in mystical terms; and wherever there is movement there is supposed to be the presence of divinity.

The social life of the Vedic songs is more in accordance with western usage. The family is instituted, and the dwelling fixed. The government is patriarchal. Every man is priest in his own house, and his own hand kindles

* Exod. xviii. 9. Num. xxii. 8.

the sacred fire. Marriage is monogamic. Woman is had in honour, and is a joint ruler, and a joint worshipper with her husband. She is seen to move freely in the market, at the well, in the place of worship, and in the palace. There then succeeds an era of greater formality and exclusiveness. Men with pleasant voices are employed to chant the hymns; the householder resigns his place of privilege; and the hierophant pretending to sanctity is entreated to present the sacrifice. These begin to form a separate class, and to claim immunities. Their pretensions are resisted; but they finally triumph, and the perfected Brahman appears, claiming to be more than saint in purity, and more than king in power.

The opinions entertained by the Hindus on the origin of the Vedas are varied and contradictory. There are no fewer than twelve different deliverances on this subject. In the following analysis the supposed source is given, and then the authority upon which the statement is made, from some sacred book, but not Vedic. 1. *The elements.* "Prajápati brooded over the three deities (fire, air, and the sun), and from them, so brooded over, he drew forth their essences—from fire the Rig Veda, from air the Yajush, and from the sun the Sáma verses." Chándogya Upanishad. 2. *The mouth of Brahma, at the creation.* "Once the Vedas sprang from the four-faced creator, as he was meditating, How shall I create the aggregate worlds as before? He formed from his eastern and other mouths the Vedas called Rich, Yajush, Sáman and Atharvan, together with praise, sacrifice, hymns, and expiation." Bhágavat Purána, iii. 12. 3. *The breath of Brahma.*

"As from a fire made of moist wood various modifications of smoke proceed, so is the breathing of this great Being the Rig Veda, the Yajush, the Sama, the Atharvan, the Itihásas, Puránas, science, the Upanishads, slókas, aphorisms, comments of different kinds—all these are his breathings." Vrihad Aranyaka Upanishad. 4. *The creative power of Brahma.* "In order to the accomplishment of sacrifice, he formed the Vedas: with these the Sádhyás worshipped the gods, as we have heard." Harivansa, v. 47. "The god fashioned the Rig Veda, with the Yajush, from his eyes, the Sáma Veda from the tip of his tongue, and the Atharvan from his head. These Vedas, as soon as they are born, find a body. Hence they obtain their character of Vedas because they *find* (vindanti) that abode." Harivansa, v. 11. 665. 5. *Sarasvati.* "Behold Sárasvati, as the mother of the Vedas!" Mahábhárata, v. 12, 920. 6. *The mystical rite Purush.* "From the universal sacrifice were produced the hymns called Rich and Sáman, the metres, and the Yajush." Purusha Sukta. 7. *Time.* "From time the Rich verses sprang; the Yajush sprang from time." Manu, xii. 49. 8. *From the residue of the sacrifice.* "The Rich and Sáman verses sprang from the remainder of the sacrifice, uchchhista." Atharva Veda, xi. 7.' 9. *The pure principle.* "The Veda constitutes the second division of the sattva-guna, Brahma being one of the first." Manu, xii. 49. 10. *Eternity.* "The Sruti derived from Brahma is eternal; these, O Brahman, are only its modifications." Vishnu Purána, Wilson's Trans. p. 285. 11. *Vishnu.* "He is composed of the Rich, of the Sáman, of the Yajush; he is the soul.

. . . . Formed of the Veda he is divided; he forms the Veda and its branches into many divisions. Framer of the branches, Sakhás, he is also their entirety, the infinite lord, whose essence is knowledge." Vishnu Purána, p. 274. 12. *Emanation.* "The Veda was not the result of effort proceeding from the conscious intelligence of any individual."

The confusion arising from the differences between one author and another is increased by the contradictions in the writings of the same author. "He who comprehends," says Manu, "the essential meaning of the Veda, in whatever order of life he may be, is prepared for absorption in Brahma, even when abiding in this lower world." This virtue is said to extend to all the Vedas. "Just as a clod thrown into the lake is dissolved, when it touches the water, so does all sin perish in the triple Veda." Yet in another place he says, "The Sáma Veda has the pitris (sprites) for its divinities, wherefore its sound is impure." In another place he asserts the impurity of this Veda, for another reason.*

By another class of writers, all of whom are regarded as orthodox, the Vedas are placed on a level with other works, or degraded below them. "First of all the Sastras, the Purána was uttered by Brahma. Subsequently the Vedas issued from his mouths." Váyu Purána, i. 56. One Purána speaks of "the errors of the Vedas," and in an Upanishad they are designated as "the inferior science," in contrast to "the superior science," the knowledge of the soul. There are other authors and schools that reject

* Muir's Sanskrit Texts: Part iii.

one Veda and not another, or parts of Vedas; and others who say that "there was formerly only one Veda, one fire, and one cast." There have been long controversies, carried on with much ingenuity, about sound, originating in the question whether the Veda is eternal or a product; reminding us, by their inconclusiveness, of one of their own sayings, that "however much a man may try, he cannot jump on to his own shoulders."

## 7. THE RISHIS OF THE BRAHMANS.

A far more important enquiry than any involved in this useless logomachy is, What did the rishis, the authors, or seers, or proclaimers, of these ancient hymns say of themselves? Do they claim for themselves the mighty and mystic powers that have been attributed to them in modern ages, and that cause myriads, even in our own day, to utter their names with reverence and awe? Now we may venture to affirm that neither eastern nor western student was prepared for the discoveries that have been made respecting them, from their own productions. I have sometimes been ready to express my regret that so much profound learning has been expended, and so much money, in the preparing and printing of Vedic texts, by different governments and societies; but when I see the use made of them by such men as Dr. Muir, and learn the wonderful results that have arisen from the quest into their interminable mazes, whereby revelations have been made, most helpful to the missionary and the philanthropist, that might otherwise have remained hid for further ages—I am more than recónciled to both care and cost.

To the following important extracts, I ask the attention of my island friends, and as there are many of them who will understand the original, I insert the Sanskrit text, as well as the translation.*

The rishis describe *themselves* as the composers of the hymns, as will be seen from the following passages.†

1. Passages in which the word kri, *to make*, is applied to the composition of the hymns.

"Ayám deváya janmane stomo viprebhir ásayá akári ratnadhátamah. This hymn, conferring wealth, has been *made* to the divine race, by the sages, with their mouth."‡ 1. 20. 1.

"Eved Indráya vrishabháya vrishne brahma akarma Bhriyavo na ratham. . . Akári te harivo brahma navyam dhiyá syáma rathyah sadásáh. Thus have we *made* a prayer for Indra, the productive, the vigorous, as the Bhrigus (fashioned) a car. . . . A new prayer has been *made* for thee, O lord of steeds. May we through our hymns (or rite) become possessed of chariots and perpetual wealth." iv. 16, 20.

* I know little of Sanskrit, except as the parent of Singhalese; and I am therefore indebted to other writers for nearly all the information I present about the Brahman and his literature; the only exception being in those cases in which illustrative reference is made to Buddhism, or extracts are made from native books.

† Yet Max Müller, one of our great authorities upon these subjects, says; "In the most ancient (Sanskrit) literature, the idea even of authorship is excluded. Works are spoken of as revealed to and communicated by certain sages, but not as composed by them." Ancient Sanskrit Literature, 523.

‡ "With their own mouth." Wilson.

2. Passages in which the word tax, *to fashion or fabricate*, is applied to the composition of the hymns.

"Esha vah stomo Maruto namasván hridá tashto manása dháyi deváh. This reverential hymn, O divine Maruts, *fashioned* by the heart, has been presented by the mind." i. 130, 6.

"Etam te stomam tuvi-játa vipro ratham na dhirah svapá ataxam. I, a sage, have *fabricated* this hymn for thee, O powerful (deity) as a skilful workman fashions a car." v. 29. 15.

3. Texts in which the hymns are spoken of as being *generated* by the rishis.

"Suvriktim Indráya brahma janayanta viprâh. The sages *generated* a pure hymn and a prayer for Indra." vii. 31, 11.

"Imá Agne matayas tubhyam játáh gobhir asvair abhi grinanti rádhah. These hymns, Agni, *generated* for thee, supplicate wealth with cows and horses." x. 7. 2.

These extracts are selected from several hundreds of a similar description, collected by the care of Dr. Muir. Further extracts, from Professor Wilson's translation of the same Veda, will throw additional light on the character of the rishis.

Thus they pray :

"May he (Indra) be to us for the attainment of our objects; may he be to us for the acquirement of riches; may he be to us for the acquisition of knowledge: may he come to us with food." Súkta, ii. 3. "May the Maruts, born from the brilliant lightning, everywhere preserve us and make us happy." xxiii. 12. "Inasmuch as all people commit errors, so do we, divine Varuna, daily disfigure thy worship by imperfections: make us not the objects of death." xxv. 2. "Destroy every one that reviles us; slay every one that does us injury: Indra, of boundless wealth, enrich us with thousands of excellent cows and horses." xxix. 7. "Come, let us repair to Indra (to recover our stolen cattle), for he, devoid of malice, exhilarates our minds; thereupon he will bestow upon us perfect knowledge of this wealth (which consists) of kine." xxxiii. 1. "Thrice, Aswins, visit our dwelling and the man who is well disposed towards us; thrice repair to him who deserves your protection, and instruct us in threefold knowledge: thrice grant us gratifying (rewards); thrice shower upon us food, as (Indra) pours down rain." xxxiv. 4. "Agni, with the burning rays, destroy entirely our foes, who make no gifts, as (potters' ware) with a club; let not one who is inimical to us, nor the man who attacks us with sharp weapons, prevail against us." xxxvi. 16. "Discriminate between the Aryas and they who are Dasyus; restraining those who perform no religious rites, compel them to submit to the performer of sacrifices." li. 8. "Agni confer excellence upon our valued cattle, and make all men bring us acceptable tribute." lxx. 5. "May thy opulent worshippers, Agni, obtain (abundant) food; may the learned (who praise thee) and offer thee (oblations) acquire long life; may we gain in battles booty from our foes, presenting to the gods their portion for (the acquisition of) renown." lxxiii. 5. "Defended, Agni, by thee, may we destroy the horses (of our enemies) by (our) horses, the men by (our) men, the sons by (our) sons, and may our sons, learned, and inheritors of ancestral wealth, live for a hundred winters." lxxiii. 9. "Thou, lord of all, knowest what are the riches of those men who make no offerings: bring their wealth to us." lxxxi. 9. "The Soma juice has been expressed, Indra, for thee; potent humbler (of thy foes), approach; may vigour fill thee (by the potation), as the sun fills the firmament with his rays." lxxxiv. 1. "Dissipate the concealing darkness: drive away every devouring (foe); show us the light we long for." lxxxvi. 10. "Come into our presence; they have called thee, fond of the Soma juice; it is prepared; drink of it for thine exhilaration; vast of limb, distend thy stomach, and, when invoked, hear us, as a father (listens to the words of his sons)." civ. 9. "Kutsa, the Rishi, thrown into a well, has invoked to his succour, Indra, the slayer of enemies." cvi. 6. "Aswins, you raised up, like Soma, in a ladle, Rebha, who for ten nights and nine days had lain (in a well), bound with tight cords, wounded, immersed, and suffering distress from the water.* Thus, Aswins, have I declared your exploits: may I become the master (of this place), having abundant cattle, and a numerous progeny, and retaining my sight, enjoy a long life: may I enter into old age, as (a master enters) his house." cxvi. 24, 25.

In the later hymns of the Sanhita, there is a continuance of the same form of supplication, and the request is still

* Rebha and Vandana (also cast into a well) are said to have been rishis. "In these and similar instances, we may possibly have allusions to the dangers undergone by some of the first teachers of Hinduism among the people whom they sought to civilise." Professor Wilson. But it seems much more likely that it was on account of some cattle raid.

presented for "food, strength, and long life." Allusions to the town and its customs, and to the cultivated field, are more frequent; but the cow and the horse are still the most prominent objects before the worshipper, and he asks for protection "from dogs and wolves." Now, as in former instances, when the rishis ask for anything, they ask it for themselves. They are not intercessors, vicariously pleading with the gods. "Conquer for *us*; fight for *us*." cxxxii. 4. "May *we* acquire riches, in the strife of heroes." clvii. 2. "May *we* overcome *our* mighty and formidable foes." clxxviii. 5. "Let *us*, through thy favour, overwhelm all our foes, like torrents of water." II. vii. 3.

As we read these extracts, the impression is made upon our minds, that they are very like the revel-songs of some band of moss-troopers, gone forth to levy black-mail; and perhaps this thought is not very far from the truth. As the Aryans descended from the mighty hills where they must for some time have lingered, and spread desolation in the plains below, nothing could be more natural than many of the sentiments and wishes here expressed. They were a young nation, full of life and hope, migrating to another land, that they might seek a richer inheritance than that of their fathers, and were opposed in their progress by powerful enemies. The rishis were undoubtedly, in some cases at least, warriors as well as makers of songs; the hand red with blood might mix the intoxicating soma; and we can imagine some of their hymns sung by the whole clan immediately previous to an attack upon the Dásyas, rich in flocks and herds, or after some successful foray, when the low of the stolen kine would mingle with the voice of praise to the power that had given them their prey. We have here more than enough to convince us that the framers of the Vedas were ordinary men, making no pretension to the wonderful powers with which they have been invested by the Brahmans. The Vedas are a purely human production; the confessions and invocations of the rishis themselves being our warrant for this conclusion. The religious element is scarcely apparent, in many of the Sanhitas; for prey, and not purity, the request is presented. There are occasionally hymns that rise above this low estimate of rishi piety, in which are passages of great poetic beauty. With some notion, however vague, of the unity of God, they address the elements as his agents or representatives. They see these elements, now for the first time in their tropical energy; and intense emotion is stirred within their souls, as they appeal to the gleaming sun, the rapid lightning, and the dark storm-cloud, lying low in the sky from the weight of the abundant treasure it contains, with which it is ready to fill the exhausted well and fertilize the parched wilderness.

The claim set up by the Brahmans for the supernatural inspiration of the rishis cannot be maintained. We speak, in common phrase, of the inspiration of the poet. All ages and nations have done the same. The poets themselves are accustomed, like Milton, to ask light and aid from heaven.

> "And chiefly, Thou, O Spirit, that dost prefer
> Before all temples, the upright heart and pure,
> Instruct me. . . . . . .
> . . . . . . . . What in me is dark,
> Illumine; what is low raise and support."

But we do not, on that account, approach the poet as we should one whom we thought was in the possession of super-human intelligence. Many of our rhymers are no more sorcerers than the dullest prose writer that ever wrote on palm-leaf or paper. Just in the same way, the rishi of the Brahman, looked at as a hymn-maker, is a harmless kind of being, respectable, sometimes religious, and somewhat austere, asking for divine guidance almost in the very words his brother poets have used in all time, for the same purpose; and claiming for himself neither irresistible power, like the wicked Mára, nor unerring intuition, like the teacher Buddha. There is thus another race of imaginary beings swept away, with the genii and ghouls of our childhood, from the dreamland that has been the dread of many generations; and the whole world will soon learn that man has been his own greatest enemy, and that he has suffered the more, the further he has wandered away from the voice of the God who loves him.

Nearly the whole of the Himalayan mass of later Sanskrit lore will have to be set aside as incredible. It is the result of wilful perversion and pretence; it tells of events that could never, by any possibility, have happened, and of beings that could never, by any possibility, have lived. It will always be interesting, as the record of man's wondrous power of creativeness, within a certain limit, and of his ability to fascinate and mislead those whom he seeks to bind and blind; but when the genius of history shall appear in her full majesty, she will allow no stately temple to the kings of the Brahman, and to his warriors no victor's crown.

We have seen what the first and the greatest of the rishis were, on the testimony of their own hymns. The character of these men, as it appears in the literature of more recent periods, is so entirely different to that which is recorded in the most ancient of the Sanhitas of the Rig Veda, that we can scarcely bring ourselves to think that the ascetic Brahman, to whom the world, and all within it, is an illusion, can be the representative, by religious descent, of the Aryans, who loved to drink the intoxicating soma, and rode on the wild horse, and lifted cattle.* By degrees, as further research is made in Vedic revelation, we shall be able to trace more clearly the manner in which this great change was effected. But when the Aryans ceased to be emigrant and nomadic; when municipal institutions had to be formed, and property protected; when a life of activity and warfare had to be succeeded by one of inertness and quiet; when those whose forefathers had dwelt amidst the everlasting snows had to yield to the enervating effects of a warm climate—it is reasonable to suppose that a new state of things would arise, which would have a correlative effect upon the race.

## 8. THE RAHATS AND RISHIS OF THE BUDDHISTS.

The Buddhists have been equally deceived with their antagonists, the Brahmans, in the estimate they have formed of the character of the rishis. The power they

* We see the modern disregard of the Vedas, in the fact that recently there was not a complete copy of these sacred works in the possession of any of the Brahmans of Calcutta, nor was there any one who had read them.

atrribute to these venerated sages is scarcely inferior to that of the rahats, which we shall have to notice at greater length by and bye. By Singhalese authors they are represented as being possessed of super-human attributes. In seeking to obtain nirwána, it is a great advantage to have been a rishi in a former birth. The rishi can tell, by his own intuitive knowledge, the nature of all diseases, and prescribe for them an infallible remedy. When he wishes for mangoes, or any other fruit, he can go through the air and take them. He can comprehend space. He can assume any form. He can destroy fifty cities, if he so wills it. He can tell how many drops there are in the ocean, and number the living creatures that inhabit it; and can tell how many spans there are in the sky, and how many atoms in Maha Meru, though it is nearly a million of miles high. He can dry up the sea, though in one place it is eight hundred and forty thousand miles deep. He can hide the earth with the tip of his finger, and shake the whole of the Himalayan forest, with all its mountains, with as much ease as if it were a ball of thread.

When the power of the rishis is presented as a comparison, which is a common practice with native authors, it is spoken of, if possible, in still more extravagant terms. The gods are sometimes envious of the elevated position to which they attain, and fearing lest they themselves should be superseded, and thereby lose their high and privileged positions, they resort to the meanest and most unwarranted schemes to accomplish their downfall. The throne of Sekra (Indra) having become warm, he knew thereby that his celestial supremacy was in danger; and when looking to see whence it proceeded, he discovered that it came from the meritorious observance of the precepts by the rishi Lómasa Kásyapa. To induce the sage to take life, by slaying the animals at a sacrifice, and thus commit evil, the déwa persuaded the king to call him to the performance of this rite, by sending his daughter to the forest in which he lived. Spell-bound by the beauty of the princess, he consented to accompany her to the city for this purpose; but when about to uplift the sacrificial knife, the plaintive cry of the animals brought him to his senses, and he returned at once to the forest, thereby preserving his great merit still intact.

The Vedas are declared by Buddha, as previously stated, to have been corrupted by the Brahmans. The aged brahman, Dróna,—who, at the sage's cremation, secreted one of his bones as a relic, in his hair, but was afterwards deprived of it by the déwas,—on visiting the teacher of the three worlds, asked him whether, if an aged Brahman were to visit him, he would rise and offer him a seat. Buddha replied that he could not do so, as it would be highly improper; and asked Dróna if he regarded himself as a true Brahman. The reply that he made was: "If one who is descended from a father and mother that are both of pure race, who can trace his descent as equally pure through seven generations, and knows the Veda perfectly, is to be regarded as a Brahman, then am I one." But Buddha denied that the Brahmans were then in the possession of the real Veda. He said that it was given in the time of Kásyapa (a former supreme Buddha) to certain rishis, who, by the practice of severe austerities, had acquired the power of seeing with divine eyes. They were Attako, Wámako, Wámadewo, Wessámitto, Yamataggi, Angiraso, Bháraddwájo, Wásetto, Kassapo, and Bhagu. The Vedas that were revealed to these rishis were subsequently altered by the Brahmans, so that they are now made to defend the sacrifice of animals, and to oppose the doctrines of Buddha. It was on account of this departure from the truth, that Buddha refused to pay them any respect.*

At another time, when Buddha resided at Jétawana, there were several aged Brahmans of the Maha Sála Kula, who came to visit him. (To belong to this kula, a Kshatriya must possess 100 kótis of kahapanas, and spend daily 20 amunams of treasure; a Brahman 80 kótis, and spend 10 amunams; and a Grahapati 40 kótis, and spend 5 amunams).† These Brahmans resided in Kosol, and were senile and decrepit, as they had lived in the reigns of several kings. They sat respectfully on one side, and said to Buddha, "Do the present Brahmans follow the same rules, practise the same rites, as those in more ancient times?" He replied, "No." They then requested, that if it were not inconvenient, he would be pleased to declare to them the former Brahmana Dharmma. He then proceeded: There were formerly rishis, men who had subdued all passion by the keeping of the síla precepts

* Anguttara Nikáya: Panchaka Nipáta.

† It is to be understood throughout, that when, in quoting from the Pitakas, words appear within parentheses, they are taken from the Commentary, and not from the Text.

and the leading of a pure life. They had no cattle, no gold (not even as much as four massas, each of which is of the weight of six mára seeds) and no grain. Their riches and possessions consisted in the study of the Veda, and their treasure was a life free from all evil. On this account they gained the respect of the people, who had always alms ready for them at their doors. They suffered no kind of annoyance or persecution, and no one sent them away empty when they approached the dwelling. Some of them remained continent until 48 years of age. They did not then, like others, seek to purchase their wives, but went to the door of some one of their own caste, and said to the inmates, "I have remained chaste 48 years; if you have a virgin daughter, let her be given to me." The daughter, if they have one, is brought to the door, in bridal array, water is poured on the hands of the Brahman and his bride (as the marriage rite), and the parents say, "This is our daughter, but we give her to you, that she may become your wife, and be by you supported." But why do these Brahmans, after refraining from marriage so long, then seek a wife? It is from a needless apprehension. They suppose that if they have no son, the race will become extinct, and that on this account they will have to suffer in hell. (There are four kinds of beings who fear when there is no danger. 1. Worms, that fear to eat much, lest they should exhaust the earth. 2. The bird kirala, the blue jay, that hatches its eggs with its feet upwards, that if the sky should fall, it may be ready to support it. 3. The kos lihiniyá, the curlew, that treads with all gentleness, lest it should shake the earth. 4. The

Brahman, that seeks a wife lest his race should become extinct.)

The Brahmans, for a time, continued to do right, and received in alms rice, seats, clothes, and oil, though they did not ask for them. The animals that were given they did not kill; but they procured useful medicaments from the cows, regarding them as friends and relatives, whose products give strength, beauty and health. The Brahmans, (not killing animals in sacrifice) had soft bodies, of a golden colour, and great prosperity. Through their abstinence from evil, other beings enjoyed a similar state of happiness and repose. But by degrees they saw and coveted the wealth of kings, as well as females richly arrayed, chariots drawn by horses of the Ajanya breed (that knew the mind of their owners, and took them whither they willed to go, without any guidance) and elegant buildings. In this way their minds became corrupted. They resolved to ask kings to make animal sacrifices. By this means the passions of the Brahmans became increased. They thought that if the products of the cow were so good, the flesh of the cow must be much better. The king Okkáka, at their instance, instituted a festival of sacrifice. When the animals were assembled, the king slew the first with his own sword, gashing them, and pulling them cruelly by the horns, though previously to this time they had remained free from injury or molestation. The Brahmans then slew the rest. Because of this butchery, the déwas and asurs cried out, "There is unrighteousness, unrighteousness, among men;" (so loudly that all over the world it was heard). Prior to this period, there were only three kinds of diseases among men; carnality, hunger, and decay. There are now 98, of various kinds. The Vaisyas and Sudras are opposed to each other. The Kshatriyas are at war among themselves. Husband and wife are at variance. And all castes mingle together in lewdness and vice. The Brahmans, when they had heard this discourse of Buddha, embraced his religion, and said they would become upásaka devotees to the end of their lives.*

It is evident, from these statements, that Buddha was ignorant of the former condition of the world; that he knew nothing about the character and circumstances of the ancient rishis; and that he spoke from imagination alone, and not with the authority of truth. Nearly every hymn of the Rig Veda contradicts his statements; and the whole array of tradition, legend, and history is opposed to his theory of the origin of cruelty and crime among men. It may be said, that if the Vedas have been corrupted, though the statements of Buddha are contrary to them, those statements are not thereby invalidated. But, how was it possible to alter the Vedas to this extent? It could not be done after they were committed to writing, and before this the Brahmans who preserved them were scattered over a country a thousand miles in breadth. Long before the time of Buddha there were rival sects and schools among the Brahmans, who would watch each other's proceedings with all jealousy, and render it impossible for them to concert any scheme to alter, in any

* Bráhmana Dhammika Suttanta.

degree, the word that they regarded as eternal and the breath of the supreme Brahm.

In the mistakes and misrepresentations of many of the Brahmans, who were contemporaries of Gotama, as to the power of the rishis, the sacred books of Buddhism partake to an equal extent. They tell us, that his father, Suddhódana, had a rishi friend, Káladèwala. After breakfast this aged sage was accustomed to visit one of the celestial worlds, and watch the ways of the déwas; and he there learnt that a supreme Buddha was about to appear among men. He could see backward 40 kalpas, and forward the same period, and know the events in each.

The following narrative is ascribed to Buddha himself, and appears in the Játakattha-kathá. There was a priest, Pindóla Bháraddwája, who went to the garden of the king of Udeni, to spend the day in retirement. The king, on the same day, went to the same garden, attended by a retinue of women, upon the lap of one of whom he placed his head, and fell asleep. When the other woman saw that the king was no longer listening to them, they put down their instruments of music and went to walk in the garden. On seeing the priest, they worshipped him, and he preached to them the bana. When the king awoke, he was annoyed that the other women had left him; and on discovering the priest, he resolved that he would tease him, by causing red ants to sting him. But Pindóla Bháraddwája rose up into the air, and after giving the king some good advice, went through the air to Jétawana, and alighted near the door of Buddha's residence, who asked why he had come; and the priest repeated to him the whole story. On hearing it, Buddha said that this was not the only occasion when he had been thus treated, and he then declared to him the Mátanga Játaka.

In a former age, when Brahmadatta was king of Benares, there was a low caste chandála, by name Mátanga, but on account of his great wisdom he was called Mátanga Pandita. He was a Bhodisat (the being who is afterwards to become a supreme Buddha). In the same city was a nobleman who had a daughter, Ditthamangaliká, who twice in the month, properly attended, resorted to one of the gardens for pleasure. On one occasion, when Mátanga was approaching the city, the young lady was emerging from the gate, accompanied by her maidens; and so on seeing them he stood on one side, lest they should be polluted by the presence of a low caste man. As she was looking through the curtains of her conveyance, she happened to see him, and asked her maidens what he was. They replied that he was a mean chandála. As she had never seen such a being before, she called for scented water, to wash her eyes, and commanded her retinue to return home. On hearing this, they insulted and beat Mátanga without mercy, as it was through him that they had lost their day's pleasure. When he came to his senses, and reflected on what had happened to him, he resolved that he would not rest, until he had obtained possession of Ditthamangaliká as his wife. At once he went and lay down opposite the doorway of her father's house, and when asked why he did so, he said that he had come to obtain the nobleman's daughter as his wife. His request was, of course, indignantly rejected; but there he remained six days, and on the seventh (to save the family from the still greater disgrace and inconvenience that would have come upon it if he had perished at their door),* she was brought and given to him; when she, respectfully, said she was willing to go to his village. But he replied that her attendants had beat him so cruelly that he could not rise, and that she must carry him on her back. She was obedient, and did as she was commanded. On the seventh day, without having had any intercourse with her meanwhile, he thought within himself, "I must enrich this maiden, by causing her to receive greater wealth and happiness than any other woman; but this cannot be unless I become a sramana priest." Then saying to her that he was going to the forest to provide the food they needed, and that she must not be uneasy until his return, he went away. On the seventh day after he had taken upon himself the obligations, and assumed the garb of a priest, he attained to samápatti (the completion of an ascetic rite that confers supernatural powers). He then returned to the village through the air. When his wife asked him why he had become a priest, he said she must inform the people of Benares, that on the seventh day from that time her husband would appear as Maha Brahma, and cleave the moon in two. On the day of the full moon he apppeared as he had said, illuminating by his brightness the whole of the city, 120 miles in extent. In the

* Had this misfortune occurred, the whole family would have lost caste for seven generations.

presence of the citizens, he caused the moon to cleave into two portions, and then descending went thrice round the city through the air.

On seeing this those who were worshippers of Maha Brahma went to the house of Mátanga, presented offerings of untold value, and ornamented his dwelling in the richest manner. He then made known to his wife, that through umbilical attrition alone she would have a son; that the water in which she bathed would be sought for with eagerness by the people, as it would free them from all disease and misfortune ever after; and that those who saw her would each offer to her a thousand (kahapanas). The followers of Maha Brahma provided for her a golden palanquin, and took her to the city, where they built for her a splendid pavilion; and as she there brought forth her son, he was called, in consequence, Mandabba. When grown up, he daily fed 16,000 Brahmans. But his father Mátanga, seeing by this means he was arriving at the wrong landing place (in his effort to obtain salvation) went through the air, and alighting at the place where the alms were distributed, took his seat on one side; but when Mandabba saw him, he commanded him to be off quickly, as there were no alms there for such as he. When the attendants were preparing to take him away, he rose up into the air, and after repeating other gáthá stanzas, said, "They who attempt anything against the rishis, are like men who attempt to scrape the rough rock with the finger nail, or to bite through hard iron with their teeth, or to swallow fire." After this Mátanga went through the air towards the east gate of the city, causing his footsteps to remain, as he went from place to place with the alms-bowl. The déwas of the city, enraged at the insult he had received, caused the head of Mandabba to be turned the wrong way on his shoulders, and the Brahmans to vomit, and then roll themselves on the ground, utterly disabled. When Ditthamangaliká heard of what had taken place, she went to enquire what was the cause; and when she had seen her son, his eyes white like those of a dead man, and his body stiff, she said that the sramana who had come to ask alms could be no one else but Mátanga, and resolved that she would go to him and ask pardon for her son. By his footsteps she discovered the place where he was. He was just finishing his meal, leaving a small portion of rice in the bowl. She poured water from a golden vessel, with which he washed his mouth, and then ejected it into the same vessel. When the mother asked pardon for Mandabba, the rishi said that the injury was not done by him; he had felt no anger when he was insulted, neither did he feel any anger then: it was the demons that had done it. "Your son," said he, "has studied the Vedas until he is intoxicated by them; but he is ignorant of that which is proper to be done, in order to produce the result at which he aims." She still pleaded in his behalf. He then said that he would give her a divine medicine; and that if she took half of the rice from the bowl, and put it into her son's mouth, and the other half into the mouth of the Brahmans, mixed with water (from the golden vessel), they would all recover. He also informed her how the persons were to be known who were proper to be the recipients of alms. The

Brahmans were revived, in the manner he had said; but as they had been recovered by eating the rice of a chandála, they were greatly ashamed, and went to live in the city of Mejjha.

There was a Brahman, Játimanta, who at that time resided near the river Wettawati, and was exceedingly proud of his high caste. To humble him, Mátanga went to reside near the same place, higher up the river. One day, after cleaning his teeth, he expressed a wish that the tooth-cleaner would fasten itself in the hair of the Brahman. He then threw it into the river, and as Játimanta was bathing at the time, it was caught in the tuft on the top of his head. Thinking it had come from some one of low caste he went up the river to see, and when he found out that it had come from Mátanga, he abused him as a mean, scurvy fellow, and told him to go and live lower down the river (that the same inconvenience might not occur again). On receiving this command, he went to reside lower down; but the thing took place again, only the tooth-cleaner this time went against the stream instead of down it. Again was Mátanga subjected to abuse; and the Brahman cursed him, and told him that if he did not depart, on the seventh day his head would split into seven pieces. Then the rishi, without any anger, resolved that he would remove his pride by a stratagem; and accordingly, on the seventh day he prevented the rising of the sun. When the people of the land came to Játimanta to entreat him to allow the light to shine, he said that he was not the cause of its being withheld; it was Mátanga. They then went to the rishi, who said that the sun might be released if Játimanta would humble himself at his feet. They therefore dragged the Brahman to the place where the rishi was; but even when he had worshipped him, Mátanga still refused to let the sun rise, because, if it rose the head of the Brahman would be split (as a punishment for the curse he had uttered). The people asked what, in such a case, was to be done; when he told them to bring clay, and therewith cover the head of Játimanta, and take him to the river up to his neck. This was done; the sun was then permitted to rise; and its rays caused the clay to cleave into seven portions (as a merciful mode of homogeneous revenge). The Brahman went down under the water; and his pride was thoroughly subdued. Then Mátanga seeing that the 16,000 Brahmans were residing in the city of Mejjha, went thither through the air, and taking his bowl proceeded to seek alms in the street where he had alighted; but when the Brahmans saw him, lest they themselves should come to nought through his influence, they persuaded the king to send messengers to put him to death. At the moment of their arrival he was eating the rice from his bowl; and as his mind was off its guard (and he was left on that account, without the protection that would otherwise have defended him from all evil) they were able to dispatch him with their swords. He was born in a Brahma-loka; but the déwas, to avenge his death, caused a shower of hot mud to fall, that destroyed the whole country. In that birth Buddha was Mátanga; and the king of Udeni was Mandabba.

In this translation, many of the minor details are omitted,

as the narrative is too long to be inserted at full length; but I have preserved nearly all that relates to supernatural endowment. One of three consequences must, of necessity, follow from the statements made in this extract: 1. The Atuwáwa Commentaries are not to be received as an authority; or, 2. This particular narrative is an interpolation; or, 3. Buddha did really say what is ascribed to him in this Játaka. The first alternative will scarcely be conceded, from the important consequences that would follow any attempt to invalidate the claim of the Commentaries to be regarded as of equal authority with the Text. It would be of no avail to allow the second, as the same statements are made in other parts of the sacred books. And if we receive the third, then the power attributed to the rishis is acknowledged, attested, and confirmed by Buddha. But that men with such powers ever lived in this world is against the entire testimony of all credible history; and in thus avowing his belief in their existence the Tathágato proclaims that he is under the control of like influences with other men. As in the present instance, he is led into mistake by the errors of his age. That the narrator of the Játaka believed in the power attributed to Mátanga, we have evidence in the following stanza, uttered as his own thought in reference to a previous stanza:

Having said this, Mátanga,
The rishi, truly powerful,
Went through the sky
Whilst the Brahmans were looking on.*

* Appendix, Note B.

## 9. THE CREDIBILITY OF THE HISTORICAL RECORDS OF THE WEST.

It is a question often asked by the natives of India, "Why are our books not to be believed just as much as yours are? It is only book against book; and we maintain that our books contain the truth, and that yours do not." Our reply is, that when we see the ola leaf and the printed page lie side by side, there may not be much apparent difference in the credibility of their evidence; but we must go back some two thousand years, and then the difference is not between book and book, but between book and memory, or between book and tradition.

In the Scriptures of the Hebrews, the art of writing is continually referred to, even in the earliest books. In Job we have reference to three different kinds of writing; in a book, on lead, and in the rock (Job xix. 23, 24). In Genesis v. 1, we read of "the book of the generations of Adam." In Exodus xvii. 14, Moses is commanded to "write this for a memorial in a book." The ten commandments were written upon tables of stone "with the finger of God" (Exod. xxxi. 18). Moses prays that if the people were not forgiven, his name might be blotted out of the book which God had written (Exodus xxxii. 32). In the book of Joshua, who lived about a thousand years before the time of Buddha, we read of Kirjath-sannah, or "the city of letters," and of Kirjath-sepher, "the city of books" (Josh. xv. 15, 49). In Psalm xl. 7, we have the passage, "Then said I, Lo, I come: in the volume of the book it is written of me." It is thus evident that writing must have been known to the Hebrews, and in common use, long before the time at which the most ancient of the Vedic Hymns were composed, if Max Müller's Chronology be taken as our guide. The Egyptians were probably acquainted with writing at as early a period as the Israelites. There is no reference to writing in the poems attributed to Homer; but the Greeks are supposed to have become acquainted with the art in the eighth century B.C., though the laws of Zaleucus, B.C. 664, are the first that are known to have been written. There is an inscription on a vase brought from Athens to England, "which cannot be later than 600 B.C." A public library was established at Athens, about 526 B.C., by Hippias and Hipparchus. The father of secular history, Herodotus, was born 484 B.C., only 59 years after the death of Buddha. From this time we have a regular succession of authors, belonging to various nations, without any long interval between one and the other, whose works have come down to our own time. The events of their own day are recorded by them, as well as those of preceding ages.*

From the statements and narratives of these successive authors, in many instances for a time contemporary, we have evidence that the men we revere among the Greeks and other nations, are not imaginary names, and that the acts attributed to them are real events. The proofs we possess of the genuineness and credibility of early western

* In the list of authors prefixed to Liddell and Scott's Greek-English Lexicon, there are the names of thirty-three persons who flourished before the beginning of the fifth century B.C., and of sixty-seven who flourished in that century.

literature will be seen, by referring to the circumstances under which the New Testament was originally penned, and has since been preserved. 1. There are quotations from it, and references to it, in various books, from the present time up to the time of the apostles. These quotations are so numerous, that "the whole of the New Testament might have been recovered therefrom, even if the originals had perished." 2. There are numerous manuscripts of ancient date now preserved in the libraries of Europe, the oldest of which is in the Vatican at Rome, and is supposed to have been written nearly 1500 years ago; and this would, no doubt, be copied from the oldest and best authenticated MS. within reach of the transcriber. 3. There are ancient versions in several languages, the oldest being the Syrian, which was translated either in the first century of the Christian era, or immediately afterwards. From these facts we can be certain that the New Testament was written immediately after the death of our Lord, to whom be "the kingdom, the power, and the glory, for ever and ever;" and that they have come down to us in their original form, without addition, or diminution, or corruption, beyond the usual mistakes of the most careful copyist. The same mode of argument can be used in relation to the age and uncorrupted preservation of other works, though it may not be applicable to them to the same extent as to the Scriptures. "The antiquity of the records of the Christian faith," says Isaac Taylor, "is substantiated by evidence, in a ten-fold proportion, more various, copious, and conclusive, than that which can be adduced in support of all other ancient works."

## 10. THE INCREDIBILITY OF THE LEGENDS OF INDIA.

When we turn to Brahmanical and Buddhist literature, we find that similar evidences of credibility are either entirely wanting, or are presented to a very small extent. Max Müller tells us, that in the 1017 hymns of the Rig-veda there is not a single reference to any kind of writing, nor in any work attributed to the Brahmana period; and in the Sutra period "all the evidence we can get would lead us to suppose that even then, though the art of writing began to be known, the whole literature of India was preserved by oral tradition only." "The pure Brahmans never speak of granthas, or books. They speak of their Veda, which means knowledge. They speak of their Sruti, which means what they have heard with their ears. They speak of Smriti, which means what their fathers have declared unto them. We meet with Brahmanas, i.e. the sayings of Brahmans; with Sutras, i.e. the strings of rules; with Vedangas, i.e. the members of the Veda, with Pravachanas, i.e. preachings; with Darshanas, i.e. demonstrations; but we never meet, with a book, or a volume, or a page." The names and divisions of the Pitakas are of a similar character; but there are in them several undoubted references to writing. "There were in Rajagaha seventeen children who were friends, Upáli being the principal one; his parents thought much of a profession for him, by which he might obtain a livelihood after their death. They thought of his being a scribe, but remembered that writing would tire his fingers."* It is supposed by some orientalists that the earliest reference to writing in India is in relation to Buddha, of whom it is said in the Lalita Vistara, that when the young prince had grown he was led to the writing-school, lipsála; but this is a comparatively modern work, of little authority, and in Ceylon known only by name.

The art of writing cannot have been known in Ceylon at a period much earlier than in India, as it was evidently introduced into the island after the language in present use was formed. The words tínta, ink, and páena, a pen, shew that the people were taught to write on paper by the Portuguese. When we examine the materials connected with their own mode of writing, the words we meet with are adapted words, or words formed by combination; as pota, a book, is from potta, plural potu, the bark of a tree, like the English word book, from a root that signifies primarily bark, the Latin liber, of the same meaning, and the Greek biblos, the inner bark of the papyrus; pus-kola, a blank leaf, is the strip of talipot leaf upon which they write; liyanawá, to write, meant originally to cut, to engrave, to make an incision; ul-katuwa, the stylus, is literally a sharp thorn; akura, a letter, is from akka, a mark; kundaliya, ෴ the sign that a sentence is finished, answering to our full stop, is a bracelet, or collar; and kiyawanawá, to read, is literally, to cause to say.

That the alphabet of Ceylon was derived from a western source, will be seen from a comparison of the following Phœnician and Singhalese letters:—

* Rev. D. J. Gogerly, Journ. Ceylon Branch Royal As. Soc. vol. ii. p. 124.

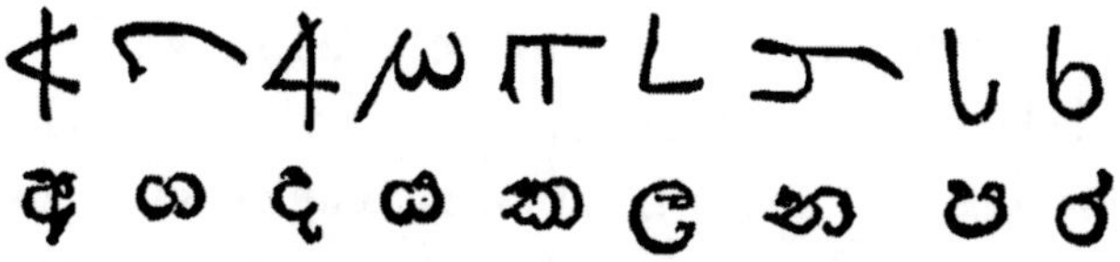

The outline of the shape, the elementary form, is the same in both the series. We might have introduced other letters, but these will be sufficient for our purpose; and if we had other specimens of the ancient alphabet from which to choose, it is probable that we should be able to trace the similarity further still. The letters g, y, ṅ, and r, are either reversed or turned upside down; but this is readily accounted for. The most ancient mode of writing, as we learn from inscriptions now extant, was from right to left, which was followed by the boustrophédon order, in alternate lines from right to left and from left to right, after the manner in which oxen plough, "in which the letters were reversed."* The Greek epsilon for instance is found in four different positions, ε ɜ ω ɷ. Among the primitive nations there appears to have been no fixed rule for the direction of their writing. The direction of the sculptured figures is said to be the guide in the monuments of Egypt. In the confusion arising from this practice, the permanent inversion of the above letters may have taken place. The Singhalese alphabet is arranged on the Nágari system, which in itself would indicate an Aryan origin: but the principal characters may have come to us from one source, and their arrangement and completion from another. I know too little about the character in which the ancient inscriptions on our rocks and other places are cut, to allow

* Newman, Kitto's Biblical Cyclopædia, art. Alphabet.

of my giving an opinion as to the relation which the two alphabets of Ceylon bear towards each other. The view I have taken of the origin of the Singhalese alphabet is not without interest, in reference to the supposition of Sir Emerson Tennent, that Galle is the Tarshish of the Scriptures, with which the Phœnicians traded. There are other Indian alphabets in which a similar resemblance can be traced, but not to the same extent. Mr. James Alwis, the editor and translator of the Sidath Sangarána, has noticed the affinity between the Tamil and Singhalese alphabets; and remarks that "the vowel signs with which the consonants are inflected agree in a wonderful manner." There may be some alliance, not in shape but in origin, between the Hebrew points and the vowel-symbols of the Aryan languages.

We therefore conclude, from the above facts, that the art of writing was unknown in India when it was in common use on the eastern coasts of the Mediterranean; and that the people of this island are indebted to some nation there resident, most probably the Phœnicians, for a knowledge of the art, and for many of the characters of the alphabet. I am thus particular in establishing what might otherwise seem to have little reference to our main subject, from the fact, that the natives of India give to every thing connected with themselves an immeasurable antiquity, and thereby foreclose any attempt that may be made to shew them their real position.

In India there is scarcely any trace of that kind of literature that has ever been the heritage of the western nations, except in what are called the middle ages, when "gross darkness covered the people." We have no contemporary history of any Aryan nation, except in fragments that are small in themselves, and separated from each other by long intervals. Though there are, it is supposed, ten thousand different Sanskrit works now in existence, with the exception of the Rája Tarangini, there is hardly one from which the historian can extract a sure date or a real event. No occurrence has had a greater effect upon the interests of Bráhmanism, both as to caste and creed, than the rise and spread of Buddhism; but the notices of the system in Sanskrit works are so few, that the most learned of all Englishmen in this language, Professor Wilson, judging from this stand-point, seriously questioned whether Buddha ever existed at all.

There is the same want of all that is real and trustworthy, and the same absence of fact, in the writings of the Buddhists. In that which takes the place of history in their sacred books, they carry us back many myriads of years, and give us long details about nen who lived to the age of 10,000 years, and sages who had an attendant retinue of 400,000 disciples. The Maháwanso is not a religious authority, and it presents a smaller portion of the incredible than the Pitakas; but even this work, upheld for its comparative truthfulness, tells us that Gótama Buddha was near the banks of the Ganges, and in the Himalayan forest, and in Ceylon on the same day; that finding the island filled with demons he spread his carpet of skin on the ground, which became effulgent, and extended itself on all sides, until the demons stood on the outermost shore (we suppose, like the cocoa-nut groves of the present day, but without their beauty); and that he caused the island Giri to approach, to which he transferred them, and then put the island back again in the deep sea, with all the demons on it; thus rendering Lanká habitable for men; and that then, as if this was not enough for one day's wonders, when his work was so far done, he quietly folded up his carpet and preached to the déwas, when more than a myriad myriad beings "received the blessing of his doctrines." If it be said that this was done by Buddha, the all-powerful, and the acknowledged vanquisher of demons, and is therefore out of the pale of ordinary occurrence, we may watch, as one of every-day sights of those times, and within the limit of humanity, the priest Anando come through the air, enter a pavilion by emerging from the floor without touching it, and assist in the holding of a convocation, at the close of which "the self-balanced earth quaked six times from the lowest abyss of the ocean." Again, if it be said that this was in a far-away country, about which we can know little, we may return to our own land, and we are told that in the 307th year of Buddha, or thereabouts, by virtue of the piety of the then king, many miraculous phenomena took place; the riches and precious metals buried in the earth came up therefrom, and appeared on the surface; the treasures buried in the sea came to the land; and the eight kinds of precious pearls rose up from the ocean, and stood in a ridge on the shore.

This is the manner in which the easterns write history! But the effects of this constant effort at exaggeration have been most disastrous to the interests of India. The every day incidents of common life, though it is of these, almost exclusively, that a nation's happiness is composed, are regarded, in consequence, as too trivial to be of any interest. The Aryan wants the marvellous and the miraculous, if he is to listen to what has been said or done in other ages; and so, for more than two thousand years, he has been crammed to satiety with the puerile and impracticable, if it be possible to satisfy a craving so morbid and unnatural. It is not necessary that further proof should be presented, in order to convince the intelligent natives of India that the events recorded in their histories, so called, are monstrous and incredible; and that before we can believe any of their statements, we must have some other evidence to convince us that what is said is true.

We are now prepared to understand the difference between the historical works of Europe and India, as to their truthfulness and credibility. All the most important events in European history were recorded by authors who lived at the time the events took place, or immediately afterwards; whilst in India there is often a vast, and almost limitless, interval between the supposed happening and its being recorded in a book. When the art of writing was introduced into the east, a tempting opportunity was presented for the exercise of a power that has bound, as as with a spell more powerful than was ever feigned of ancient rishi, all its generations, from that time to the present. Brahman and Buddhist seized on the opportunity with like fatality to the well-being of their deluded votaries. There were no musty rolls or dust-covered parchments, to start up from obscurity, like the Bible found by Luther in the library at Erfurth, and reveal the imposition that had been palmed upon the world. The past was all before them; they could people it as they willed, and make it speak any language, or tell of any event, that best suited their purpose.

The Buddhists were not so forward as the Brahmans to embrace the opportunity thus afforded, if we may rely upon what we learn from themselves; but in wild invention they have outstripped all competitors, of whatever age, race, or sect. They have writings that they regard as sacred, to which they pay the same reverence that the Brahman gives to the Veda. These writings are called, in Pali, Pitakattaya; or in Singhalese, Pitakatraya, and to the whole there are Commentaries, called in Pali, Attakathá, or in Singhalese, Atuwâ. The principal sections into which they are divided are three:—Winaya, Suttan, and Abhidhamma. The Text and Commentaries contain, according to a statement in the Saddharmálankáré, 29,368,000 letters.* There are three events, connected with the transmission of these works, that we must notice. 1. We are told that the Pali Text and the Commentaries were first brought to the island as the unwritten Dharmma, in the mind or memory of Mahindo, son of the then reigning monarch of India, B.C. 307, who came through the air, with six other persons, "instantaneously," and alighted at Mihintalla, near Anurádhapura; and that not long after

* We learn from a statement in the Journal of the Bengal Asiatic Society for May, 1847, communicated by Dr. J. Muir, that in the four Vedas there are 56,000 slokas, and in the Commentaries 460,000. It is said that in the entire English Bible there are 3,567,180 letters.

his arrival, in the space of a few minutes he converted the king and 40,000 of his attendants, whom he met when out hunting; but no wonder, if "his voice could be heard all over Lanká." He is said to have translated the Commentaries into Singhalese. But for Mahindo to have retained in his memory the whole of the Text and the Commentaries, would have been almost as great a miracle as the mode by which he is said to have reached Ceylon. If Mahindo brought any part of the Pitakas, he could not have brought them in the extended form in which we have them now; and, therefore, as the Buddhists of the island cannot tell what portion is ancient, and what is new, what part was brought by the priest, and what has been added by others, they can have no confidence that the word they now receive as primitive truth is not the invention of a later age. 2. We are told, again, that the whole of the matter now composing the sacred books was orally transmitted, from generation to generation of the priesthood, until the year B.C. 90, without being committed to writing. "The profoundly wise priests had theretofore orally perpetuated the Pali Pitakattaya and the Attakathá. At this period these priests, foreseeing the perdition of the people (from the perversions of the true doctrine), assembled; and in order that the religion might endure for ages, recorded the same in books."* Then, even allowing that the whole of the Pitakas were brought to the island at the time of the establishment of Buddhism in it, what surety is there that they were remembered exactly for so many years, and that they were recorded correctly at last?

* Mahawanso, cap. xxxiii.

There were heresies abroad at the time, and we have no proof that those who are called heretics were not the orthodox Buddhists, and the writers of the Pitakas heretics. 3. The Commentaries, as we have them now, cannot be the same as those that are said to have been brought over by Mahindo. We learn from the Mahawanso that in the year 432 A.D., nearly a thousand years after the death of Buddha, a Hindu priest, Réwato, was the means of the conversion of a Brahman, called Buddhaghóso, "the voice of Buddha," from his eloquence, whom he commanded, in the following terms, to repair to Ceylon, and there to translate the Commentaries into Pali. "The text alone has been preserved in this land: the Attakathá are not extant there; nor is there any version to be found of the wádá (schisms) complete. The Singhalese Attakathá are genuine. They were composed (made) in the Singhalese language by the inspired and profoundly wise Mahindo, who had previously consulted the discourses of Buddha, authenticated at the three convocations, and the dissertations and arguments of Sáriputto and others, and they are extant among the Singhalese. Repairing thither, and studying the same, translate (them) according to the rules of the grammar of the Mágadhas. It will be an act conducive to the welfare of the whole world." On his arrival in Ceylon, Buddhaghóso first made an abridgement of the sacred books, which he called Wisuddhimargga. "Having assembled the priesthood, who had a thorough knowledge of Buddha, at the bo-tree, he commenced to read out (the work he had composed). The déwas, in order that they might make his gifts of wisdom celebrated among men, rendered that book invisible. He, however, for a second and third time recomposed it. When he was in the act of reproducing his book for the third time, for the purpose of propounding it, the déwas restored the other two copies also. The (assembled) priests then read out the three books simultaneously. In those three versions, neither in a signification, nor in a single misplacement by transposition; nay even in the théra controversy, and in the Text, was there, in the measure of a verse, or in the letter of a word, the slightest variation. . . . Then taking up his residence in the secluded Ganthákaro wiharo (temple) at Anurádhapura, he translated, according to the grammatical rules of the Mágadhas, which is the root of all languages, the whole of the Singhalese Attakathá (into Pali). This proved an achievement of the utmost consequence to all the languages spoken by the human race,"* It is not a little singular, that having been at first translated into Singhalese by a stranger from India, when the Commentaries were again translated into Pali, it was a Brahman who did it. The Singhalese Commentaries are not now in existence; but this may be accounted for from the fact that the whole of the literature of Ceylon was destroyed by the Tamils, and had to be renewed from Burma or Siam. The priests of those countries, not knowing the language of Ceylon, were probably never in possession of the Singhalese version.

It is said in the same chapter of the Mahawanso: "All the théros and achárayos held this compilation in the same estimation as the Text." This follows, almost of

* Mahawanso, 250.

necessity, if the preceding statements are to be believed; for if Mahindo was a rahat (and therefore incapable of falling into error on any subject connected with religion), the Commentaries he translated must have been as free from error as the original; if the priests who afterwards committed them to writing were rahats, as the Singhalese affirm, they could not err; and if Buddhaghóso wrote out the whole of the Wisuddhimargga three times from memory, without the slightest variation, "even in the letter of a word," we may conclude that his Commentary was equally free from mistake. When the late Mr. George Turnour had an interview, in Kandy, with the two high priests of the Malwatta and Asgiri establishments, and their fraternities, to discuss the question of an "apparently fatal discrepancy," between the Text and the Commentary, they replied that "the Pittakatthá only embodied the essential portions of the discourses, revelations, and prophecies of Buddha; and that his disciples, some centuries after his nibbánan, were endowed with inspiration, and that their supplements to the Pitakatthá were as sacred in their estimation as the text itself." The Commentaries, then, it is to be remembered, are of equal authority with the Text, on the testimony of the author of the Mahawanso, and of the high priests of both the establishments in Kandy.

## 11. WILSON, MAX MÜLLER, AND TURNOUR ON BUDDHISM.

We shall be better prepared to enter upon some of the questions we have yet to consider, if we notice before proceeding further, the opinions formed on Buddhism by the learned men of Europe who have studied this subject. The name of Professor Wilson is well-known, and greatly revered, in Ceylon, from the vast erudition he has displayed in his Sanskrit Dictionary and Grammar. The following extracts are taken from an Essay, read as a Lecture, "On Buddha and Buddhism," before the Royal Asiatic Society, April 8, 1854, and published in the Society's Journal, vol. xvi. art. 13. The Professor supposes that the Pali books of Ceylon are not so ancient as the Sanskrit Buddhistical writings of India Proper. "Their subsequent date may be inferred from internal evidence; for, although they are in all respects the very same as the Buddhist works of India—laying down the same laws and precepts, and narrating the same marvellous legends—they bear the characteristics of a later and less intellectual cultivation, in their greater diffuseness, and the extravagant and puerile additions they frequently make to the legendary matter." After reference to the accounts that are current among various nations as to the principal events connected with the life and death of Buddha, he thus proceeds: "These accounts of Sakya's birth and proceedings, laying aside the miraculous portions, have nothing very impossible, and it does not seem improbable that an individual of a speculative turn of mind, and not a Brahman by birth, should have set up a school of his own in opposition to the Brahmanical monopoly of religious instruction, about six centuries before Christ; at the same time there are various considerations which throw suspicion upon the narrative, and render it very problematical whether any such person as Sákya Sinha, or Sákya Muni, or Sramana Gautama, ever actually existed. In the first place, the Buddhists widely disagree with regard to the date of his existence. In a paper I published many years ago in the Calcutta Quarterly Magazine, I gave a list of thirteen different dates, collected by a Tibetan author, and a dozen others might be easily added, the whole varying from 2420 to 453 B.C. They may, however, be distinguished under two heads, that of the northern Buddhists, 1030 B.C. for the birth of Buddha, and that of the southern Buddhists, for his death B.C. 543. It is difficult, however, to understand why there should be such a difference as five centuries, if Sákya had lived at either the one or the other date.

"The name of his tribe, the Sákya, and their existence as a distinct people and principality, find no warrant from any of the Hindu writers, poetical, traditional, or mythological; and the legends that are given to explain their origin and appellation are, beyond measure, absurd.

"The name of Sákya's father, Suddhodana, 'he whose food is pure'—suggests an allegorical signification, and in that of his mother, Máyá, or Máyádeví, 'illusion, divine delusion,'—we have a manifest allegorical fiction; his secular appellation as a prince, Siddhártha, 'he by whom the end is accomplished,'—and his religious name, Buddha, 'he by whom all is known,' are very much in the style of the Pilgrim's Progress, and the city of his birth, Kapila Vastu, which has no place in the geography of the Hindus, is of the same description. It is explained, 'the tawny site,' but it may also be rendered, 'the substance of

Kapila,' intimating, in fact, the Sánkhya philosophy, the doctrine of Kapila Muni, upon which the fundamental elements of Buddhism, the eternity of matter, the principles of things, and final extinction, are evidently based. It seems not impossible, after all, that Sákya Muni is an unreal being, and that all that is related of him is as much a fiction as is that of his preceding migrations, and the miracles that attended his birth, his life, and his departure."

These conclusions of Professor Wilson were come to without any reference to their religious bearing, from the insight he gained into Buddhism by the study of Sanskrit authors, and of such works in Pali as had then been translated or published; and he examines, and determines upon, the character of the system, in the same manner in which he would carry on any secular or scientific investigation. "The process of conversion," he says in the last sentences of the Essay, "is unavoidably slow, especially in Central Asia, which is almost beyond the reach of European activity and zeal, but there is no occasion to despair of ultimate success. Various agencies are at work, both in the north and the south, before whose salutary influence civilisation is extending; and the ignorance and superstition which are the main props of Buddhism, must be overturned by its advance."

No one has done more than Max Müller to render subjects connected with the languages and religions of India popular in England. He has raised language into a science, and by his terseness of style, power of analysis, and richness of resource in illustration, he has also made

Sanskrit lore part of the literature of the world. In his able work "On Ancient Sanskrit Literature," he makes frequent reference to Buddha, and supposes that the virulence with which he was assailed, arose from his opposition to the exclusive privileges and abuses of the Brahmans, rather than from his religious speculations. The bitterness of the Brahmans, and the mode in which they assailed their opponents, may be learned from the following extract from Kumárila's Tantra-varttika. "These Sákyas (Buddhists), Vaiseshíkas, and other heretics, who have been frightened out of their wits by the faithful Mimánsakas, prattle away with our own words as if trying to lay hold of a shadow. They say that their sacred books are eternal; but they are of empty minds, and only out of hatred they wish to deny that the Veda is the most ancient book. And these would-be logicians declare even that some of their precepts (which they have stolen from us), like that of universal benevolence, are not derived from the Veda, because most of Buddha's other sayings are altogether opposed to the Veda. Wishing, therefore, to keep true on this point also, and seeing that no merely human precept could have any authority on moral and supernatural subjects, they try to veil their difficulty by aping our own arguments for the eternal existence of the Veda. They know that the Mimánsakas have proved that no sayings of men can have any authority on supernatural subjects; they know also that the authority of the Veda cannot be controverted, because they can bring forward nothing against the proofs adduced for its divine origin, by which all supposition of a human source has been removed.

Therefore, their hearts being gnawed by their own words, which are like the smattering of children, and having themselves nothing to answer, because the deception of their illogical arguments has been destroyed, they begin to speak like a foolish suitor who came to ask for a bride, saying, 'My family is as good as your family.' In the same manner they now maintain the eternal existence of their books, aping the speeches of others. And if they are challenged, and told that this is *our* argument, they brawl, and say that we, the Mimánsakas, have heard and stolen it from them. For a man who has lost all shame, who can talk away without any sense, and tries to cheat his opponent, will never get tired, and will never be put down!" Kumárila afterwards tells the Buddhists, that "they who ascribe to everything a merely temporary existence, have no business to talk of an eternal revelation:" but, upon their own principles, they would refute this argument, by saying, that what seems to be temporary is the repetition of an eternal series. With the other argument they would have greater difficulty; that the words of Gótama, who was born like other mortals, and breathed like them, and who afterwards died and was burnt, could not be allowed to supersede the revelation of the gods, as presented in the unerring Veda.

We are told by Max Müller, from whom the preceding extract has been taken, that the Buddhists have no history previous to the time of Asóka, except "what was clearly supplied from their own heads and not from authentic documents." Until the adoption of Buddhism as the state religion by that king, there was no object in connecting the lives of Buddha and his disciples with the chronology of the Solar or Lunar dynasties of India. We possess more than one system of Buddhist chronology, but to try to find out which is "the most plausible seems useless, and it can only make confusion worse confounded if we attempt a combination of the three." Until new evidence can be brought forward to substantiate the authenticity of the early history of Buddhism as told by the Ceylonese priests, it would be rash to use the dates of the southern Buddhists as a corrective standard for those of the northern Buddhists or of the Brahmans, as before the year 161 B.C. their chronology is "traditional and full of absurdities." Vijaya, the founder of the first dynasty, means "conquest," and such a person most likely never existed. To give renown to the temples of Ceylon, the statement was invented that they had been visited by Buddha. These are the conclusions of another orientalist; who regards the legends of Buddha as "absurd," and its chronology as "confusion."

From the attention paid to Pali literature by the late Mr. Turnour,—the most prominent name among the few civilians of the island who have interested themselves in the study of its languages, history, or religion—it is believed by many of the natives that he was in reality a Buddhist; with what reason, we may learn from the following extracts. "According to the Buddhistical creed, all remote, historical data, whether sacred or profane, anterior to Gótama's advent, are based upon *his* revelation. They are involved in absurdity as unbounded, as the mystification in which Hindu literature is enveloped. . . . . It would be inconsistent with the scheme of such a creed, and absurd on our part, to expect that the Buddhistical data comprised in the four and a half centuries (subsequent to the advent of Gótama), should be devoid of glaring absurdities and gross superstitions."* "In regard to the 236 years which elapsed from the death of Gótama to the introduction of Buddhism in Ceylon, in B.C. 307, there is ground for suspecting that sectarian zeal, or the impostures of superstition, have led to the assignment of the same date for the landing of Wijayo, with the cardinal Buddhistical event—the death of Gótama. If historical annals did exist (of which there is ample internal evidence) in Ceylon, anterior to Mahindo's arrival, Buddhist historians have adapted those data to their falsified chronology."† "Both the chronology and the historical narrative, prior to the advent of Gótama Buddha, are involved in intentional perversion and mystification; a perversion evidently had recourse to for the purpose of working out the scheme on which he based that wonderful dispensation, which was promulgated over Central India, during his pretended divine mission on earth of forty-five years, between 588 and 543 before the birth of Christ."‡ There are other passages of a similar description scattered throughout Mr. Turnour's writings. No missionary has been more explicit than he, in declaring Buddhism to be a pretence and superstitious imposture, though he was better acquainted with its history and character than any other civilian who has resided in the island.

The inhabitants of India, who have among themselves

* Mahawanso, xxviii. † Mahawanso, li.

‡ Journal of the Bengal Asiatic Society, vol. vii. 686.

few examples of men who study, for years and years, a religion they regard as false, for the sake of the general information they thereby gain, take it for granted, when they see a European poring over one of their sacred books with intense interest, that it must necessarily be because he admires its contents, and believes its doctrines. But let them know, that this is a conclusion that has no foundation in truth.

## 12. DIFFERENCES IN THE CHRONOLOGY OF THE BUDDHISTS.

It will have been noticed that there is one subject referred to alike by all the writers we have just named—the extraordinary differences in the chronology of Buddha's appearance, as adopted by the various nations that have embraced his faith. This difference amounts to nearly two thousand years. The Chinese have the following dates for this event: B.C. 640, 767, 949, 950, 1045, and 1130. From the Tibetan books fourteen different dates have been collected, by the learned Hungarian, Csoma de Korosi: B.C. 546, 576, 653, 752, 837, 880, 882, 884, 1060, 1310, 2139, 2135, 2144, and 2422. The Japanese date is about B.C. 1000. Fa Hian, a Chinese traveller who visited Ceylon in A.D. 410, says that ten days before "the middle of the third moon" the king of this island was accustomed to send a preacher to proclaim the austerities and mortifications of Buddha, at the conclusion of which he declared: "since his Ni houan 1497 years have elapsed;" which would make the death of Buddha to be in the year B.C.

1077.* Hiun Thsang, another Chinese pilgrim, who wrote A.D. 640, after his return from India, says that the accounts differ about Buddha's death, it being fixed at 900, 1000, 1200, 1300, and 1500 years before his time. The Mahawanso fixes the same date for the death of Buddha and the landing of Wijaya in Ceylon; but this date, B.C. 543, is never found in the sacred chronology of Buddhism, before it was borrowed from the profane chronology of Ceylon.† It was the opinion of Mr. Turnour that "sectarian zeal, or the impostures of superstition," had led to the assignment of the same date for both these cardinal events. Professor Wilson founded one of his reasons for questioning the existence of Buddha upon the fact of these numerous discrepancies; and the Buddhist will do well to ask himself, If the being I worship, and in whom I trust, once lived, how has it come to pass that the differences of opinion about the date of his death are so many, and extending to so vast a period?

* Laidlay's Pilgrimage of Fa Hian.

† Max Müller, Ancient Sanskrit Literature.

## CHAPTER II.

## THE COSMICAL SYSTEM OF THE BUDDHISTS.

In the preceding chapter we have prepared our way, gradually, for a more direct and immediate notice and refutation of the various statements put forth by Buddhist writers that are not "historically true;" in which I include everything that is contrary to facts known, proved, and universally acknowledged, in European literature or science. I confine myself, almost exclusively, to Pali authorities; and in the few instances in which I have deviated from this course, I have given notice that my information is taken from some more modern work.

### PART FIRST.—THE BUDDHIST UNIVERSE.

The Buddhists are taught that the universe is composed of limitless systems or worlds, called Chakka-wála, or Sakwalas. They are scattered throughout space, in sections of three and three,*—and incomprehensible as is their number, they can all be seen by Buddha; who can know whatever takes place in any one of them,† if he turns his

* Appendix, Note C.

† Note D. The Sára Sangaha, from which this information is gained, is a compilation from the Text and Commentaries, by the priest Suddattha. The statement here made is taken by him from the Commentary on the Buddha Wanso, which is not in the Mission Library.

attention towards it, or wills to know it. In the centre of each system there is a mountain called Sinéru, or Maha Méru. It is 1,680,000 miles from its base to its summit; half of which mass is below, and half above the surface of the ocean. It is the same size, or 840,000 miles in length and breadth.* On each side it is of a different colour, being like silver towards the east, and like a sapphire towards the south.† But though its sides are spoken of, it is round, not square. If it were square, like a house, it would be spoken of as having a north wall, or a south wall. Its side means its aspect, whether north or south; and by its size is meant its diameter. It is supported on the three-peaked Trikuta rock, like a vessel upon a tripod. If it were square it would require four rocks upon which to stand, instead of three. Where these rocks rise to the elevation of 40,000 miles, there Maha Méru rests, and it is firmly clasped by them as by a pair of pincers. When it is said in the Lóka-pannyap-tip-prakarana that it lies in the ocean only 800,000 miles deep, it is because the elevation of the rocks is not included. The three rocks rest upon a World of Stone. The Chatumaharájika, déva-lóka, or celestial world, extends from the summit of the Yugandhara rocks to Sakwala-gala. On the summit of Maha Méru is Tawutisá, the heaven of Sekra. There are six déwa-lókas in all. There are sixteen rúpa-brahma-

* There is some uncertainty about the length of the yójana, by which all great distances in India are measured; but to be rather below, than above, the supposed length, and for convenience of calculation, I have reckoned it at 10 miles. The native reading for the size of either half of Maha Méru would be 84,000 yójanas, or yodunas. Note E.

† Note F.

lókas, in which there are no sensuous pleasures, and four more in which there is no bodily form. The residence of the asúrs is under Maha Méru. There are eight places of suffering situated in the interior of the earth. At the circumference, or outer circle, of the system, there is a ridge of stone, called the Sakwala rock, 12,034,500 miles in diameter, and 36,103,500 miles in circumference.*

Between Maha Méru and the Sakwala ridge there are seven circles of rocks, with seven seas between them.† They are circular because of the shape of Maha Méru. The first, or innermost, Yugandhara, is 210,000 miles broad; its inner circumference is 7,560,000 miles, and its outer 8,220,000 miles. From Maha Méru to Yugandhara is 840,000 miles. Near Maha Méru the depth of the sea is 840,000 miles, from which its depth gradually decreases, until near Yugandhara it is 420,000 miles. The second, Isadhara, is 210,000 miles high, and 105,000 broad; its inner circumference is 11,340,050 miles, and its outer 11,970,000. The width of the sea between Yugandhara and Isadhara is 420,000 miles. Near Yugandhara the depth of the sea is 420,000 miles, and near Isadhara 210,000. The third, Karawíka, is 105,000 miles high, and 52,500 broad; its inner circumference is 13,230,000 miles, and its outer 13,540,050. The width of the sea between Isadhara and Karawíka is 210,000 miles. Near Isadhara the depth of the sea is 210,000 miles, and near Karawíka 105,000. The fourth, Sudassana, is 52,500 miles high, and 26,250 broad. Its inner circumference is 14,175,000 miles, and its outer 14,332,500. The width

* Appendix, Note G.

† Note H.

of the sea between Karawíka and Sudassana is 105,000 miles. Near Karawíka the depth of the sea is 105,000 miles, and near Sudassana 52,500. The fifth, Nemindara, is 26,250 miles high, and 13,125 broad. Its inner circumference is 14,647,500 miles, and its outer, 14,726,250. The width of the sea between Sudassana and Némindhara is 52,500 miles. Its depth near Sudassana is 52,500 miles, and near Némindhara 26,250. The sixth, Winataka, is 13,125 miles high and 6,562½ broad. Its inner circumference is 14,883,750 miles, and its outer 14,923,120. The width of the sea between Némindhara and Winataka is 26,250 miles. Its depth near Némindhara is 26,250 miles, and near Winataka 13,125. The seventh, Aswakanna, is 6,562½ miles high, and 3,281¼ broad. Its inner circumference is 15,001,860 miles, and its outer, 15,711,700. The width of the sea between Winataka and Aswakanna is 13,125 miles. Its depth near Winataka is 13,125 miles, and near Aswakanna 6,562½. From Maha Méru to the Sakwala rock the distance is 5,597,250 miles; and the rock itself is 1,640,000 miles high, half below the water and half above.* Buddhaghóso names Yugandhara first; but Buddha himself mentions them in the following order; Sudassana, Karawíka, Isadhara, Yugandhara, Némindhara, Winataka, and Aswakanna. But the discrepancy is to be reconciled thus. On a certain occasion Mátali, the charioteer of Sekra, showed king Nimi the infernal regions. As their return was delayed, Sekra sent the swift Jawana to

* There is a discrepancy between these numbers and those given in other places; in some instances arising from errors of transcription in copying the native olas.

enquire what was the reason. The chariot was at once turned towards the heaven whence they had come, Tawutisá. When they rose above the water, they were near Sudassana, and the king, looking before and behind, enquired what rocks they were that he saw; and the charioteer, looking first before him, said, Sudassana, Karawíka, Isadhara, and Yugandhara; and then looking behind him, said, Némindhara, Winataka, and Aswakanna. Buddha, referring to this occurrence, mentions them in the same order, whilst the author of the Wisuddhi Margga takes them in their local order, beginning with the innermost first. But there is no disagreement between the one statement and the other; like the waters of the Yamuna and Ganga they become united. When the author of the Atuwáwa on the Nimi Játaka defines what Sudassana is, he says that the outermost circle of rock is Sudassana; but he wrote this from carelessness, or want of thought.*

The seas between the circles of rock are called Sídanta, because their waters are so light, or unbuoyant, that the feather of a peafowl would not float in them.† There are also seas that have their names from the colour of the rays that fall on them from Maha Méru, or from the gems that they contain. The rays are like the respective sides of the mountain; and the silver rays from the east, mingling with the sapphire rays from the south, cause the seas and skies in those directions to be of the same colour. The rays pass across the circular rocks and seas, until they strike against the Sakwala ridge.‡ The waters of the seas

* Jinálankára. † Appendix, Note I. ‡ Note J.

do not increase on account of rain, or diminish on account of heat.*

The Great World is 2,400,000 miles in vertical thickness. At its base is the Gal Polowa, or World of Stone, consisting of hard rock, serving the same purpose as the boards at the bottom of a tub, and impervious to water, 1,200,000 miles thick; and above that is the Pas Polowa, or World of Earth, also 1,200,000 miles thick. Underneath the World of Stone is the Jala Polowa, or World of Water, 4,800,000 miles thick; and below this the Wá Polowa, or World of Wind, 9,600,000, miles thick.†

In the great sea between the Aswakanna and Sakwala rock there are four continents. 1. Jambudípa, in shape like a chariot, is 100,000 miles in length and breadth. 2. Aparagóyána, in shape like a mirror, 70,000 miles. 3. Pubbawidéha, in shape like a half-moon, 70,000 miles. 4. Uttarakuru, in shape like a seat, 80,000 miles. Around each continent there are 500 islands. The faces of the inhabitants are of the same shape as the continents in which they live.‡

From Maha Méru to the Aswakanna rocks is 2,083,600 miles; from Maha Méru to the centre of Jambudípa is 2,798,600 miles; and from Jambudípa to the middle of the Sakwala rock is 2,798,000 miles, a little more or a little less, as the odd yójanas are not reckoned. This continent is situated in the centre of the Blue Sea.§

If it were not for the circular rocks, all the waters

* Sára Sangaha. Anguttara Nikáya Wannaná, the 8th Nipáta. Paháráda Suttanta. Wisuddhi Margga.

† Note K. ‡ Sára Sangaha. § Jinálankára, Appendix, Note L.

would form one great ocean; then, when the great wind strikes against Méru and the Himála-wana, and the Sakwala is shaken, the waters would be shaken too, and all running to one side, would overflow the continents and islands, and the Sakwala would be destroyed. When the Sakwala is shaken, the waters within it are shaken too, and this causes the sea to ebb and flow. In the Maha Parinibbána Suttanta, Buddha enumerates to Anando eight causes of earthquakes. The first he mentions is on this wise: "The earth rests on the Jala-polowa, or World of Water, and the water rests on the Wa-polowa, or World of Wind. The wind rests on the Akása, air, or space. Anando! whenever the great wind blows, it causes the water to shake, and when the water shakes, the earth shakes."* The Aluwáwa says: "When the wind blows that shakes the Sakwala, it makes an opening in the World of Wind, by which the water descends, and the earth descends too; but when the wind returns to its own place, the water rises, and the earth rises with it. Thus, when the water shakes, the earth shakes too, and this shaking continues to our own time, but because the earth is so large, its rising and descending are not perceived." The Tíká says that the Gal Polowa, or World of Stone, and the Sakwala ridge are joined together like (the timbers of) a ship, and are one; only, to make a distinction, that which is under is called Gal Polowa, and that which is round, Sakwala Gala. The Gal Polowa, which prevents the World of Water from overflowing the World of Earth, is like the bottom of an iron vessel,

* Appendix, Note M.

the Sakwala ridge is like the rim of the vessel, the continents are like the rice (put in to be eaten), and the oceans are like the sauce poured around the rice.*

Each Sakwala has a sun and moon. The sun is 500 miles in height, length, and breadth, and its circumference is 1,500 miles. The moon is 490 miles in height, length, and breadth, and its circumference 1,470 miles. Their orbits are horizontal with Maha Méru, at an elevation of 420,000 miles above the surface of the earth. The orbit of the moon is lower than that of the sun by ten miles. It is one thousand miles from the lowest part of the moon to the highest part of the sun. The inside of the sun is gold, and the outside is covered over with crystal. Both within and without it is hot. The inside of the moon is a gem, and the outside is covered with silver. Both within and without it is cold.† On the day of the dark moon, the moon is immediately under the sun. The sun and moon travel on together, but as the moon does not move so rapidly as the sun, the distance between them increases continually, until, on the day of the full moon, it is 15,000,000 miles from the sun.‡ In the space of one month it moves towards the north, and then towards the south, as the sun does in one year. The planets travel on the two sides of the moon. The moon moves towards them, as a cow towards her calf. It never leaves the twenty-seven lunar mansions. When the sun travels crosswise, from south to north, or from north to south, it moves more slowly than when its course is straight. On the day after the dark moon, the sun has passed away

* Jinálankára. † Appendix, Note N. ‡ Note O.

from the moon a million miles, on account of its greater swiftness. The moon then appears like a streak, or line. On the second day the distance has increased a million miles more. And thus it continues, day by day, until, on the day of the full moon, when the sun is at the greatest distance from the moon, and the sun's shadow entirely removed from the moon, the whole of the moon's surface appears. The same process then goes on as before; the distance between the sun and moon being altered by a million of miles each day; but it now diminishes, instead of being increased. On the day of the dark moon, the sun being the higher of the two, overshadows the moon, like the covering of a small vessel by a larger, or the overpowering of the light of a lamp by the sun's rays at mid-day.*

There are three paths, and to each of the paths there are four signs (of the Zodiac), in which the sun and moon constantly travel; they are the Goat, the Bull, and the Elephant.† When they are in the first there is no rain; when in the second, there is a moderate quantity, neither too much rain nor too much heat; and when in the third the rain is excessive, and pours down as if the heavens were opened. The sun and moon, during six months of the year, move from Maha Méru towards the Sakwala rock, and during the other six months from the Sakwala rock towards Maha Méru. When the path of the sun is not cross-wise but straight, it gives light to three of the continents at once. In each direction its rays remove the darkness for the space of 9,000,000 miles. When the sun

* Sára Sangaha.

† Appendix, Note P.

is rising in this continent (Jambudípa), it is mid-day in Pubbawidéha, sunset in Uttarakuru, and midnight in Aparagóyána; when it is rising in Pubbawidéha, it is mid-day in Uttarakuru, sunset in Aparagóyána, and midnight in this continent; when it is rising in Uttarakuru it is mid-day in Aparagóyána, sunset in this continent, and midnight in Pubbawidéha; when it is rising in Aparagóyána it is mid-day in this continent, sunset in Pubbawidéha, and midnight in Uttarakuru; and when it is mid-day in this continent, half the sun appears in Pubbawidéha, as if setting, and half appears in Aparagóyána, as if rising; thus the sun illuminates three continents (at the same time).*

Are the sun and moon swallowed by the asur Ráhu?† Yes. This Ráhu is 48,000 miles in size; his breadth between the shoulders is 12,000 miles; his thickness, from breast to back, is 6,000 miles; his head is 9,000 miles in size; his forehead 3,000 miles; from eyebrow to eyebrow is 1,500 miles; his nose is 3,000 miles long, and his mouth 3,000 miles deep; the breadth of his palm and of his foot foot is 2,000 miles; and one joint of his finger is 500 miles long. When Ráhu sees the shining of the sun, he descends towards the path in which it moves, and there remaining with his mouth open, the sun falls into it, as if into the Awichi hell. The déwas resident in the sun bawl out, trembling with fear. He sometimes covers the sun and moon with his hand; sometimes hides them under his jaw; sometimes licks them with his tongue; and some-

* Note Q. Sára Sangaha, Sárattha Dípani, Agganya Sutta Wannaná.
† Note R.

times moves them up and down in his mouth, like an animal chewing its cud. But he is not able to prevent them from moving onward. Were he to attempt to keep them in his mouth, saying, "I will kill these (bawling) déwas," they would escape through the crown of his head.*

The waters of the sea in which the Walabhámukha is formed, rise up towards the sky, appearing in all directions like a lake with its embankments broken down. When the waters thus rise, one side appears like a precipice, and the other like a valley; and they rush impetuously towards the Aswakanna and Sakwala rock. They rise in waves the height of ten or a hundred miles, causing a hollow like the infernal regions, and making a noise sufficient to break the drum of the ear. There is a great whirlpool in one part of the sea. It is thus caused: the gates of the Awichi hell (underneath Jambudípa), are continually opening and shutting, by which a great flame arises, so that the water boils for many miles below the surface, which is thereby greatly agitated. It is this terrible place that is called Walabhámukha.†

The waters become deeper as they recede from the continents, on both sides, gradually, according to the following scale; an inch, two inches, a span, a cubit, a yashtiya, an isbá, a half gawuta, a gawuta, a half yójana, a yójana, and so on, until, near Maha Méru they are 840,000 miles deep, and near the Sakwala rock 820,000 miles. From the bottom upwards, for 400,000 miles, they are

* Sára Sangaha. Sanyutta Wannaná.

† Sára Sangaha. Suppára Játaka. Théra Gáthá Wannaná.

agitated by large fishes; and from the surface downward, for 400,000 miles, they are agitated by the wind. In the 40,000 miles that intervene between the two agitations, there is a perfect calm. There are waves 600 miles high, called Mahinda; others 400 miles high, called Pórána.* The carcases of elephants, horses, and other animals, are cast on shore, as if thrown by the hand, and no impurity whatever attaches to the waters. In them there are fishes called Timinda, 2,000 miles in size; Timingala, 3,000 miles; and Timira Pingala, 5,000 miles. There are four others, Ananda, Timinda, Ajáróha, and Maha Timi, each 10,000 miles in size. When the Timira Pingala shakes his right or left ear, the waters are agitated for the space of 5000 miles around, and it is the same when he shakes his head or his tail. When he moves his head and tail together, the waters are agitated for the space of 8000 miles. It requires water more than a thousand miles deep to cover his back.†

In the continent of Jambudípa, there are 40,000 miles that have been swallowed up by the ocean, because the merit of those who were to derive benefit from the land was exhausted; 30,000 miles are covered by the Himálawana; and 30,000 miles are inhabited by men.‡ In the part in which men live there are fifty-six ratnákaras (places where gold, and the other ten kinds of treasure, are found); 99,000 seaports, from which customs are levied; and 189,000 cities.

The Himála-wana is so called, because it is covered with

* Appendix, Note S. † Sára Sangaha. Maha Nidana Sutta Wannaná, in the Digha Nikáya. Appendix, Note T. ‡ Note U

hima, or snow; or because in the hot season the snow melts. There are 500 rivers in it, each of which is 500 miles in length, breadth, and depth. There are seven large lakes: Anotatta, Kannamunda, Rathakára, Chhaddhanta, Kunála, Mandákini, and Síhappapáta, each of which is 1500 miles in extent. Around Anotatta are five mountains: Sudassana, Chitta, Kála, Gandhamádana, and Kailása. Sudassana is golden, and 2000 miles high; its rocks hang over, like the bill of a crow; Chitta is throughout of gold; Kála is of antimony; Gandhamádana is of the colour of mung seed, and there grow upon it ten different kinds of fragrant creepers or trees: kalu-wæl, with the fragrance in the root; sandun, in the wood; hora, in the outer integument; lawanga (cinnamon?), in the bark; dhulu, in the layers; sarja, in the milk; tamála, in the leaf; kungkuman, in the flower; játiphala, in the fruit; and ghanda-ghanda, in every part; with various kinds of medicinal plants. There are also caves: golden, gem-like, and silver. At the entrance of the gem-like cave, there is a tree called Munjúsaka, ten miles high and ten broad, on which grow all kinds of plants, whether aquatic or terrene; and a wind arises that removes all impurities, now making smooth and even the comminuted gems of which the surrounding sand is composed, and now sprinkling water from the Anotatta lake, that has the fragrance of all sweet-scented trees. Seats are at all times prepared for the reception of the Pasé-Buddhas, when any appear. When one Pasé-Buddha takes his seat, all the others assemble there at the same time; and if any one has recently attained this privilege, he tells how he became possessed of it. All the mountains are of the same height and form. All are 500 miles broad, and in length and height 2000 miles. The water in the lake is clear as crystal, and there are bathing-places in it well divided from each other, to which those resort who have merit; the Buddhas, Pasé-Buddhas, the rishis who have the power of irdhi, the déwas, and yakshas. From its four sides proceed four rivers, called after the mouths from which they issue: Singha, lion; Hasta, elephant; Aswa, horse; and Wrashabha, bull. These animals abound upon their banks. Each of the rivers goes three times round the lake, and then passes onward to the sea. The river at the south proceeds in a straight line over a bed of stone 600 miles, then strikes against a rock, rising about ten miles in all directions, and becoming like a lake ten miles in size, then passes 600 miles through the air, and in its fall breaks the rock Tiyaggala in pieces. It then becomes a lake 500 miles in extent, proceeds 600 miles on a bed of stone, and 600 miles underground, and after striking against the rock Windhya, changes into five streams, like the fingers on the hand. As the river goes three times round Anotatta, it is called Awartta (coiling); for the next 600 miles, Krashna; when rising into the sky, Akása; after striking the rock, Tiyaggala; after passing the rock, Bahata Ganga; and when going underground, Uman. The five rivers are the Ganga, Yamuna, Achirawati, Sarabhu, and Mahi. In the centre of the lakes the water is clear, and there are then circles, ten miles broad, of vegetation, each circle having its own kind of plant or tree.*

* These are described in the original with great minuteness; but I have not thought it necessary to insert the description at length.

Between the eastern and northern mouths of Chhaddantha there is a nuga, or banian tree, the trunk of which is fifty miles round and seventy miles high; it has branches on its four sides sixty miles long; from the root to the highest part is 130 miles; and from the tip of one branch to that of the opposite one is 120 miles. It has 8000 roots, shining like the mountain Munda Mani.* On the eastern side of the same lake there is a cave 120 miles in size, to which the chief of the elephants, with 8000 others resort in the rainy season, whilst in the hot season they lie among the roots of the banian tree. Near the lakes, the sugar cane grows as high as an areca tree. There are plantains as large as an elephant's trunk, and lotus flowers the size of the head of a plough.†

There are lions in the Himála-wana of four kinds: trina, kála, pandu, and késara. The trina is dove-coloured, and in shape like a cow. It feeds on grass. The kála is like a black cow, and feeds on grass. The pandu is of a yellow colour (like a priest's robe,) and in shape is like a cow; it feeds on flesh. The késara has its mouth, the tips of its nails, and the extremities of its feet, red, like sealing-wax; three lines run from the head along the back, as if drawn by the pencil of a painter; his mane is of thick hair, like a rough mantle worth a laksha of money; and in other parts of his body his colour is like fine flour or the powder of chanques. He is called murga-rája, or the king of beasts. Issuing from a golden, silver, or gem-like cave, he goes forth, either because he is tired of darkness and wishes for light, or for purposes of nature, or in search of food, or

* Sára Sangaha, Sárattha Dípani.

† Sára Sangaha.

prompted by passion. When going in search of food, he stands on a rock, or some other elevation, places his hind legs evenly, spreads his front legs before him, draws forward the hind part of his body, bends his back, breathes with a noise like the thunder, and shakes the dust from his body. In the same place he runs to and fro, like a young calf, at this time appearing like a fire-brand whirled round in the night. In compassion towards other beasts, he looks round and roars; at which time the elephants, bulls, and buffaloes, which are on mountains, or near ponds and lakes, fall down the precipice into the water. But can there be compassion in one that feeds on another's flesh? Yes. Thus he thinks: Of what use will it be to kill many? I must not destroy the smaller beasts; and so he has compassion. At his first roar he can be heard thirty miles, in every direction. No biped or quadruped that hears this roar can remain in the same place. When he sports himself, he can leap, to the right or left, an isba, and when he leaps upward, four or eight isbas. If he leaps on even ground, he can leap twelve or twenty isbas; if from a rock or elevated place, sixty or eighty isbas. If his course is intercepted by a tree or rock, he passes an isba round, in order to avoid it. When he roars the third time, he moves thirty miles, as rapidly as the sound of the roar, and at that distance he overtakes the echo of his own voice.*

In the same forest there is a Jambu, or Damba tree, from which Jambudípa, or Dambadiwa, derives its names. From the root to the highest part is 1000 miles; the space covered by the outspreading branches is 3000 miles in cir-

* Sára Sangaha, Appendix, Note V. Anguttara Nikáya Wannaná.

cumference; the trunk is 150 miles round, and 500 miles from the root to the place where the branches begin to extend; the four great branches are each 500 miles long, and from between these flow four great rivers. Where the fruit of the tree falls, small plants of gold arise, which are washed into the river, and carried onward to the ocean.*

---

This summary of what we may call the geography and astronomy of the Buddhists, is taken from works that are considered as authoritative by the followers of the Tathágato; but nearly every one of the propositions therein contained is proved to be false, unfounded, and unreal, by the demonstrations of science. On reading them, the European, or the native of India who is acquainted with European literature, is ready to say, "What nonsense! these things are too absurd to require to be refuted;" but, though they may appear in this light to those who have received superior instruction, it may be well to remember, that errors which have been regarded as revealed truth during thousands of years, are not to be set aside by an utterance of surprise or an expression of contempt. I shall, therefore, examine, one by one, the statements attributed to the Bhagawá; who is called sarwagnya, the all-knowing; buddha, he who knows all that can be known, and lókawidú, he who knows all worlds.

* Sára Sangaha. Note W. Wisuddhi Magga. Sárattha Dípani.

## PART SECOND.—THE ERRORS OF THE SYSTEM.

### 1. THE CHAKKA-WALA, OR SAKWALAS.

It was the thought of Buddha that there are numberless worlds on a plane level with the world in which we live. When he resided in the Nigrodhuáráma temple, at Kapila-wattu, his native city, he was asked by Anando about a certain sráwaka, called Abhibhu, who, whilst resident in one of the brahma-lokas, could cause his voice to be heard at the same time in a thousand worlds; and he was further requested by Anando to inform him whether he himself possessed a similar power. Buddha replied; "The Tathágato is unlimited, appameyya (in the exercise of this power.") The same question was asked by Anando three times. Buddha then enquired if he knew what chúlaní lókadhátu meant? And as he intimated, in reply, that this would be a proper time in which to instruct the priests upon the subject, the sage proceeded: "The space illuminated by one sun and moon is a lókadhátu, or world. A thousand of these are a chúlaní lókadhátu, or inferior series of worlds; so that in one chúlaní lókadhátu there are a thousand suns and moons, a thousand Maha Mérus, a thousand of each of the four continents, four thousand great oceans, and a thousand each of the déwa and brahma lókas; this is a chúlaní lókadhátu. Two thousand of these make a majjhimika lókadhátu, or middle series. Three thousand of the middle series make a maha sahassi lókadhátu, or superior series. Anando! if the Tathágato is wishful, he can cause his voice to be heard in all these worlds, or even a greater number. And it is in this way. By the glory proceeding from the Tathágato, all these worlds are enlightened, and when the enquiry is made, whence this brightness proceeds, he speaks with his voice, (so that in all these worlds it can be heard).*

At another time, when Buddha resided in the Jétawana wihára, near the city of Sáwatthi, a certain déwatá, called Róhatissa, came to him by night, illuminating the whole place by his presence, and respectfully asked him, "Is it possible to know, see, or arrive at, the limit (of the worlds), or a place where there is neither birth, jayati; existence, jiyati; death, miyati; or re-production, chawati?" Buddha replied, "I do not say there is such a limit;" but he repeated a stanza to this effect:

By journeying (one) cannot arrive at
The limit of the lóka:
(But) without arriving at the limit
There is (yet) freedom from sorrow (dukkha).

The déwatá afterwards said; "In a former birth I was a rishi, of the same name as now. I had the power of irdhi, and could go through the air. How? As the arrow of the skilful archer cuts through the shadow of a tall tree, with the same ease and rapidity I could step from the eastern to the western boundary of the Sakwala. Being possessed of this rapidity of motion, and length of step, a desire arose in my mind to travel to the end of the world. In this way, and for this purpose, I travelled for the

* Anguttara Nikáya. Appendix, Note X.

period of one hundred years, never stopping unless for eating, drinking, sleeping, or the purposes of nature; but in that space of time I had not arrived at the end of the world; and I then died."*

No one but the Tathágato can know the extent of the infinite worlds. The Sakwalas are not the stars, as is sometimes supposed; they are tub-like masses, of the same shape as our own Sakwala, floating as ships in the great universe of waters, which is everywhere extended, and is itself supported by the air, everywhere extended also. But though the telescope of the astronomer has swept through every part of the heavens, north, south, east, west, above, and below, and revealed the existence of thousands of worlds never seen by the naked eye, he has not discovered anything like a Sakwala. It is not strictly correct that Buddha teaches that the Sakwala is itself a plane. The four continents and the great seas are on a level; but from Aswakanna to Maha Méru there is a series of rises, culminating in the heaven of Sekra. Yet no fact in science is more certain than that the earth is of a shape entirely different to that which is given it by Buddha. There is scarcely any part of it in which Europeans are not found, at any given moment, either as sailors, travellers, or colonists; and as no limit to it has been discovered by them, it is proved thereby that its shape is like that of an orange; not merely round like a circle, but globular like a ball or sphere. It is, therefore, of the same shape as the other worlds that travel through the sky, and can have no limit like a sakwala gala, or wall. To a line there are

* Anguttara Nikáya, Note Y.

limits; to a circle there is no limit; and if the whole surface of a sphere be traced to find a limit, the effort will be in vain. This limitlessness is not from its being infinitely extended, but from its globularity. The various beings on the surface of the earth, whether they walk with their heads upwards or downwards, are attracted towards the centre of the earth by the law of gravity, or the tendency that everywhere exists, in a smaller or lighter body, to be attracted towards a mass that is larger, or of greater weight. Upwards and downwards are relative terms, varying with the position of the object about which we speak.*

* It may not be out of place to insert here the reasons usually given for the rotundity of the earth.

1. Nearly every part of the earth has been visited, but no limit has been found to it.

2. By sailing always in an eastern direction without ever turning to the west, or, by sailing always in a western direction, without ever turning to the east, ships arrive at the same place whence they departed. Not many weeks pass over without the arrival in England of ships that have sailed round the world. This, it may be said, is not absolutely impossible upon Buddhist principles; but then, as the Aswakanna rocks, outside which is the nearest way we could go, are 15,111,700 miles in circumference, it would require more than 200 years to accomplish the voyage, sailing at the rate of 200 miles every day.

3. When there are tall objects at a distance, we can see only the top, but as we approach them, we see gradually the parts that are lower. The most satisfactory test of this law is at sea, because there we have no inequalities of any consequence to intercept the view. By ascending to the top of the mast, sailors can see distinctly things that they could not see at all from the deck of the vessel. In every part of the earth and sea similar effects are observed. When looking at a ship approaching the shore through a telescope, whilst it is yet in the horizon, the upper parts of the mast are seen distinctly, so that the colour and shape of the flag can be distinguished, but the deck, the vessel itself, cannot be seen at all.

4. The shadow of the earth is circular, as seen when thrown on the moon during an eclipse.

An objection is sometimes raised by the Buddhists that as there are some parts of the world not yet visited by Europeans, these parts, if visited, might prove that the Buddhist is right, and the European wrong. But this cannot be. There are probably some parts of the province of Bintenne, in this island, not yet explored by the white man; but he has been on every side of it, and knows that it can only be of a certain size; and it is the same with other unvisited lands; he has been all round them, and can tell exactly their extent. Except the interior of Africa and Australia, and the north and south poles, nearly every part of the earth has been seen by the eye of the traveller or navigator; and if we could sift the evidence they would give, under an examination on these subjects by a board of scientific men, it would all tend to prove that Buddha was ignorant of the true figure of the earth, and that all he says about it is unscientific and false.

## 2. MAHA MERU.

1. There are proofs afforded by mathematical astronomy of the non-existence of this mountain, more certain than any I can make plain to those who are not acquainted

5. By ascending an elevation, we can see near the horizon, stars that are lower in the heavens than the lowest we saw when we were on level ground. We then see more of the sky than half a circle. When the sky has been ascended in a balloon after sunset, the sun has again come into view, appearing first to rise, and then to set a second time.

6. In one part of the earth the stars that are seen are entirely different to those seen in another part; and the manner in which they seem to change their places can only be accounted for on the supposition that the earth turns on its axis, and is spherical in shape.

None of these things could take place if the earth were of the shape it is said to be by Buddha. It *must* be a sphere.

with the science upon which its conclusions rest. But I may state, that there is a general law in existence, that all the parts of the universe, whether large or small, influence each other, and are dependent on each other. I will explain what I mean by an illustration. Until the invention of the telescope, the number of known planets was six: Mercury, Venus, the Earth, Mars, Jupiter, and Saturn; but since then no fewer than fifty-five others have been discovered, the existence of which was entirely unknown previously to this period. In 1781, Sir William Herschell discovered the planet now called Uranus. This planet was closely watched from that time, and as certain irregularities were observed in its motion that could not be explained by the action of the planets then discovered, two young men, Adams of Cambridge, and Le Verrier of Paris, unknown to each other, set themselves to the task of calculating the cause of this irregularity. Each arrived at the same conclusion, that the cause must be the existence of a planet outside the orbit of Uranus; and they then sought out the position in which the planet would be found. When Le Verrier had completed his calculations, on the 23rd Sept., 1846, he wrote to Dr. Galle, one of the Astronomers Royal in the Observatory at Berlin, informing him that the longitude of the planet he was to seek for would at that time be 326 degrees, and requesting him to look for it there. The astronomer did as he was requested, and found the planet "that very night." The name of Neptune was given to it. It is 2,864,000,000 miles from the sun, and 35,000 miles in diameter. It is evident, then, that if the astronomer could tell the existence of an object one twenty-fourth of the size of Maha Méru, and nearly nine hundred times more distant from us, he could easily ascertain the existence of that mountain, if there is such a place, even though it were impossible to see it; but the same science that told of the existence of Neptune, and its exact position, though human eye had never seen it from the foundation of the world, tells us, with equal certainty, that it is impossible for a mass like Maha Méru to exist at all in the present economy of the universe.

2. If there were such a mountain as Maha Méru, we ought to see it from Ceylon, on the principles of Buddhism, as its rays are said to strike the Sakwala rock, which is much more distant from it than the continent in which we live. This will be seen from the figure on the next page, if A represent Maha Méru, B Jambudípa, and C the Sakwala rock. The same diagram, in which the proportions are drawn according to the heights and distances given in the text, shews also that there is no object coming between Jambudípa and the summit of Maha Méru. Perhaps it will be said that its rays do not give the kind of light by which objects are seen. But are we not told that these rays give colour to the seas, as well as the skies, connected with our continent? Again, we are told that the eastern side of Maha Méru is of silver and its southern of sapphire. But is not the moon said to be of a similar substance? Then, if we can see the welcome face of the moon, formed of crystal and silver, why cannot we see the face of Maha Méru, which is formed of sapphire and silver, according to Buddhist science? And if it be said that it is too distant for us to be able to see it, I ask, how is it, then, that we

*The Form and Arrangement of a Buddhist Sakwala.*

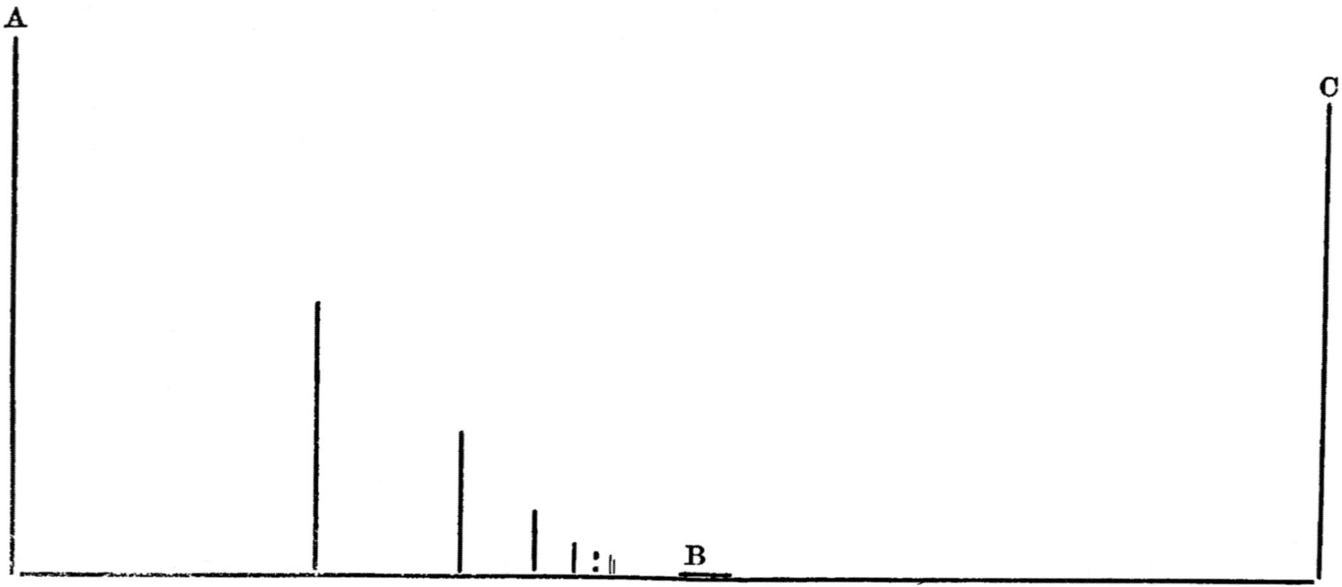

can see so plainly the planet Saturn, which we are told by the astronomer is ten times less in size, and three hundred times more distant from this continent, than the size and distance given to Maha Méru by Buddha?

3. All the objects upon the surface of the earth are attracted towards its centre, and partake of a motion, it is proved to possess, by which it turns round once in about twenty-four hours. The turning of the earth upon its axis may not be capable of proof from ocular evidence like that afforded of the turning of the sun and planets by the observation of the spots upon their surface, but either the earth must thus turn, or the whole universe of sun, moon, planets, comets, and fixed stars, must move round the earth every twenty-four hours, which, from their immense distances, and the consequent rapidity with which they must travel, would be a greater wonder than the rotation of the earth, however marvellous it may seem. I have sometimes been told that if the earth turns round, I have only to leap up, and the ground from which I leaped would pass from under me. But we will take the instance of a person in a railway carriage, which sometimes goes at the rate of a mile in one minute. By the law it is now attempted to establish, if the person in the carriage were to let anything fall from the roof, it would strike against the back of the carriage, or at least fall obliquely; but the experiment can be tried in Ceylon, not many months hence, and it will be found that the object will fall perpendicularly, whatever may be the rapidity of the train, just as if the carriage were perfectly at rest. The reason is, that the motion of the carriage is communicated to everything in it; and, for

the same reason, an arrow sent perpendicularly into the air would return to the place whence it was shot from the bow, because the motion of the earth would be communicated to the air and the arrow. There must also be some reason why the arrow returns to the earth, and does not fly away into space. It has been discovered that its fall is occasioned by what is called the attraction of gravitation, a property by which, as we have already noticed, every particle of matter has a tendency towards every other particle of matter, so that all bodies not only attract other bodies, but are themselves attracted; and the property is mutual and universal. This force increases in known proportion to the nearness of bodies to each other, and by the same law it decreases as they recede from each other. Every two portions of matter within the universe attract each other with a force proportional directly to the quantity of matter they contain, and to the inverse square of their distances. The force is also in proportion to the quantity of matter contained in the body; the more massive body exerting the greater power of attractiveness. The sun attracts the earth, the earth the moon, and the moon the waters of the ocean; and all act upon each other. The earth, then, being a far larger mass than any object near it, everything upon it is attracted towards its centre in a straight line; and it is for this reason that the arrow returns from the sky and falls to the ground. But there is another force of a different kind, affecting everything upon the surface of the earth. It acts in this way. If a piece of lead, attached to a string, be turned rapidly round, and the string breaks, the lead will fly off to a considerable distance. There is the same tendency to fly off in all things whirled round by the turning of the earth; but this tendency is counteracted by the other force, the force of gravitation. There are thus two forces acting upon everything near us; one force pulling things towards the earth, and the other tending to send them away from it. Now at the height of 26,000 miles from the earth,* the off-flying force counteracts or overcomes, the force by which objects are attracted to the earth; and, therefore, everything connected with the earth, and carried with it as it turns round day by day, must be within that distance. There cannot, therefore, by any possibility, be a mountain like Maha Méru upon this earth, or connected with it, as it is said to be 840,000 miles high; a height that would necessitate its being hurled into space.

4. We know exactly at what place it is midnight, and at what place it is noon, at any given moment, and the exact distance also between the two places; and we can thereby prove that there can be no mountain between the two places of the size of Maha Méru, as taught by Buddha.

5. The Buddhists seek to place Maha Méru in some part of the world unvisited by Europeans; and the North Pole especially is one of their favourite positions. But the poles of the earth are not 7,000 miles from Ceylon; so that if the centre of Maha Méru were at the North Pole, it would not only reach to Ceylon, as the semi-diameter of this mountain is 420,000 miles, but it would reach nearly twice as far as the moon. As Maha Méru is fifty times larger than the earth, it is evident that it cannot be

* Maury's Physical Geography of the Sea.

upon the earth; and when some adventurous man of the coming time shall succeed in reaching the North Pole, we are certain that he will not find there a mountain like Maha Méru.

There can be no doubt that Buddha taught the existence of Maha Méru. These are his very words: "Sinéru, Bhikkhawé, pabbatarájá chaturásíti-yójana-sahassáni áyáména; chaturásíti-yójana-sahassáni wittháréna; chaturásíti-yójana-sahassáni maha samuddé ajjhógálho; chaturásíti-yójana-sahassáni samuddé achchuggato."* "Priests! the great mountain Sinéru is 84,000 yójanas in length; 84,000 yójanas in breadth; 84,000 yójanas sunk in the great ocean; and 84,000 yojanas above the great ocean." An attempt may be made to set aside the consequences of this exposure of Buddha's ignorance, by saying, that this is a kind of mistake that does not invalidate his doctrines; Buddhism may still be true as a religious system. But this is a fallacy that I am most anxious to set aside. If Buddha said that which is false, under the supposition that it is true, he betrays ignorance, imperfect knowledge, and misapprehension. He cannot, therefore, be a safe teacher; there may be some things about his religion that are true, as there are about every religion; but it is not a revelation; its author was a mere man, with limited and imperfect knowledge; and to receive it as the pure unmixed truth, is a mischievous and fatal mistake.

When the existence of Maha Méru was denied some years ago, a writer calling himself Kahagallé Mohattála, said that Buddha intended all he taught about Maha Méru

* Satta Suriyuggamana Suttanta: Anguttara Nikáya; the 7th Nipáta.

as an allegory.* But if Maha Méru falls, it does not fall alone. The heaven of Sekra, and the other celestial and brahma worlds must fall with it. And if all these things are an allegory, the hope of the Buddhist is indeed vain. According to his own system, he knows not what sins of former births he may have yet to expiate in births to come; he may now be a religious and truth-loving man, but he can tell nothing about his next birth, whether it will be one of happiness or misery; he cannot aim at anything higher or nobler as the end of existence than to become nothing; and now a professor of his own religion takes away from him all hope founded on the intermediate states of happiness to which he has been permitted, heretofore, to look forward as his temporary reward.†

## 3. THE SAKWALA ROCK.

The same arguments that prove the non-existence of Maha Méru prove the non-existence of the Sakwala rock. From its massiveness, it could not exist without being known to the astronomer, even though it were impossible

* Gogerly, Evidences and Doctrines of the Christian Religion.

† "Absurdities do not strike the people of India as they would the inhabitants of another land; and, if pointed out, sometimes rather strengthen than weaken their conviction of a divine origin. The statements about the size of Maha Méru present to them no incongruity, and are gravely received, as if they were a well-known axiom. A mortal, they say, could not put the greater into the less, and therefore, by doing it, God gives a signal proof of the greatness of his power. In proportion as a statement, or doctrine is absurd its credibility is not diminished, but augmented; and the more it outrages reason and common sense it is regarded as the more worthy of the Deity." Among the matters regarded as incapable of demonstration by Kapila is the existence of "the golden mountain Méru."—Christian Work, Sept. 1863.

to see it. But if it exists, it ought to be seen, as it is nearly as high as Maha Méru, and about the same distance from us. Three of the Sakwalas are always contiguous to each other, as we learn from the Commentary on the Dígha Nikáya, Mahapadána Suttan; in which we are told that three of the Sakwalas touch each other, like three wl eels, or three hoops, and that between the three there is the Lókántarika hell, 80,000 miles in size. All the Sakwalas are alike in their arrangement, each having a Maha Méru, sun, moon, etc. But every object of the size of a Sakwala, in whatever part of visible space, has been examined by the telescope. Bodies have been discovered with phases like the moon; others with dark spots, or with belts, upon their surface; and another with a luminous ring near it, 30,000 miles broad. Several are scen to have moons revolving round them as the moon revolves round the earth, and some stars revolve around each other; but anything like the appearance presented by the Sakwala of Buddhism, has not yet been discovered, and we may venture to say, never will, if the analogy presented by numberless facts is to be regarded.

## 4. THE CIRCLES OF ROCK AND SEA.

The argument from the calculations of the astronomer is applicable to all the seven circles of rock and sea, with equal fatality to their existence. And besides that, if the mighty steps that arc said to form the pathway toward the heaven of Sekra really exist, they ought, according to the common laws of vision, to be seen from Ceylon, as being onc of the islands attached to Jambudípa.

## 5. THE SUN AND MOON.

We have learnt what the ideas of the Buddhists are as to these luminaries. But what are the facts, as taught by incontrovertible science? Instead of the sun going round the earth, it is the earth that goes round the sun. If the sun and other objects in the heavens go round the earth, such is their immense distance from it, that the sun must travel 400,000 miles in a minute, the nearest stars must rush through the sky at the rate of 1,000,000,000 miles in a second of time, and the more distant stars, all of which are much larger than the earth, with a rapidity that no numbers can express. The sun is upwards of 90,000,000 miles from the earth, when it is the nearest to us. The mode in which these numbers are found out may be learnt from any work on practical astronomy; there is no mystery about them; they may be calculated by those whom I now address. As we know the size of the Sakwala, we are certain that, by native computation, the sun can never be much more than six millions of miles from us, when visible; and science tells us that it is 882,000 miles in diameter, and not 500, as stated in the native books. From the earth to the moon is 240,000 miles, and this luminary is about 2000 miles in diameter and not 490, as given by native authors. According to European astronomy, founded upon known and proved data, the distance from the moon to the sun is never less than 90,000,000 of miles, but according to the Buddhists, who found their numbers upon imagination only, it is, in some instances, within the distance of one yójana, or ten miles. We may easily learn that the native numbers as to the relative distances of these two bodies from the earth, cannot be right. When we look at the sun through a telescope its apparent size is very little altered, on account of its immense distance; it is much the same in appearance as when seen by the naked eye. But when we look at the moon through the same instrument, it is like looking at another world; rocks and valleys can be seen and measured, and the shape of an object as small as the fort of Colombo can be distinguished. The moon is almost as near to us in reality, as the height given to the Yugandhara rocks; and it is evident, therefore, that if these rocks exist, the moon must strike against them, in her passage through the sky, from the force of gravitation, acting according to its invariable law. It is further evident that the principles of Buddhism are wrong altogether, because, if it were possible for the moon to approach so closely to Maha Méru as to come within a distance of 420,000 miles, she would be so powerfully attracted towards the mountain, from its immense massiveness, that her motion would be entirely disarranged. The moon is not a luminous body in itself, but is visible because it reflects the rays of the sun; and when a smaller portion of its surface appears, it is not from any covering as by a vessel, or from any overpowering by a superior light, but from its illuminated portion being turned away from the earth. The half of its surface is always bright, except during an eclipse; but from our position on the earth we can only see the whole of its brightness when it is opposite the sun.

The outer side of the sun is said, in the Sára Sangaha and other works, to be of crystal. But this statement is proved by the telescope not to be correct. There are spots on the sun, some lighter and some darker than the general surface, which are continually changing their position and appearance; and from them we learn that the sun turns round once in a little more than twenty-five days, as the earth turns round in one day. The numerous observations made on these spots, since they were discovered, led at first to the conclusion that the sun is a solid, non-luminous body, covered over by two layers of gaseous matter, the one nearest the sun being also non-luminous, but the other luminous gas, or flame; and that the spots are like openings in the clouds of our own sky, revealing the dark surface of the solid globe. Subsequent discoveries have somewhat modified this idea; but no one can look at the sun, through an instrument of even moderate power, without being assured that the sun is not composed of either crystal or gold.

The surface of the moon is said, by the same authorities, to be covered over with silver, and to be cold; but the telescope again teaches us a different lesson. When seen through it, the surface of the moon appears to be thickly covered with mountain masses, of various forms and size, tinted white and gray, many of them extremely abrupt and steep, and separated from each other by immense ravines and extensive valleys. There is no vapour of any kind on its surface, so that when visible it is always bright and clear. The marks upon it are so well defined as to allow of maps being made to represent its appearance, with names for the ridges and valleys, as in a map of the countries of the earth. In 1856 Professor Smyth visited the island of Teneriffe, for the purpose of making experiments on various disputed points connected with the heavenly bodies. His observations were made at 8,840 and 10,700 feet above the level of the sea. At both elevations he ascertained the warmth of the moon's light.

It is thus proved that nearly every one of the propositions made in the native books, as to the sun and moon, is contrary to truth. The astronomers of the west were nearly in equal ignorance with those of the east until the invention or improvement of the telescope, by Galileo, about two hundred and sixty years ago. This instrument at once upset all the old notions about an earth at rest and a revolving sky; and it now becomes an agent of destruction to the supremacy of Buddha, more fatal than the arrow of the archer who tried to take his life at the instigation of his brother-in-law, Déwadatta, or the stone hurled against him from the Gijhakúta rock.

## 6. THE THREE PATHS.

The statements that appear in the native books respecting celestial phenomena all lead to the conclusion that they who made them were unacquainted with any other country besides India. The speculations about the different degrees of rain when the sun is in different paths can only be true of one region; because, when it is cold and rainy in one part of the world, it is warm and dry in another; and in some parts of the world, as the coasts of Peru and Mexico, and the deserts of Africa, Asia, and Australia, there is no rain at all, in any season of the year. Of these things the native authors were ignorant; they were guided by what they themselves saw, in their own locality; and from not having the benefit of the enlarged observation of travellers to other portions of the earth, they have fallen into the errors they set forth as religious truth. It is difficult to arrive at certainty as to what they say about the motions of the sun, the explanations given by the native pundits being contradictory: but if I am not mistaken, there are three: 1. The sun is in different paths, according to the season of the year, each path being at a different elevation from the earth. 2. There is the (apparent) motion we see daily from east to west. 3. There is an annual motion, answering to our declination, in the passage of the sun from Maha Méru to the Sakwala rocks, and its return from the rock towards Maha Méru. About the last motion there can be no doubt, as it is referred to in nearly all the works that treat on these subjects. When near Maha Méru, its position is called anto; when mid-way between Maha Méru and the Sakwala rock, majjhima; and when near the Sakwala rock, bahi; or inner, central, and outer. On this system, the sun must appear to *all* the inhabitants of Jambudípa, to be sometimes to the north, sometimes overhead, or in the zenith, and sometimes to the south. But this is contrary to fact, as every one who has come to Ceylon from Europe by way of the Cape of Good Hope can testify. In England, the sun is never overhead, and never to the north; near the Cape it is never overhead, and never to the south. But, as in India and Ceylon it is sometimes to the north, sometimes overhead, and sometimes to the south, the Buddhist writers have so spoken of it that it must necessarily be the same in all countries of Jambudípa, upon their principles. This is another proof that their information is confined and local, and that what they assert with confidence, as the revelations of men they call rahats, has no foundation in truth, and brings down the intelligence of the rahats, upon these subjects, to a lower level than that of the schoolboy, in the present age.

## 7. THE RISING OF THE SUN.

In what is recorded by Buddhist writers as to the position of the sun, there is the same betrayal of a want of scientific or experimental knowledge: a local occurrence is regarded as if it were universal. The sun is always, in every moment of the twenty-four hours of the day, rising in some part of *this* world, and always setting in another part of *this* world, the world in which we live, and that we can personally visit. The worlds in which the inhabitants have square or half-moon faces, or in which they never grow old, must be other and separate worlds to this; and about the rising of the sun in them I can say nothing. The sun is said to set on passing beyond Yughandara, by which it is hid. But if so, why does it remain behind the mountain so long? What is it doing during the ten hours of darkness, the length of the night in Ceylon? And how is it that in the north of Scotland, where I have lived, and know of what I affirm, at midsummer the light of the sun is seen during nearly the whole of the twenty-four hours of the day, in mid-winter the days being proportionately short? And how is it, again, that near the north and south poles, for months together, the sun never sets, but goes round and round in the sky, and is always visible? It is one glory of Britain that the sun never sets upon its territory; the meaning of which is, that during every moment of every day and night the sun is visible in one part or other of her Majesty's dominions. It was an unfortunate day for Buddhism when its founder was made to assert the existence of Maha Méru. This figment of a wild imagination has led the native writers into errors that are apparent to the inhabitants of all countries not tropical, on the testimony of their own every-day experience.

## 8. THE ASUR RÁHU.

The eclipses of the sun and moon are caused, according to Buddha, by this monster, who is said to be nearly 50,000 miles high. He sometimes covers them with his hand, and sometimes hides them in his mouth. But how can a being, with a mouth only 3,000 miles deep, swallow the sun, which is 800,000 miles in diameter, according to the calculations of science. If the sun be of so hot a nature as is represented, why does not he bawl out, as well as the déwas, during the operation; and as even a burnt child shuns the fire, why does he repeat the experiment so frequently, when he knows what must be the consequence? As to the moon, we are quite sure that there must be some mistake. In the maps of its surface, the detached masses of matter thrown down the sides of its mountains bear a considerable resemblance to the mounds of sand, hollow in the centre, piled up and thrown down with so much industry by the ants in the cinnamon gardens near Colómbo and other places. If Ráhu licks the moon with his tongue, how is it that immediately afterwards its surface is as bright as ever, and not a fragment in its hollows or heaps displaced? And how is it that scientific men, and even the naksæstrakárayás of the island, can tell to so exact a period as a second of time, for hundreds of years beforehand, that the seizure will take place? Is Ráhu a living machinery that has life like a man, and yet is obliged to move with more regularity than a clock or a watch, and this for thousands of years? Then, there is not another being like him in the whole universe. What does he do it for? Does he suppose that he can stop the course of the sun or the moon? If he could, what would be the benefit? And when he has tried, and tried in vain, for so many years, what a simpleton he must be to renew the attempt! And, lastly, how is it, except upon the principles of European science, that the solar seizure always takes place at the time of the dark moon, when the moon is between the earth and the sun; and that the lunar seizure always takes place at the time the moon is full, when the earth comes between the moon and the sun, and intercepts his rays?

I am told that my labour here may be spared, as there is scarcely any one who will read these pages that really believes in the existence of Ráhu. But is not this a declaration and confession, that Buddha either told a wilful untruth, or that he was himself deceived? There can be no doubt as to what I affirm; because every time the Pirit exorcism is read by the priests, they proclaim the damaging fact that Buddha believed in the existence of Ráhu, and in his attempt to swallow the sun and moon. Here are his words, as they appear in the Sanyutta Nikáya, Sahá Gáthá Waggá.

"Thus I heard. Bhagawa was living in Sáwatthi, in the garden of Anátha Pindiko. At that time, the moon-god was seized by the asúr Ráhu. Then the moon-god, remembering Buddha, spake this stanza:

> "Namó té Buddha wíratthu
> Wippamuttósi sabbadhi,
> Sambádhapatipannosmi
> Tassa mé saranan' bhawáti.

"'Adoration to thee, great Buddha! Thou art free from all impurities. I am distressed. Become thou a refuge to me.' Then Bhagawá, in behalf of the moon-god, addressed Ráhu thus:

> "Tathágatan' arahantan'
> Chandima saranan' gátó,
> Ráhu chandan' pamunchassu,
> Buddhá lókánukampakáti.

"'In the rahat Tathágato, the moon-god has taken refuge. Ráhu! Release thou the moon. The Buddhas are merciful to the world.' Then the asur Ráhu, having released the moon-god, went in great haste to the place where the chief asur, Wépachitti, was, and after approaching him, stood in great terror on one side. The chief asur said to him:

> "Kinnu santaramánówa,
> Ráhu chandan pamunchasi,
> Sanwiggarúpó ágamma,
> Kinnu bhítówa tittasiti.

"'Why, Ráhu, trembling, hast thou released the moon?

In terror having come, why dost thou stand thus, afraid?'
The asur Ráhu replied:

"Sattadhá mé phalé muddhá,
Jéwanto na sukhan' labhé,
Buddha gátábhi gitómhi,
Nóchi muncheyya chandimanti.

"'If I do not release the moon, my head would be split into seven (pieces); and were I to live, I could have no enjoyment, as Buddha has recited stanzas (of prohibition).'"

This is the Chanda Pirit. The Suriya Pirit is the same, substituting sun-god for moon-god, with this exception, that in speaking of the sun-god Buddha says, "Ráhu! swallow not the traveller through the skies, who, with the splendor of the heat of his shining orb, dissipates the darkness."

These words, about which there can be no doubt as to their being attributed to Buddha, are worse than weak. They are not the result of ignorance alone; they contain what must be an intentional misguidance. We cannot blame the prince Gótamo for not knowing more about these things than the rest of mankind in that age; but to say that the sun-god or the moon-god applied to him for protection from an asur, and that he professed to grant this request, is to charge him with the utterance of what he must have known to be untrue, and with the false assumption of powers that he did not possess.

## 9. THE WORLDS OF WATER AND WIND.

The native authors do not often venture upon a scientific demonstration in proof of any of their propositions; but in

Milinda Panha there is one in favour of the resting of the World of Water on the World of Wind. When Milinda, king of Ságal, said that he could not believe that this was possible, the priest Nágaséna replied, by taking a syringe, and pointing out to him that the water within the instrument was prevented from coming out by the external air; which reply was satisfactory to the king. But the reason of the retention of the water within the syringe is, that whilst there is the pressure of the air from below, there is none from above, upon the water that has entered into the space made by the drawing up of the handle. Were the sucker not air-tight, the water would instantly rush out, notwithstanding the pressure from below of the exterior air. The reply of Nágaséna does not, therefore, apply to the case in question, and entirely fails to present an adequate reason for the support of the World of Water by the World of Wind, or Air.

## 10. THE SEA.

1. *Its Waves.* We are told that there are waves 100 miles, or more than three million feet, high. This is a great exaggeration. There are no waves that are 100 feet high, and not often any that are half that height. In the wildest parts of the sea, and in the strongest gale, the waves are seldom more than forty feet high. We are told, again, that the water of the sea is agitated by the wind 400,000 miles from the surface; whereas, in the most violent storms, the ocean is not moved by the wind in the least at the depth of 100 feet.

2. *Its Depth.* Near the Sakwala rock the sea is said to

be 820,000 miles deep. This must be the sea to which we have access, because it is said to deepen gradually to this number of miles from the shores of Jambudípa, where it is one inch deep. But what is the truth of the matter, as ascertained by experiment, a thousand times repeated? The sea has nowhere been found to be more than eight miles deep, and few soundings have told of a depth of more than five miles, the average not being more than three or four. The statement that the sea gradually increases in depth from the shore of the continent, is another great mistake. There are maps of the principal oceans of the world, on which the depth of the water in different places is marked; and from these it is seen, that in some instances the water is deeper near the shore than it is in the middle of the ocean. In the bed of the Atlantic there is a deep valley, averaging in depth five miles; but the depth between Ireland and Newfoundland does not generally exceed one mile.

3. *Its Stillness.* We are told that between the 400,000 miles that are agitated by the wind, and the 400,000 miles that are agitated by the fishes, in the Great World, there is a stratum of still water 40,000 miles in thickness. But the Timira Pingala could not agitate the waters in which it is said to live, for the space of 8,000 miles, without affecting the waters above, especially if, at the time, it was near the top of its own waters. Besides, no part of the sea is ever still. Were there not a constant interchange between the particles at the bottom and the top, the sea would lose its balance and its counterpoises. Not being able to preserve its status, the water at the bottom would

grow heavier and heavier, whilst that at the top would become lighter and lighter, until the one became all salt, and the other entirely fresh. By currents, and other means, again, there is a general circulation in the sea, by which, in process of time, water from one part is conveyed to another part, and by which a general commingling and interchange of the waters takes place.*

4. *Its Fishes.* We are told that in one part of the sea there are mermen, with bodies like human beings, and noses as sharp as razors, who rise up and down in the water. This is a fabulous creature, formerly supposed to exist by nearly all nations familiar with the sea; but though ships are now sailing upon every part of the ocean, no instance is recorded of a merman or mermaid having been met with by any one whose word can be believed. But what are we to say as to fishes 10,000 miles in size? By what are they sustained? They must eat, or they are not fishes. They must be in absolute darkness, as light does not penetrate more than a few hundred feet below the surface of the sea. Then, again, water is compressed by pressure, or weight. At the depth of ninety-three miles it would be twice as close or compressed as at the surface. Where the sea is 3000 fathoms deep, upon every foot of water there is a pressure equal to 1,296,000 pounds. The reason of this I shall be able to explain more clearly, when, in reference to the trees that are said to grow in the Himála-wana, I shall have to speak of the properties of air; but I may here mention, that I have more than once seen the following experiment tried at sea. An empty

* Maury's Physical Geography of the Sea.

bottle, closely corked, its mouth covered over with cordage and wax, is let down into the séa, during a calm. When it is brought up again it is full of water, with the cork reversed, shewing the immense pressure there must be to force the cork into the bottle. At the depth of 440,000 miles the water would become solid, and the body of the fish would become crushed with a weight so inconceivably great, that it would be impossible for it to move, and, therefore, it could neither shake its ear or its tail, as the Timira Pingala is said to do. Thus, all that is said about the sea is as untrue as the statcments about the Sakwalas and the sun and moon.

## 11. THE GEOGRAPHY OF THE WORLD.

1. *Land and Water.* By native geographers, professing to write by the guidance of the unerring Bhagawá, the proportion of water connected with our continent is represented as being immensely greater than that of land. But if the *surface* of the earth were divided into 200 equal parts, about fifty parts would be land, and the rest water; and if the *mass* of the earth were divided into 1786 equal parts by weight, the sea would be equivalent to only one of them.

2. *The Continents and Islands.* Nothing answering to the four continents has been discovered upon the face of the earth; nor can they exist, because, if existent, they must have been seen by European mariners, who are continually visiting every sea and shore. The faces of men are not of one shape in one part of the world, and in another of an entirely different shape. Except where artificial

means are used to produce distortion, as among the Indians of North America, there is not anywhere a greater difference than can be seen among the residents in Ceylon, where we have the flat face of the Malay, and the oval profile of the Singhalese. The five hundred islands said to be attached to each continent, exist in the imagination only. Near Jampudípa there are few islands; at some distance from it there are the Laccadives and Maldives, but they are more than 40,000 in number, and in the South Seas also the islands are numbered by thousands.

3. *Jampudípa.* This continent, inhabited by men, is said to be 100,000 miles in length and breadth, including the portion submerged for the want of merit in its inhabitants. But it is difficult to tell what to make of Jambudípa, as mentioned by native writers. If it is intended to include the entire portion of the earth inhabited by men, in the 30,000 miles that are given to Jambudípa as it now exists, the description of it is imperfect, and like previous statements that we have noticed, is put forth by persons whose opportunities of observation have been limited, and who can have had no intercourse with any part of the world away from India and the countries on its immediate borders. Its comparison in size with the Himála-wana, and the names given to its principal provinces, cities, and rivers, teach us that it includes no more than the country now called India, and that the knowledge of the earlier Buddhists was confined to this region. And yet, though it is so small a portion of the earth, they believed that it was the whole of the world of men. The rishis and rahats are said to have visited other worlds, and yet the account

they give us of their own is entirely wrong; and when they refer to any place out of the limits of their own country, they give us fiction instead of truth, the imaginary instead of the real. In this conclusion Buddha himself is to be included. He mistook a small part of the world for the whole, and beyond what he learnt from others of places at a distance from his native country, he was as ignorant as the rest of the subjects of Suddhódana. But the 30,000 miles, as applied to India, are not correct, as it is in no part more than 2000 miles from east to west, or 1500 miles from north to south, whilst the surface of the whole earth contains nearly two hundred millions of square miles.

4. *The Himála-wana.* This forest is within sight of places said to have been visited by Buddha in his reputed wanderings from city to city; and if we are to believe the legends of his life, it was no more trouble to him to go to it through the air, than to take the alms-bowl through the streets of any city near which he happened to live. Its own name, the names of its mountains, its position, its size in comparison with Jambudípa, and the rivers that are said to rise within it, all point it out as being the wild and mountainous region north of India. We should have thought that whatever mistakes might be made with regard to other countries of the world, there could be none in relation to so near a land. But the errors about this forest are as numerous, and almost as monstrous, as those about Maha Méru and the seven circles of rock. It is said to have in it seven lakes, each of which is 1500 miles in length and breadth; though its whole length is only 1000 miles, and its breadth much less. All kinds

of flowers and trees are said to grow there, though several of those enumerated are never seen out of the tropics, unless protected by artificial means. It is said to have mountains 2000 miles high, though the highest mountains in it, and there are none higher in any other part of the world, are not five miles high. From the descriptions of it, and the allusions to it, in almost every part of Buddhist literature, we should conclude that the forest is more like the Paradise of the Scriptures than any other spot upon the face of the earth. Prákrama Báhu, from hearing of its fame, wished to visit it; and when he died, on account of his great merit he was born there as a bhúmátu-déwa, there to remain until the appearance of the next Buddha, Maitrí. But that my Singhalese friends may see the kind of place to which the spirit of their former king has been transported, I will make a few extracts from the Journal of an English gentleman, who visited it about eighteen years ago. "The prospect was dreary in the extreme; the quantity of snow upon the mountains was continually increasing; a keen north blast pierced through tent and blanket; and the ground was everywhere hard and parched.—The people driving yaks looked miserably cold and haggard, and their eyes, much inflamed, testified to the hardships they had endured on the march.—For miles continuously we proceeded over snow; there was scarcely a trace of vegetation, and the cold was excessive.—We met a small party going to Tibet, all of whom appeared alike overcome by lassitude, difficulty of breathing, a sense of weight on the stomach, giddiness, and head-ache.—I found it almost impossible to keep my temper under the aggravations of pain in the forehead, lassitude, oppression in breathing, a dense drizzling fog, a keen wind, a slippery footing, where I was stumbling at every few steps, and icy-cold wet feet, hands, and eyelids.—Sometimes, when the inhabitants are obliged from famine to change their habitations in the winter, the old and feeble are frozen to death, standing and resting their chins on their staves; remaining as pillars of ice, to fall only when the thaw of the ensuing spring commences.—There is no loftier country on the globe than that embraced from the Donkia Pass, and no more howling wilderness; well might the Singtam Soubah describe it as the loftiest, coldest, windiest, and most barren country in the world. Never in the course of all my wanderings, had my eye rested on a scene so dreary and inhospitable. The 'cities of the plain' lie sunk in no more death-like sea than Cholamoo lake, nor are the tombs of Petra hewn in more desolate cliffs than those which flank the valley of the Tibetan Arun."* There are brighter spots in the Himalayas, but they are pleasant from contrast, rather than from reality, and to an inhabitant of the luxuriant island of Ceylon would appear to be most undesirable places for a residence. The native writers refer more especially to the parts where there are high mountains and extensive caves, and to the great lakes from which the rivers of Jambudípa take their rise; and of these regions this is the character—cold, barren, and comfortless, to a degree that has few parallels on earth.

* Hooker's Himalayan Journals.

## 12. THE ANOTATTA LAKE.

No sheet of water answering to the description given of this lake has been found in the Himalayas, though several adventurous travellers have visited them, in order to find out the sources of the great rivers of India. It is certain that there is no lake, in any accessible part of the whole range, from which all the four great rivers can take their rise, nor any that has four rivers running round it. It is generally supposed that by the Anótatta lake is meant the Rawan Hrad, or Langa, near which, and some say communicating with it, is the Mansarawar, or Mapang. The traditions of the natives of the Himalayas somewhat differ from the statements of the Buddhists. According to them, the four mouths are known by the name of the lion, the peacock, the bull, and the horse; the four rivers are the Indus, Sutlej, Káli or Gogra, and the Brahmaputra; and the legend is, that the first river takes its name from the bravery of the people who dwell on its banks, the second from the beauty of its women, the third from the turbulent wildness of its waters, and the last from the excellence of its horses. The streams are supposed to rise from the sacred hill Gangri, north of the lake Rawan Hrad, and the general opinion is, that the lake has no outlet. The country through which the Indus runs at its commencement, is described as "one of the most dreary regions in existence." The Buddhist authors seem to have blended into one narrative several different traditions, mingling with them a few facts. The underground course of the Ganges may refer to the places where its stream is covered by snow; the passage through the sky to some lofty waterfall; and the breaking of the rocks to a rapid rush of the waters after some temporary obstruction by glaciers and other causes; but the five rivers of our day, "the Punjaub," are the Jailum, Chenaub, Rawi, Beas, and Sutlej, none of which have any connexion with the Ganges, and all that is said about the size of the river near its source, and its course around the lake, is contrary to fact.*

## 13. THE JAMBU AND NUGA TREES.

There are several remarkable trees recorded in the Buddhist annals, but I shall confine myself to the two I have just named. The Jambu tree is said to be a thousand miles high, and the Nuga seventy miles; the first is in the centre of Jambudípa, and the other in the Himálawana. But it is utterly impossible that such trees can exist. The process by which I shall prove it may seem tedious, but it is sure, and will show the fallacy of many other assertions of the Buddhists. In order to live, trees, as well as animals, must have a certain amount of air. Air is elastic, and has weight; it may be compressed into a smaller space than it occupies under ordinary circumstances, to an extent immensely greater than water, to which I have previously referred. It is, therefore, much thicker at the surface of the earth than it is above; and it becomes lighter, gradually, the higher we rise. The air near the surface of the earth is pressed down by the air

* Thornton's Gazetteer, art. Indus. Journal of the Bengal Asiatic Society, vol. viii. p. 232.

above it, with a force of fifteen pounds to the square inch. In this way. There is a small heap of cotton, scattered lightly; if we throw more cotton upon it, the heap will be pressed, and become thicker in proportion to the quantity of cotton we throw; and if we could throw as much as would make a mountain, the original cotton would be pressed down to a firm and solid mass. It is in the same way with air; the air near the surface of the earth is pressed down, and becomes thicker, from the weight of the air above. We know, too, that the air does not extend many miles above the surface of the earth. We cannot tell exactly how high, but from the reflection of the sun's rays after sunset, it is concluded to be about 40 or 45 miles. Beyond that distance we are certain that there cannot be any air the existence of which is appreciable. The air, at a certain distance up, becomes too thin to sustain life. Thus when persons ascend high mountains, as we have seen with the travellers in the Himalayas, or rise to a greater height in balloons, there is great difficulty in being heard, though speaking loudly; birds are unable to support themselves; there is an oppression in breathing; the veins swell; the blood rushes to the nose; the forehead throbs; and a sleepiness creeps on that, if not arrested, would end in death. In the elevated plains of South America the inhabitants have larger chests than those of lower regions—an admirable instance of the animal frame being enabled to adapt itself to its peculiar circumstances. A person breathing upon the top of Mount Blanc, although extending his chest in his usual way, takes in only half as much air as he does at the foot of the mountain.* There is an analogous effect upon plants. As we ascend the mountain side, there are certain kinds of plants that grow near the foot, which soon disappear; the plants that succeed them at a little higher elevation, disappear in their turn; the number of kinds that will grow becoming less and less; until at last an elevation is reached in which nothing can grow. The higher we rise the greater is the cold, for the same reason, the rarity or thinness of the air, and from the distance above the surface of the earth, where the heat is greatest. In the Himála-wana, when we rise to the height of about 15,000 feet, there is perpetual snow, and neither animals nor plants can live at these elevations, on account of the extreme cold. We can suppose that at the same height, away from the mountains, the air will be colder still. It is not possible, therefore, that there can be trees reaching into these heights, where the cold is so intense, and the air is too thin to sustain life.

There is a kind of breathing or respiration going on in plants, as well as in animals. They drink in one kind of air, oxygen, and give out another, carbonic acid, continually, by night and by day, in sunshine and shade. They also obtain from the atmosphere a large proportion of what they require as food; and this they procure by decomposing the carbonic acid of the air, absorbing or fixing its carbon, and setting free its oxygen, by means of their green parts, and under the influence of light. For these processes air is indispensably necessary. There are other reasons why trees cannot reach above a certain

* Arnot's Elements of Physics.

elevation. They would fall in pieces by their own weight. Were a piece of wood of a given thickness to be placed erect, it would snap across for the same reason; and though a living tree might have greater strength, the same effect would be produced, in similar circumstances. Trees above a certain size and height would be unable to procure the quantity of food by their roots necessary to sustain them; there would be no air to stir their leaves, without which they would droop; and there would be no rain to sprinkle and refresh their leaves. It is, therefore, impossible that there can be trees, in any part of this earth, like the Jambu or Nuga of the Buddhists.

The largest tree seen in the Himalayas by Dr. Hooker, who visited this region solely for botanical purposes, was an oak, 47 feet in its girth, and 200 feet high. The largest tree known to exist in the world is the Wellingtonia gigantea, a native of California, which is said to attain to the height of between 300 and 400 feet. But trees that are miles high never existed anywhere but in old tales; and these tales are now only listened to by children, or by the uninformed and superstitious.

## 14. THE LIONS OF THE GREAT FOREST.

The description given us in the Sára Sangaha of the lions in the Himála-wana is confirmatory of the supposition I have ventured to make, that the Commentaries must have been composed, as well as written, in this island, and by persons who have known little of India but by report. Nearly all the references to the continent are like the record of one who attempts to describe, from imperfect sources, scenes of which he has heard, connected with other people and lands, and has written down what has been told him, with all its exaggerations. We cannot think it possible that any one who had lived in the north of India could write about lions that are in shape like a cow, and eat grass. It may be the yak or the bison that is intended, as these animals answer somewhat to this description, and are found upon the Himalayas; but no one acquainted with even the rudiments of natural history would class them with lions. Then as to the lions themselves. Who but a Buddhist ever talked, in sober earnest, of lions that could leap 80 isbas, which would be 11,200 feet, or of lions that could keep pace with the sound of their own voice, for the distance of 30 miles? The furthest distance that a lion can leap is not much more than 20 feet, according to the testimony of those who have watched its habits in its native jungles.

We have now had colossal proportions in nearly every department of nature, but our records of the enormous are not yet exhausted. The horse Kantako, upon which Buddha rode, when he fled from the palace to become an ascetic, was 36 feet long (from its neck to its tail); in the same night it proceeded 300 miles, and could have gone much further, if its progress had not been impeded by the number of flowers thrown in its pathway by the déwas; and at one leap it crossed the river Anoma, a distance of 210 feet. When Anando told Buddha that the understanding of the circle of existence was not difficult, the sage replied that he was not to speak in that manner, as it was because of his being accustomed to it that it appeared to be easy. The Commentary says, among other examples, that, in a similar manner, the ocean appears deep to others, but not to the Timara Pingala; and that the sky appears vast to others, but not to the Supanna-rája. Now this bird is 1500 miles in size; each of its wings is 500 miles; its tail 600 miles, its neck 300 miles, its mouth 90 miles, and its legs 120 miles. It requires a space of 7000 or 8000 miles in which to flutter its wings. This creature, if it exists, must be the king of birds, without any dispute. The roc seen by Sinbad, the worthy sailor, was no bigger than a cloud, and therefore very insignificant when compared with the supanna-rája.

In this enumeration of the errors of Buddhism that are contrary to fact, as taught by established and uncontroverted science, I have been guided in my selection by those that are the most extravagant, and the existence of which involves the most important consequences. There are many others, of a similar kind, that I might notice; but by this means my work would be extended to an inconvenient length; as the errors contained in the writings of the Buddhists are almost as numerous as the leaves on which they appear. When I commenced my Pali researches, I had not the most distant idea that I should meet with these absurdities and extravagances in the sacred books. I had read several of them, many times over, in Singhalese; but supposed that they were the misrepresentations of some isolated dreamer in one of the wiháras of the interior, who had lived all his days amidst the reveries and phantoms arising from a weak and confused intellect. But what has been my surprise, and I may say my humiliation too, to find that they are regarded as the revelations of the rahats—men in whom the Buddhists place the utmost confidence, as they suppose that they could literally turn the world upside down, divide the moon into two pieces, stop the course of the sun, and do a thousand other things equally wonderful.*

This ever-recurring defect, of a want of simplicity, and a straining after that which is extravagant, vitiates all Buddhist writings, even the most sacred. We are continually told of things that are either impossible in themselves, or so exaggerated by the narrator, that they become impossibilities from the manner in which they are said to have taken place. I do not include in this notice any of the tales that are related about the déwas and their doings. I deny the whole of the numerous statements that are recorded, as to the visitation, assistance, and approbation of these beings, said to have been given to Buddha and his associates; because, if they existed, which I also deny, they must have known that the Tathágato had no claim to receive such marks of reverence at their hands, inasmuch as they would learn from his sermons, that either he himself was deceived as to many of his statements and doctrines, or that he was wilfully deceiving the people whom he addressed; neither does it seem a very dignified position in which to place the supreme ruler of a celestial world, to represent him as holding an umbrella twelve

* In this section my scientific authorities, in addition to those I have already named, have been—in astronomy, Herschell, Mosely, Lardner, and Breen; and on general subjects, the London and Penny Cyclopædias.

miles in height, or blowing a chanque shell twenty cubits long. I deny all that is said about the passing through the air of Buddha and his disciples, or of their being able to visit the déwa and brahma worlds. They were men, and no mere man was ever in the possession of such powers as are attributed to the son of Máyá and to the rahats. The age in which these wonderful beings are said to have lived is within the limit of history, and the testimony from this authoritative source is most unquestionably and conclusively against their existence. I select a few examples of the kind of statement to which I refer, from an extended series of a similar description.

We are told that when the prince Gótama was named, 80,000 of his relatives were present, and that when he was sixteen years of age "the Sakya tribes sent their daughters superbly decorated (that they might become his wives). There were 40,000 dancing girls. The princess who was (afterwards) the mother of Ráhulo, became the principal queen." When returning from the pleasure garden, at the time he was about to become an ascetic, he took from his person a pearl necklace, worth a laksha of treasure, and gave it as a present to the princess Kisá-gótami. His royal father, Suddhódana, at an agricultural show, held a golden plough, whilst his state officers had ploughs of silver. There are many other statements about the population and wealth of Kapila-wattu of the same kind. But it is said that there were, at that time, 63,000 kings in Jambudípa, Rajagaha being the metropolis of Magadha, and Bimbisára the lord paramount. The city of Kóli, the residence of another king, was only a few miles from Kapila-wattu, as the inhabitants of both cities were accustomed to meet together for pastime in the Lumbini garden, which was about half way between the two places. With so small a territory as the one over which Suddhódana reigned as an inferior king, and with his own court to provide for, how did he find means to provide for the 40,000 women in the palace of his son; and whence came the wealth that the royal family must have possessed, if the king could plough with an implement of gold, and his son give away an ornament worth a laksha of treasure? And what are we to say about the 40,000 women themselves? How could so great a number of women be taken from so confined a population? Again, the numbers represented as being present on different occasions of importance in the history of Buddhism are equally incredible, as when it is said that Bimbisára visited Buddha accompanied by 120,000 Brahmans and householders, and that 6,000,000 priests were present in the city of Patali-putta, when the third convocation was held.*

The tales that are told about the acts performed by Buddha, and the wonders attendant on these acts, need only be stated, in order to be rejected at once from the realm of reality and truth. A moment after his birth, he stepped upon the ground, and called out, with the voice of a lion, "Aggóhamasmi lókassa; jetthohamasmi lókassa; setthóhamasmi lókassa; ayamantimá játi; natthi dhám punabbawóti. I am chief in the world; I am principal in

* The statements in this and the former paragraph are taken from the Commentary on the Buddha Wanso, except the last, which is taken from Turnour's extracts from the Dípawanso.

the world; I am supreme in the world; this is my last birth; hereafter there is to me no other existence."* When five months old he sat in the air, without any other support, at a ploughing festival. At an exhibition of his strength before his assembled relatives, prior to his marriage, he sent an arrow from his bow which split a hair at the distance of ten miles, though at the time "it were dark as if it were night." The following occurrences took place at the time he received the supreme Buddhaship. "When meditating on the paticheha samuppáda circle of existence, the ten thousand sakwalas (in any of which Bódhisat may be born) shook twelve times. When he attained to the pre-eminent wisdom, the whole of these sakwalas were ornamented (as a festive hall). The flags on each side of the sakwala rocks, north, south, east, and west, reached to the opposite side, south, north, west, and east. Those that were raised on the earth reached to the brahma-lóka, and those that were raised in the brahma-lóka reached to the earth. All the flower trees in the various sakwalas put forth blossoms; and to the same extent the fruit trees became laden with fruit. On the trunks and branches there were lotus flowers, whilst garlands were suspended from the sky. The rocks were rent, and upon them flowers appeared, in ranges of seven, one above the other. The whole space of the sakwalas appeared like one wide mass of flowers, as everywhere they were spread. The Lókántarika hells, 80,000 miles in extent, in all these sakwalas, were illuminated by a more brilliant light than could have been made by seven suns. The waters of the

* Mahapadána Suttanta, Játakatha-katthá.

great ocean, 840,000 miles deep, became fresh. The streams of the rivers were arrested. The blind from birth saw, the deaf heard, the lame walked, and the bound prisoner was set free." Again, after he had preached his first sermon, it is expressly said that "then the foundations of 10,000 worlds were shaken, and moved about tumultuously, and a great and brilliant light was presented."* These things *are* too absurd to require serious refutation; and the students at present in even the smaller educational establishments of Ceylon, would feel themselves aggrieved, were I to make the attempt.

There are endowments and powers claimed for the ancient ascetics, and for Bódhisat in his various forms of existence, of the most extraordinary character. We have seen that the rishi Mátanga prevented the sun from rising, and bisected the moon. Bindumati, a courtezan, turned back the stream of the Ganges. The chakrawartti kings had horses and elephants on which they could ride through the air, and visit any of the four great continents.

When there was a famine in Wéranja, Moggalan, one of the two principal disciples of Buddha, asked permission from him to turn the earth over, that, as its under surface is like virgin honey, the starving population might thereby be fed; and when he was asked what would become of the inhabitants of the earth, he replied that he would cause an extension of one of his hands, and collect in that all the people, whilst he inverted the earth with the other. As

* Játakattha-katthá. Dhamma-chakkappawattana Suttanta. I could multiply the record of these marvels to an indefinite extent, from numerous other works; but it is not necessary, as I found on them no argument.

this was not permitted, he wanted to take the priests to Uttarakuru, but this proposition also was disapproved of by Buddha;* not from the act being impossible, but from its not being necessary that it should be performed.

* Gogerly: translated from the Párájiká. Journal of the Ceylon Branch of the Royal Asiatic Society, vol. i. p. 79.

# CHAPTER III.

## THE ONTOLOGY OF BUDDHISM.

In exposing the errors of Buddhism that in the preceding pages have passed under our review, we have been aided, in most instances, by the sure deductions of science. We now turn to another order of error, in the overthrow of which we shall require assistance from a different source, or the application of former principles in a new form.

### 1 FORMER STATES OF EXISTENCE.

The constancy with which reference is made to former states of existence is one of the first things that strikes us in looking into the writings of the Buddhists. The personal character of the Tathágato is invested thereby with an apparent sublimity of abnegation and self-sacrifice. The resolves of the imaginary Buddhas of past ages have nothing to equal them, for disinterestedness, in all the annals of heathenism. Myriads upon myriads of years ago, according to his own fictitious narrations, he might have released himself from the pains and penalties of successive existence; but he voluntarily continued in the stream of repeated birth, that he might attain to the privilege of being able to teach sentient beings the way to the city of peace; though he knew that he could only gain it by passing through innumerable births, and enduring reiterated privations and hardships. But it takes away from our admiration of the thought, when we remember that the city of peace, to which he would lead mankind, is nothingness; and that in many of his births his recorded actions are unworthy of so great an aim, as that which he professes to have set before him. With his own circumstances, and those of others, in the most distant ages, he professed to be as familiar as with the events of the passing moment; and the sacred books would lose much of their attractiveness, if the apologues and tales having a reference to the past were taken from them. There can be no transmigration, in the usual sense of the term, according to the principles of Buddhism, but there is the repetition of existence; and this idea enters into every part of the system. It is more frequently referred to by Buddha than any other of his tenets, and has produced a greater influence upon the people professing his religion than any other of its speculations.

The pretensions of Buddha to a perfect knowledge of the past is set forth in the following terms: "The rahat is endowed with the power, called pubbéniwásanánan′, of revealing his various former existences. Thus, I am acquainted with one existence, two existences, three existences, four existences, five existences, ten existences, twenty existences, thirty existences, forty existences, fifty existences, a hundred existences, a thousand existences, and a hundred thousand existences; innumerable san′watta-kappé, innumerable wiwatta-kappé; innumerable san′-watta-wiwatta-kappé.

"I know that I was born in such a place, bearing such a name, descended of such a race, endowed with such a complexion; that I subsisted on such an aliment, and was subjected to such and such joys and griefs, and was gifted with such a term of existence; and who, after death, was regenerated here. Thus it is that he who is endowed with the pubbéniwásanánan' is acquainted both with his origin and external appearance (in his former states of existence)."*

The Atuwáwa on the above extract has this further explanation: "There are six kinds of beings who exercise this power. . . . Among these the titthiyá (the professors of other religions) have the power of revelation over forty kappé, and not beyond, on account of their limited intelligence; and their intelligence is limited, as they recognize a limitation to corporeal and individual regeneration. The ordinary disciples (of Buddho) have the power of revelation over a hundred and a thousand kappé, being endowed with greater intelligence. The eighty principal disciples have the power of revelation over a hundred thousand kappé. The two chief disciples over one asankheyyan and a hundred thousand kappé, their destination being fulfilled at the termination of these respective periods. To the intelligence of the supreme Buddho alone there is no limitation."

It might be difficult, by mere reasoning, apart from the

* Turnour: translated from the Patisambhidan', the 12th book of the Khudaka Nikáyo. Journal of the Bengal Asiatic Society, vol. vii. p. 691. The same sentences, nearly word for word, are scattered throughout the sacred books, and may be found, among other places, in the Sámannya Phala Suttanta and the Mahá Padána Suttanta.

Scriptures of God, to prove that there is no such thing as transmigration. But without entering into any argument on the general question, we may safely assert, that Buddha knew much less about the past than any one may learn in the present age, who understands any language in which there is a modern literature. There are facts of recent discovery, unknown to Buddha, that powerfully teach one of his favourite doctrines, the impermanence of all things. By the pursuits of the geologist many phenomena have been brought to light, that were undiscovered at the beginning of the present century. We now learn that a continual change is taking place in everything connected with the earth, the nature of which it is not difficult to understand. Wind, rain, light, heat, frost, the tides, earthquakes, electricity, with other powers and forces, affect almost every object, from the single atom to the mighty mountain, and from the small rain-drop to the extended ocean. We live in the midst of universal change. One thing is melted, another becomes solid, and a third seems to pass away entirely, by being changed into air, or by being burnt. Rivers roll down their beds great masses of rock, and remove them to considerable distances. Ice forces its way down the sides of the mountain, and alters the appearance of the plain. From the polar seas vást masses of rock are floated to warmer regions, by ice-bergs, and are there deposited when the ice melts. In some countries there are numerous jets of boiling water, that as they rush upwards throw out large blocks of stone. Volcanoes are at work, sending forth streams of fire, that when they cool become like metal in hardness. The rivers are powerful agents, in producing similar effects upon a mightier scale. It has been calculated that the Ganges brings down daily into the Bay of Bengal, during the rainy season, 400,000,000 tons of mud. The sea wears away the coast in one place, and enlarges it in another; and its waters insinuate themselves among crags and hills, until they are so undermined that they fall. The same power that formerly depressed the valleys we now cultivate, and upheaved the hills we climb, is continually exerting its force. The south and west coasts of England are gradually rising above the sea. The coast of Norway has been elevated 200 feet within a recent period. In South America there are tracts of country extending thousands of miles, in which the rising and lowering of the land has been observed, whilst in Mexico hundreds of square miles have been thrust upwards, and a hill a thousand feet high has been formed in a short space of time. In the great Chilian earthquake a mass of earth equal to an immense number of cubic miles was raised. The smallest creatures are adding to the re-arrangement of the geography of the world. Coral insects have built a reef along the shore of New Caledonia, four hundred miles long, and another a thousand miles long on the east coast of Australia, in some instances their works being several hundred feet high.

These effects may be observed in Ceylon, by those who are willing to make geology their study, and watch the changes that are taking place around them; but it must be with a patience like that of the old ascetics, when they practised dhyána, and a perseverance like that of Bhódhisat, when, as a squirrel, according to the fable, he sought to dry up the sea, by lading out its waters with his bushy tail. "The land (of Ceylon) has for ages," we are told by Sir Emerson Tennent, "been slowly rising from the sea, and terraces abounding in marine shells imbedded in agglutinated sand occur in situations far above high water-mark. Immediately inland from Point de Galle, the surface soil rests on a stratum of decomposing coral; and sea shells are found at a considerable distance from the shore. Further north, at Madampe, between Chilaw and Negombo, the shells of pearl oysters and other bivalves are turned up by the plough more than ten miles from the sea. These recent formations present themselves in a still more striking form in the north of the island, the greater portion of which may be regarded as the conjoint production of the coral polypi, and the currents, which for the greater portion of the year set impetuously toward the south. Coming laden with alluvial matter collected along the coast of Coromandel, and meeting with obstacles south of Point Calimere, they have deposited their burthens on the coral reefs round Point Pedro, and these raised above the sea-level, and covered deeply by sand drifts, have formed the peninsula of Jaffna and the plains that trend westward until they unite with the narrow cause-way of Adam's Bridge—itself raised by the same agencies, and annually added to by the influences of the tides and monsoons.

"On the north-west side of the island, where the currents are checked by the obstruction of Adam's Bridge, and still water prevails in the Gulf of Manaar, these deposits have been profusely heaped, and the low sandy plains have been proportionally extended; whilst on the south and east, where the current sweeps unimpeded along the coast, the line of the shore is bold and occasionally rocky. This explanation of the accretion and rising of the land is somewhat opposed to the popular belief that Ceylon was torn from the main land of India by a convulsion, during which the Gulf of Manaar and the narrow channel at Paumbon were formed by the submersion of the adjacent land. The two theories might be reconciled by supposing the sinking to have occurred at an early period, and to have been followed by the uprising still in progress. But on a closer examination of the structure and direction of the mountain system of Ceylon, it exhibits no traces of submersion."*

A gentleman well known for his scientific attainments informs me, that every stone in the Jaffna peninsula is composed of hardened sand and shells, furnishing some very beautiful fossil specimens. The shells, in most instances, particularly in the interior of the peninsula, have been petrified by the gradual substitution of calcareous or flinty particles for the particles of the shell inside the stone; but, bordering on the sea, the shells themselves are still to be traced in the rocks. The peninsula is *visibly* growing and extending into the sea about Point Pedro.

Nearly the whole of our present lands and continents were formerly under the sea, as is proved by the remains of marine animals and plants that are found deposited below the surface of the earth; and it is not only in the

* Sir J. Emerson Tennent's Ceylon, vol. i. p. 12.

material of which the earth is composed that these things are taking place; changes equally striking have taken place in the world of living existence. Leaves, fruits, stems, and roots of trees, and skeletons of animals, very different to any that now live, have been found in thousands of instances, in nearly all parts of the world. Not only in the earliest ages was the animal and vegetable life of a kind different to that which is now seen; but this was succeeded by new races, to be in turn displaced by creatures of another form and habit, but in every instance adapted to the condition of the earth at the period in which they lived. At one time the atmosphere was of a higher temperature than at present, on which account the productions of the vegetable world were then most luxuriantly abundant. To this we are indebted for our present supply of coal, which is composed of vegetable remains that by pressure and other agencies have been converted into a mineral substance. It has been calculated that at Saar Rivier the coal stratum must be 22,015 feet below the surface of the earth. "Hence," says Humboldt, "from the highest pinnacle of the Himalayas to the lowest basin containing the vegetation of an earlier world, there is a vertical distance of 48,000 feet."*

There is a singular uniformity about the arrangement of the strata in which the fossil remains are found. If we are told the character of a stratum, we can know from that the character of the one above it, and of the one below it, in most instances. If we know the form of an animal or a plant that formerly existed, we can tell in what kind of

* Humboldt's Cosmos, by Otté; vol. i.

earth or rock it will most probably be found; and if we know the earth or rock, we can tell what kind of form will be the most abundant in its fossil remains. Of many of the curious creatures that formerly existed, only a few fragments have been found. Among them are birds of all sizes, from an ostrich to a crow, and lizards with a bird's beak and feet. Near the shore, in the ocean, were fishes with a pavement of teeth covering the palate, and enabling them to crush and eat the crabs, lobsters, and other shell fish that there abounded. Further out at sea were large and voracious sharks. Reptile-like animals were at one time the most numerous and powerful. The plesiosaurus united the characters of the head of a lizard, with the teeth of a crocodile, to a neck of immoderate length, so that it has been compared to a serpent threaded through the shell of a turtle. On the land were crocodiles in great variety. One animal was taller than an elephant; but instead of a trunk it had a long narrow snout, armed with strong and sharp tusks; and another had a body half as long again as an elephant, with feet so large and strong that a crocodile would be crushed by it at a single blow. The Himalayas contain the remains of a gigantic land tortoise, twelve feet in length and six in height. The megatherium lies in the vast plains of South America. It is larger than an Indian bull, and has claws of immense length and power. The length of the body is eighteen feet, and its girth fourteen feet; and the thigh bone is nearly three times the size of that of an elephant.*

* The geological facts I have recorded, are principally taken from Lyell, Ansted and Mantell.

There can be no doubt that the condition of the world, in the ages of which we are speaking, was very different to anything that is presented in our day. Now if Buddha lived in these distant ages, and had a perfect insight into their circumstances, as he tells us he had, how is it that we have no intimation whatever, in any of his numerous references to the past, that the world was so different, in these respects, to what it is now? We have exaggerations of present forms of existence; a thousand arms given to Mára, and a height higher than the moon to Ráhu; but of the innumerable creatures that then lived, and are now found in a fossil state, he says not a word. According to his discourses, there were, at that time, the same kinds of trees, of reptiles, of fishes, of birds, and of beasts, as in his own day. He was himself, as we learn from the Játaka Wannaná, an elephant, a lion, a horse, a bull, a deer, a dog, a guana, a jackal, a monkey, a hare, a pig, a rat, a serpent, a frog, a fish, an alligator, a hansa bird, a peafowl, an eagle, a cock, a woodpecker, a water fowl, a jungle-fowl, a crow, a snipe, and a kindurá, or merman, which is a fabulous creature, commonly met with in old tales, but never seen in this age of universal observation and enquiry. How is it that in his numerous births he was never any kind of creature except those that are common to India? The only conclusion we can come to is, that he knew nothing about the beasts that roamed in other lands, or the birds that flew in other skies; and that as he was ignorant of their existence he could not introduce them into his tales. As we are told that he was never born in any smaller form than a snipe, it might have been an indignity to him to be one of the organisms found at Bilin, so small that there are forty-one thousand millions of their shells in a cubic inch; but it would have been none to be a giraffe in the present kalpa, or a megatherium among the creatures that are extinct. It will be said that he was never born but in Jambudípa, and that therefore, he could not be any creature not found in India; but it is evident that by Jambudípa he meant the whole of the space inhabited by men, or man's earth, about the size and shape of which he was as ignorant as all the other men who then lived.

Then again, how are we to believe his statements when he speaks of Benares and other cities as having existed for many myriads of years, when we know that an entire change in the very formation of the countries in which they are situated has taken place? That the region now called India has partaken in the general interchange of land and water, we have proof in the fossil remains that are plentifully and extensively found in the peninsula. Remains of the sivatherium and mastodon, large animals that once haunted its plains, and of the hippopotamus that once frequented its rivers, may now be seen in museums. The remains of the vegetable world tell us of the difference between its present and former atmosphere and temperature. At Chirra Ponji, north of Calcutta, there is a bed of coal, 4300 feet above the level of the sea; and there are evidences, in the same neighbourhood, of great upheavement from igneous action. The hills not far distant are covered with a stratum of marine shells, and in some places there are the remains of an ancient coast, as is seen by extensive deposits of shingle. Not far from Benares coal has been found, and it is certain that no city could have existed in this country at the time these deposits were formed.*

These facts are sufficient to convince every observant mind, that what Buddha says about his past births, and those of others, is an imposition upon the credulity of mankind, without anything whatever to support it from fact. The earth, in every part of its vast bosom; in the burning plain and the ice-bound sea; from the highest elevation ever trod by human foot, to the lowest depth ever seen by human eye, has cherished proofs infallible, which she now reveals, that every word spoken by the Tathágato about his former states of existence is a fabrication and an untruth.

## 2. FORMER AGES.

The Mahawanso, and other works written in Ceylon that profess to be historical, tell us that the first twenty-eight kings of the earth lived an asankya each. An asankya is thus numerated. Ten decenniums make one hundred; ten hundreds, one thousand; one hundred thousands, one laksha; one hundred lakshas, one kóti; one hundred lakshas of kótis one prakóti; one kóti of prakótis, one koti-prakóti; one kóti of kóti-prakótis, one nahuta; and so on, for fourteen times more, each time multiplying by ten millions, until the number reaches a unit with

* The statements in relation to the geology of India are taken from the Journal of the Bengal Asiatic Society.

thirty three cyphers. I have not met with any confirmation of kings living an asaṅkya in the Text of the Pitakas; but in the commentary it is said to have been declared by Buddha that men lived to this astounding age.

The Buddhawanso is a history of the twenty-four Buddhas who preceded Gótamo, and was delivered by Buddha himself in the first year of his supremacy, in order to convince his relations that the course he was taking had high authority in its favour. In speaking of Kakusandha, the third Buddha before himself, he says: "In this kappo the Bhagawá Kakusandha was born, whose allotted term of existence was forty-thousand years. That term of existence gradually decreasing was reduced to ten years; and subsequently increasing again to an asankheyyan, and from that point again diminishing, had arrived at the term of thirty-thousand years." It is in this manner that the decrease and increase in the term of human life takes place. It commences with an asankya and goes down gradually to ten years; and it then rises again, until it reaches an asankya. In the same commentary we are told that when the term of human existence is 100,000 years or upwards, it is not a proper time in which for a Buddha to appear, because "under so protracted an existence the human race have no adequate perception of birth, decay, or death." Nearly at the end of the commentary we have this statement: "Aparimeyyé ito kappé, chaturo ásinsu nayaká. Infinite kalpas before this, there were four great ones (Buddhas)." A Chinese legend tells that before the present kalpa "ten quadrillion times a hundred quadrillions of kalpas, each kalpa consistɪg of 1344 millions of years, there was a chakrawartti ing."*

The book of the Dípawanso,† after enumerating the ynasties of all kings from the commeneement of royalty, ud then referring to the Okkáka, or Sákya, race, to hieh Buddha belonged, says: "The whole of these ɩonarchs, who were of great wealth and power, were in umber onc laksha, four nahutans, and three hundred 40,300). Sueh is the number of monarehs of the ynasty from which Bódhisat is sprung."‡ From Maha ɪmmata, the first king, to Suddhódana, the father of uddha, there were 706,787 kings, who reigned in ninc- cn different eapitals, all of whieh were known in the me of Bhagawá; but several of them have sinee become ɜsolate, and even their sites forgotten, among whieh we ust inelude his own native city, Kapila-watthu. But .e length of these dynasties, the monarchs of whieh lived r all periods from an asankya to the present age of man, ɩs no analogy in real oceurrenee. There are kings now igning who regard themselves as the successors of the esars, and others who are called the children of the sun; ɩt this is merely an honorary form, and though repeated not received as fact. There is no dynasty now, on any rone, that exercised the functions of royalty in the time Buddha.

The periods to which we are taken back by the authori- ɜs of Buddhism are so remote as to be beyond the power

* Laidlay's Pilgrimage of Fa Hian.

† This is not one of the sacred books.

‡ Turnour: Journal of the Bengal Asiatic Society, vol. vii. p. 922.

of numbers to express them. Yet in the most distant of these ages, the same languages were spoken as in the time of Buddha; there were the same manners and customs, the same kinds of dress and ornaments, and the same kinds of food; men had the same names, and followed the same occupations; there were the same modes of government, the same castes, the same forms of religion, the same modes of travelling, the same denominations of coin, the same species of grain, and the same diseases and medicines. But how is it possible for this unchangeableness to have continued so long? Does not Buddha himself teach us the impermanence of all things? There is not at the present moment a single country upon the face of the earth occupied by the same people that lived in it three thousand years ago, if we except the Arabs, and perhaps the Ceylonese and Chinese. The men of Israel, who existed then, exist now, but they are exiles from their fatherland. It cannot be, that in myriads of years, and with intervals of myriads of years as well, there has been so little change in the economy of the world as is represented by Buddha; and so little difference, as to the manners and customs of mankind, between these distant times and the times in which Buddha is said to have lived.

It will be said that this sameness is a necessity, as the world exists in successive series, one of which most intimately resembles another; and that, therefore, the history of any given period must necessarily be like other and distant periods. Then, we reply, the present age, as well as those that preceded it, must have had its prototype in repeated and limitless cycles. And, by the same law, there must have been in former ages, as now, the art of printing; the manufacture of telescopes, clocks, and watches; the use of gas, gunpowder, and fire-arms; and the establishment of steam-boats, railways, and electric telegraphs; and all the other inventions of modern science (as we, in our ignorance, it seems, call them). How is it that none of these things are ever referred to by Buddha, even in the shadow of an allusion, or the most distant hint? We need not wander far for the true answer. It is, that all that is said about past existence in Buddhist works has no more reality about it than "the baseless fabric of a vision," to pass away before the influence of truth, as the mist of the mountain before the sun-ray of the morning.

But we have not yet done with the evidence against Buddha from the same source. He tells us that myriads of years ago men lived in this world, and as he represents their story, in far greater numbers than at the present time. But reliable tradition and truthful history take us no further back, in the story of man, than the time attributed to the deluge; and we are led to seek the origin of our race, by the aid of the same guides, not only in that particular age, but in some part of Central Asia, in conformity with the declaration of Scripture, that the ark of Noah rested upon mount Ararat. We can trace man to no more distant age, and to no other country or place. And further, among all the fossil remains that have been found, no bone that can be proved, without doubt or controversy, to have belonged to the human species, has been discovered; but even if the perfect skeleton of a man were found in some old drift, clothed with flesh, and having about him still the raiment in which he lived and the weapons with which he fought, and with a legible inscription around his place of burial, so as to make it certain that he was a real man, and no mistake, this would prove nothing in favour of Buddhism. It would only show that there were men upon the earth at an earlier period than is generally supposed, but the argument we have adduced would still remain in its full force; because man could not possibly have lived in the ages to which Buddha takes us, as the world was not then prepared for his reception, and its circumstances were antagonistic to the existence of any being with an organism like that of man. All analogy teaches us that the position in which God places his creatures is always adapted to their frames and faculties. Then, what becomes of the numerous tales about "the days of yore," when Brahmadatta was king of Benares, or some other king reigned in some other city? The sum of the ages given to these monarchs takes us back more years than the whole of the present generation of men could count before their death, giving each man, woman, and child, five hundred thousand to do in a day. To a demonstration, the statements of the Tathágato are "not historically true;" and they ought, therefore, to be set aside as unworthy of further notice, or handed down to posterity as examples of the foolish things that men are led to believe when they lose the guidance of the oracles of God.

## 3. PRESENT EXISTENCE.

There was error in all that Buddha taught in relation to past existence, and when he spoke to his disciples of the germ of present being, in many instances he was equally far from the truth. No one but himself, according to his own account, knew the manner of the origin of the universe, and as it would have been of no benefit to his disciples to understand it, he did not reveal it to them, and says that all speculation upon this subject is profitless and vain. But in his teachings on the manner of the origin of the present race of men, he is much more communicative. He taught, correctly, that the first inhabitants of the earth were pure, and free from evil; but he said, in addition, incorrectly, that they first appeared by the apparitional birth, and could soar through the air, and live without food; their fall taking place through the tasting of a substance, like boiled milk, that then grew temptingly upon the surface of the earth. This may have been a perversion of an old truth, and a wrong mode of expressing what in its main principle was correct—the rectitude of primitive man, and his fall by eating something that was the means of leading him away from his original purity. On the origin of the individual man, Buddha leads his followers still further astray; but into this subject I may not enter at any length. It may suffice to say, that he attributes human conception to the most absurd and impossible causes. Though born as men, we may be subject to the most extraordinary transformations. We may change our sex, not only in passing to the next birth, but now. We may be born as men, for part of our lives, and when the power of our merit is exhausted, we may change to the inferior condition of women. We may have to expiate some former misdeed, and on that account be born as a female; but we may live to accomplish the expiation, and then be changed, in the same life, from a woman into a man.* We may be the one and the other alternately; for a time man, and then woman, in the present life, and then return back again to our original condition.

In the Dhammapada Wannaná, there is an account of a setthi, resident in the city of Soreyya, the father of two children, who was changed into a woman, because of a foolish and irreverent thought in relation to a priest, and as a woman had two more children. But as forgiveness was afterwards asked from the priest, and granted, the same person was restored to the former sex, and became a rahat. That this change took place, and that the children were born, was acknowledged by Buddha, according to the story; but all these things are pure inventions, and there is, throughout, the assignment of consequences to impossible causes. The first change took place without even the knowledge of the priest, no one can tell how; and though the second took place in consequence of the priest's forgiveness, as it is not ascribed to his interference or influence, it is simply confession of having done wrong that in itself, without any other instrumentality, wrought a miracle of the most extraordinary character; and one

* Gogerly: Journal of the Ceylon Branch of the Royal Asiatic Society, vol. i. p. 87.

that could only have been thought of in connexion with a system that regards the state of womanhood as a punishment, and the privileges she is permitted to enjoy as greatly inferior to those of the other sex. The thought of the setthi was not a crime, and scarcely a fault; but it was visited in this exemplary manner, because formed in relation to a priest; and we can only account for the invention of the story by supposing that it arose from a wish to exalt the priesthood.

We learn from the same authorities, that men and women may be produced by the apparitional, opapátika, birth, thereby starting at once into the full maturity of being; and that others are generated by touch, by look, by perfumes, by flowers, by food, by the garment, by the season, and by the voice. Beings not human receive their existence from perspiration and putridity, from wind, from warmth, and from the sound of rain. Beings not human may have human children. The Nágas have naturally a serpentine form, but they can assume the shape of men, and have been known to have children as such, and to have become priests; and it is only when, by inattention, they have lost the assumed form, that it has been discovered they were reptiles. Further search into these matters I must leave to the physiologist, who will find many strange fictions, but no new facts, in the science of life, as taught in the sacred books; I mention them that their absurdity may be seen, and as further proof that the framers of Buddhism were fanciful in their notions; and that they are, therefore, unsafe as guides, whether in science or religious truth.

## 4. MAN.

We have seen that the voice, or a look, may produce the germ of human existence, according to Buddhism, from which we should conclude that the nature and constitution of man must be something eminently subtle and ethereal. But instead of this, everything about him, after his birth, is represented as being material, or the effect of causes that are material; and as his existence is only the result of certain constituents under certain circumstances, a mere collection and continuance, at the separation or breaking up of these constituents he ceases to be, in the same way that the cloud ceases to be when its particles are separated and scattered in the shower, or the cart when it is broken up and made into bundles of firewood for the market. To continue the last illustration; the cart is only a name; it is nothing in itself but an idea; it refers to a collection of things of a certain form and size, and when they are together we call them a cart; but if we ask what the cart is, as it is evident that neither the axle-tree, nor the wheel, nor the shafts, nor any other separate portion, is the cart, we are unable to tell what the cart is, except that it is a name. In like manner if we ask what the man is, as neither the hair, nor the nose, nor the arm, nor the foot, nor any other separate member is the man, we are unable to tell what the man is, except that there is a name. These five khandas are the essentialities of sentient being. 1. Rúpa, the organised body. 2. Wédaná, sensation. 3. Sannyá, perception. 4. Sankhára, discrimination. 5. Winyána, consciousness. Besides these five khandas there is no other constituent that forms part and parcel of man as a sentient being. There is therefore, belonging to man, no soul, nor anything equivalent to what is commonly understood by the soul. It cannot form any part of the organized body, the twenty-eight elements and properties of which are all defined. The soul may be attached to an organism, but it cannot be connected with it, and cannot be one with it; as body is one thing and soul another. And it is equally evident that the soul cannot be in any of the other khandas; not in sensation, nor in perception, nor in discrimination, nor in consciousness. These may be faculties of the soul, but they cannot be the soul itself. Then, if the soul is in none of these things, and they are the whole of the constituents essential to existence, there being no other, according to Buddhism, there is no soul.*

This system tells man that he is a heap, a collection, an accumulation, an aggregation, a congeries, an increment, and nothing more. To develop light there is the lamp, the wick, the oil and the flame; and to develop the man there must be the organised body and the four other khandas. When the flame is extinguished, the light ceases to be; when the khandas are broken up, the man ceases to be; and no more, eventually, remains of the man than of the light. There is great ingenuity exercised in the treatment of this abstruse subject by native writers; but to follow them through all their classifications and distinctions would require an extended volume. The absence of originality, or the reverence they have paid to some authoritative model, causes their expositions to be consistent with each

* Appendix, Note Z.

other; and on this account, as we are not perplexed in our investigations by varied and discordant views, we can rely with the greater confidence on the conclusions to which we have come as to their ontological doctrines.

The absence of the soul seems to render it impossible that there can be any moral retribution after the present life; but the Buddhists profess to evade this consequence, by saying that when man ceases to exist, the principle of upádána, or cleaving to existence, causes the production of another being, to which the karmma of the producer,—the aggregate of all his actions, in every state of existence in which he has lived, in their ethical character, as good, or bad, or neither good nor bad,—is transferred intact. When existence ceases, the karmma still lives, and it passes over to its new possessor, with all its interests, properties, obligations, and liabilities, whether of punishment or reward. In the same way, one flame produces another flame, with the same properties; and one tree another tree, of the same nature as itself, by means of its fruit. The apostle Paul tells us, "That which thou sowest is not quickened, except it die." But in this illustration of the doctrine of the resurrection, we are permitted to see the manner of the revivification, and in some degree understand it; a nexus can be traced between the grain, dead and decaying, and the living stalk, as it carries nourishment from the decomposed particles it "swallows up" to the opening flower or the bending ear of corn. And then, above all, we are to remember that "God giveth it a body as it hath pleased him." But when existence ceases, Buddhism presents us with no medium by which the influence of the deceased being reaches the being that, of necessity, he causes to be produced. When man dies, as he has been no more than a heap, a machine, or a piece of curious mosaic; as there is nothing that passes away from him but an abstract principle, nothing soul-like; how can he produce another being, and that being, perhaps, a déwa on the summit of Maha Méru, or a Timira Pingala, myriads of miles beneath the surface of the deep? The man who, during his life, could not produce an atom of sand or a blade of grass, at his death, of his own inherent energy, and not as an instrumentality employed by another, may cause the existence of the highest and most glorious of the brahmas, or may pass onward an influence that in the course of ages will produce a supreme Buddha. The potentiality of being is not put forth until its dissolution; and man thus becomes, though not in the sense intended by the poet, "most vigorous when the body dies." But this method of retribution is imperfect, and altogether unsatisfactory. It is one being that does good, and another that is rewarded. It is one being that commits evil, and another being that is punished. The Buddhist may say, "Why need I care about the being who is to succeed to my merit? When he is, I shall not be. His existence involves my non-existence. I can never know anything about him, and he will never know anything about me. And as, when he lives, I shall be broken up, gone out, and non-sentient, what matters it to me whether the heir of my acts be a seraph or a sprite? Let us eat and drink, for to-morrow we die."

Upon these principles, there can be no transmigration,

in the usual acceptation of the term. That which transmigrates is not the spirit, the soul, the self; but the conduct and character of the man, something too subtle to be defined or explained. The analogy of the flame and the tree is misleading and defective. The flame produces another flame of the same nature, but the existence of the one does not involve the going out of the other; and from one flame a thousand flames may be produced, all burning simultaneously. The tree lives, in some instances many hundreds of years, after it has begun to produce fruit, and it always produces its like, something after "its kind;" from a mango fruit comes a mango tree, and not a goraka, as from the goraka fruit comes a goraka tree, and not a mango. The tree is one, but its fruits are many. But on the principles of Buddhism, when the man dies, he only produces one other being, and the being that he produces is most generally a being of a nature entirely different to himself; it may be an ant, a crow, a monkey, a whale, a nága, an asur, an evil spirit, or a deity. The number of sentient beings in the universe must ever remain the same, if each being inherits one separate and unbroken series of karmma, unless it be in the period in which men can receive nirwána. And by what means does it happen that just as one being dies another is always beginning to exist, as the new being is produced, not by the upádána of the former being alone, but through the agency of other causes, entirely separate from itself, but required to act in unison with it. And how is it that these causes are always in simultaneous operation at the very moment they are required? There must not only be these causes in operation at the very moment of the death of the being that produces the new being; but the result, the position of the new being, must be of such a character as to give opportunity for the reception of the karmma that has to be transferred, with all its inherent properties, and afford facilities for its exercise, in its own essential character, whether of good or evil. To these grave difficulties, Buddhism offers no solution.

I can give no further explanation of the mysterious upádána, except that it forms one link in the patichcha samuppáda, or causes of continued existence. "On account of awijjá, ignorance, sankháro, merit and demerit are accumulated; on account of these accumulations, winyyánań, the conscious faculty is produced; in consequence of the faculty of consciousness, námarúpa, the sensitive powers, the perceptive powers, the reasoning powers, and the body are produced; on account of námarúpa, the body and sensitive faculties, the sadáyatanań, the six organs of sense (the eye, the ear, the tongue, the nose, the body, and the mind), are produced; on account of the six bodily organs, phassa, contact (the action of the organs) is produced; on account of contact, wédaná, sensation is produced; on account of sensation, tanhá, desire is produced; in consequence of desire, upádána, attachment is produced; in consequence of attachment, bhawa, existence, is produced; in consequence of a state of existence, játi, birth, is produced; in consequence of birth, decay, death, sorrow, weeping, grief, discontent, and vexation are produced. Even thus is the origin of the complete catenation of sorrow." By the same rule, when one of these constituents ceases to be, the next in the series ceases to be, until "the whole combination of sorrow ceases to be produced."

This is a theory of causation, or of a series of causations, to which we cannot assent. We can understand how demerit may arise from ignorance; but how the conscious faculty is produced by merit and demerit we cannot tell. The conscious faculty once in existence, from it perception may arise. But how does perception *produce* the body and sensitive faculties? Where these are, there will be the organs of sense, and then contact, and sensation, and desire, in the prescribed order. But the great mystery still is, how desire produces existence. Physiologists tell us, when they want to put away God's hand from God's "handy-work," that desire may produce instincts, change the shape of a bodily member, or develop new instrumentalities. Through desire, a race of birds that live in marshy places may in time put forth longer legs and bills, to help them in their search for prey. Even allowing this to be true, it would only be another proof that God adapts the powers of his creatures to their circumstances and wants. But upádána is not a desire to produce life, but a desire to enjoy life; and for the above rule to be applicable here, the desire of enjoyment ought to produce the power of enjoyment; but that it does so is contrary to all experience. There is a further law to be taken into the account, that where there is no possibility of communication, there can be no consequence or effect; and as it is utterly impossible for upádána to act in places with which it cannot communicate, it must be powerless as to the act of production, in the manner claimed for it by Buddha. On another and separate count, therefore, Bhagawá is proved to be mistaken; and it is seen that the doctrines he teaches are inimical to morality, when carried out to their logical result.

## 5. NIRWÁNA.

The breaking up of the khandas is not the extinction of being. This is produced by a distinct and different process. The root of existence is not destroyed until nirwána has been seen or received. There are contradictory opinions as to the meaning of this term. In Europe, until recently, it was supposed to mean absorption. No thought of this kind could arise from the study of Buddhist writings; but from its frequent repetition by men who on other subjects are regarded as authorities, it is possible that it may have been assented to by some of my native readers, whose knowledge of men and things is derived from English literature, rather than the perusal of works written by their own countrymen; and I, therefore, think it necessary to prove that this conclusion cannot possibly be correct.

For absorption to be effected, there must be some greater being into whom the inferior being is received, merged, or lost. In Buddhism, there is no such being; as all sentient existence is homogeneous, and is always composed of one or more of the five khandas. There are three bhawo, or phases of being. 1. Káma. In the worlds belonging to this division, which includes the places of punishment, the earth, and the six déwa-lókas, there are the pleasures and pains resulting from sensuousness, or the possession and exercise of the senses. 2. Rúpa. In the worlds belonging to this division, there is the retention of the organised body; the intellectual powers are also retained, and are active; but the senses are not exercised or possessed. It is a kind of objective existence, without anything subjective. The eleventh déwa-lóka, called Asannyasattá, is an exception to this rule, as there is in it only the bodily form, without the consciousness of existence. 3. Arúpa. These worlds are four in number, and in them there is no bodily form; but there are the four other khandas, sensation, perception, discrimination, and consciousness. In the fourth of this class of worlds, Néwásannyánásannyá, there is a kind of dreaminess, in which there is neither consciousness nor unconsciousness. It is a nearer approach to nirwána than any other state. The performance of the dhyána rites secures an entrance into one or other of these worlds. Were a sentient being to pass through all these states of existence, in all these worlds, the period would extend to 231,628 maha kalpas, and 12,285,000,000 years. Then, if all existent beings are composed of one or other of the five khandas, and all possible forms of existence are included in one or other of the three series of worlds, in none of which there is permanence of being, there can be no all-pervading and infinite existence, from which all inferior and finite existences are derived, to which they belong, and in which they may again be lost.

The idea of the Brahmans is, that there is a supreme existence, paramátma, from which each individual existence has derived its being, but that this separate existence is an illusion; and that the grand object of man is, to effect the destruction of the cause of seeming separation, and to secure the re-union of the derived and the underived, the conditioned and the unconditioned. But Buddha repeatedly, by an exhaustive variation of argument, denies that there is any self or ego. Again and again, he runs over the components and essentialities of being, enumerating with tedious minuteness the classifications into which they may be divided, in order to convince his followers, that in whatever way these constituents may be placed, or however they may be arranged, there can be found in them no self. The same arguments that prove there can be no inferior or finite self, prove also that there can be no superior or infinite self, as all being is composed of one or more of the same elements.

The idea of creation, according to Buddha, arose in this way. When the inferior worlds are destroyed, many beings obtain existence in the sixth brahma-lóka, called Abassara. After living here the appointed time, eight kalpas, one of the brahmas appears again in a renewed brahma-world, of which he is the first inhabitant. He wishes that he were not alone, and that there were other beings like him, with whom he could associate. By and by other beings appear in the same world. The first being then thinks that the second being is the result of his own volition; and concludes that he is the chief, supreme; katthá, or the maker; nimáttá, or the creator; sanjitá, or the apportioner; the controller, and universal parent. The beings that subsequently appear in the same world, know that he was the first, and having no recollection of their former births, conclude that the thought of the first being is correct, and that they have from him received their existence.

The idea of eternity arises from a recollection of the past. When men are able to trace their existence backward, through myriads of years, they conclude that they have had no beginning and have existed for ever.

The whole of being is now before us; the ways of all worlds are presented to our vision; but we are told that every being in every world revolves in the round of the patichcha samuppáda, the circle of existence, and that over all and in all there is impermanency, decay, and death; and we thus learn, that as there is no paramátma, no infinite spirit or self, there can be no absorption. And yet, though there is no sentient Supreme Cause, there is a cause for all things; all existences are the result of some cause; but in no instance is this formative cause the working of a power inherent in any being, that can be exercised at will. All beings are produced from the upádána, attachment to existence, of some previous being; the manner of its exercise, the character of its consequences, being controlled, directed, or apportioned by karmma; and all sentient existences are produced from the same causes, or from some cause dependent on the results of these causes; so that upádána and karmma, mediately or immediately, are the cause of all causes, and the source whence all beings have originated in their present form.

So long as there is the upádána attachment, there will be the repetition of birth in some form or other of sentient existence, and in one or other of the three series of worlds. When this attachment is destroyed, the repetition of birth ceases; as the seed loses its fructifying principle when it has been immersed in boiling water, or the lamp no longer burns when the whole of the oil and the wick is consumed. This cessation of existence is nirwána.

The notices of nirwána in the sacred books appear to be far from numerous, and are much less frequent than we should have supposed from the importance of the subject in Buddhist estimation. The following extract is from the Abhidammattha Sangaha. "Nibbána, or nirwána, is perceived by means of the knowledge derived from the four paths (leading to itself), which are denominated lókóttara, pre-eminently excellent. To the four paths it is attached. It is called nirwána, because it is free from wána, attachment or desire. This is one view of it. It is divided into two sections, sawupádisésa, and anupádisésa. It is also sunyatá, void; animitta, unreal; and apani-hita, unexpectant, passionless. Upádisésa signifies the five khandas; and it is so called because only the five khandas are left, without any attachment or desire. It is said to be sawupádisésa, as having the five khandas. This is the state of the rahat, and is one view of nirwána. It may be said of the rahat, that he has attained to nirwána, though he still lives. He who is anupádisésa has not the five khandas. This is the state of the Buddhas, and of all who are free from the five khandas (as having neither the organized body, sensation, perception, discrimination, nor consciousness, one or other of which is essential to sentient existence). The great rishis, who are free from wána, desire, call that nirwána which is achutań, that from which there is no going (no transmigration); achchantań, that which has no boundary (neither birth nor death); asankhataṅ, that which is not affected by cause or effect; anuttara, that to which there is not anything superior; and padaṅ, that which has nothing to excel it as an advantage."

These are the characteristics of nirwána. That which is void, that has no existence, no continuance; neither birth nor death, that is subject to neither cause nor effect, and that possesses none of the essentialities of being, must be the cessation of existence, nihilism, or non-entity.* Thus dark is the pall thrown by ignorant man over his own destiny; but the thought is too sad to be dwelt upon, and we turn away from its painful associations, that we may listen to the voice of one who had seen in reality visions that were only feigned to have been seen by Buddha: "Behold, I shew you a mystery; we shall not all sleep, but we shall all be changed. In a moment, in the twinkling of an eye, at the last trump; for the trumpet shall

* "Existence, in the eye of Buddhism, is nothing but misery. It is connected with disease, decay, and death. It is subject to grief, wailing, pain, anguish, despair, and disappointment. It resembles a blazing fire, which dazzles the eye, but torments us by its effects. There is nothing real or permanent in the whole universe. 'Everything perishes.'

"Nothing, then, remained to be devised as a deliverance from this evil but the destruction of existence itself. This is what the Buddhists call nirwána.

"So far as I can understand this abstruse doctrine, it is not absorption. Viewed in every light in which the subject may be considered, and tested by all the definitions and arguments contained in the canonical works of Buddhism, nibban, to use an expression of Max Muller, is nihilism, the annihilation of existence, the same as the extinction of fire. That such is the fact appears also from the prajná paramitá and metaphysics of Kásyapa. It is, moreover, proved by the very nickname which the Brahmans apply to their Buddhist opponents, viz., nástakas, 'those who maintain destruction or nihilism,' and sunyávœdins, 'those who maintain that there is a universal void.'"—Alwis's Lectures on Buddhism, p. 29.

sound, and the dead shall be raised incorruptible, and we shall be changed. For this corruptible must put on incorruption; and this mortal must put on immortality. So when this corruptible shall have put on incorruption; and this mortal shall have put on immortality, then shall be brought to pass the saying that is written, Death is swallowed up in victory. O death, where is thy sting? O grave, where is thy victory? The sting of death is sin, and the strength of sin is the law. But thanks be to God, which giveth us the victory, through our Lord Jesus Christ.'" These are grand words, and the extract is *not* too long.

## 6. THE REVOLUTIONS OF THE UNIVERSE.

There is a periodical destruction and renovation of the universe, not of our own earth, or sakwala, alone, but in like manner of limitless (kap-laksha) sakwalas, with their Maha Mérus, suns, moons, circles of rock, continents, and seas. The destruction is by water, fire, and wind; in this order, but not in alternate succession, the destruction by wind being only at every sixty-fourth occurrence. Of the destruction by fire, which will be the next in order, Buddha thus speaks: "Priests! there is a period in which, for many hundreds of years, for many thousands of years, for many tens of thousands of years, for many hundreds of thousands of years, no rain will fall; by which all cereals, trees, and creepers, all medicinal plants, with all grasses, all nuga and other large trees, and all forests will be dried up, and will be no more: thus, priests! all existing things are impermanent; therefore, etc. After the lapse of a further immense period, a second sun appears, by which the smaller rivers, and the inferior tanks and lakes are dried up and are no more. After the lapse of another immense period, a third sun appears, by which the five great rivers are dried up. After the lapse of another immense period, a fourth sun appears, by which the great lakes whence the great rivers have their source, are dried up. After the lapse of another immense period, a fifth sun appears, by which the water in the seas, a hundred miles deep, is dried up; then a thousand, ten thousand, and eighty thousand yójanas, until only four thousand yójanas of water are left, which still further decreases until the water is only one hundred miles deep, fifty miles, a mile, a cubit (many different numbers being mentioned) until at last there is not more than would fill the feet marks of cattle, or moisten the end of the finger. After the lapse of another immense period, a sixth sun appears, when Maha Méru begins to ignite, and the whole world, from the sakwala rocks to the mansion of Sekra, sends forth one unbroken volume of smoke. At the appearance of the seventh sun, the earth and Maha Méru are burnt up, and the flame reaches to the brahma-lókas. From the hell Awichi to the brahma-lóka Abassara, there is then one dark abyss, and the whole space is void." These revelations are made that the priests may learn therefrom the impermanence of all things, and seek to free themselves from all sensuous attachments.

That the next destruction of the earth will be by fire we know from another source; but, as usual, when the sacred books of Buddhism present before us a truth, they so mar it that in their hands it becomes an untruth. How the smaller rivers still run, or the lakes have any water in them, when there has been no rain for hundreds of thousands of years, would puzzle even Buddha himself to explain. It is an axiom of science, that all natural processes are conducted by the simplest means; and there is no necessity for the appearance of seven suns to burn up the earth. Beneath its surface are molten fires of vast extent, as felt in the earthquake and seen in the volcano; and that subtle element, the electric fluid, is everywhere diffused, with its latent powers of mighty force, ready to exert themselves at once, and reduce the whole world to chaos, were God to issue the command, that they go forth and destroy.

In this section of my work, I have noticed the origin of individual being, the change of state by the repetition of birth, the cessation of existence, and the destruction of the universe; but in nearly every instance we have seen that Buddha is in error, either from mistake in his first principles, inadequacy in the causes he presents as leading to certain consequences, the contrariety of his statements to established science and known fact, or the want of logical sequence in his arguments and illustrations.

I may leave these statements without further notice, as they can be refuted by the boys on the lowest form of any well-conducted English school in the island.

## 7. MYSTIC POWERS.

There were certain powers supposed to be possessed by

the rishis and rahats that they could exercise at will. There were other supernatural endowments, that were connected with the exercise of prescribed rites, of an ascetical character. By means of pathawi (earth) kasina, being one, the faithful priest can become many. Having caused an earth to appear in the sky, or on the water, he can walk, stand, or sit on its surface. By ápo (water) kasina he can enter the earth as if it was water, and come out of it; he can cause water or rain to appear, create rivers and seas, and shake the earth with its mountains. By téjo (fire) kasina, he can send forth smoke, and cause flames to arise, and showers of burning charcoal to descend. He can subdue the light proceeding from others, by the superior intensity of his own light. He has the power to burn whatever he wills. He can cause a light by which he can see anything, as by divine eyes. By wáyo (wind or air) kasina, he can move as fast as the wind, and create wind or rain. By other kasinas he can cause darkness, turn whatever he wishes into gold, and pass through walls and ramparts without touching them.

But the principal of these mystic rites is that of dhyána or profound meditation. It was whilst engaged in this exercise that Gótama obtained the Buddhaship. In the first watch of the night, as he sat under the bo-tree, after he had overcome Mára, he received pubba-niwása-gnyána, the wisdom by which he could know the occurrences in all former births; in the second watch, he received dibba-chakkhun-gnyána, divine eyes, a vision clearer than that of men; in the third watch he received patichcha-samuppáda-gnyána, the wisdom by which he could see the whole concatenation of causes and effects—that this is sorrow, this the cause of sorrow, this the cessation of sorrow, and this the path by which the cessation from sorrow may be obtained; and again, that these are the attachments, or desires, this the cause of attachment, this the extinction of attachment, and this the path leading to the extinction of attachment; and at the dawn of the day he received sabbangnyóta-gnyána, the power of knowing clearly and fully, anything to which he chose to turn his attention.*

The priest who intends to practice the dhyánas seeks out a retired locality, as, the foot of a tree, a rock, a cave, a place where dead bodies have been burned, or an uncultivated and uninhabited part of the forest, and prepares a suitable place with his robe or with straw. He then seats himself, cross-legged, in an upright position, with his mind free from attachment and all evil thoughts, and with compassion towards all sentient beings, putting away sluggishness and drowsiness, possessed of wisdom and understanding, and leaving all doubt, uncertainty, and questioning, purifies his mind, and rejoices. Like a sick man who gains health, he rejoices; or a merchant who gains wealth, or a prisoner who gains liberty, or a slave who gains freedom, or a traveller along a dangerous road who gains a place of safety. Thus rejoicing, he is refreshed in body; he has comfort; and his mind is composed. But he retains witarka, reasoning, and wichára, investigation. This rejoicing is diffused through his whole body, as the wind entirely fills the bag that contains it, or as the oil in

* Maha Padána Suttanta. Játakattha-kattha.

which cotton has been dipped pervades every part; it comes in contact with his organised frame on all sides; there is no part of his body that does not feel it. Like an attendant who takes a metal vessel, in which he puts some of the powder used when bathing, and then mixes water with it, as much as is required, working them together, within and without, until the blending is complete; so does this rejoicing permeate through the whole body, and is diffused throughout every part.

In the second dhyána, the priest has put away and overcome reasoning and investigation, and attained to clearness and fixedness of thought, so that his mind is concentrated on one object, and he has rejoicing and gladness. There is no part of him that does not enjoy the pleasant result; as a deep lake into which no river flows, no rain falls, and no water springs up from beneath, is filled and pervaded in every part by the water, and is free from agitation.

In the third dhyána there is no rejoicing, no gladness, and no sorrow; but there is upékkhá, tranquillity, which is diffused through every part of his body, like the water that nourishes the lotus, pervading every part, and passing from the root to the petals, so that it is saturated with water throughout its whole texture.

In the fourth dhyána, reasoning, investigation, joy, and sorrow, are overcome, and he attains to freedom from attachment to sensuous objects, and has purity and enlightenment of mind. These envelope him, as a man when he is covered by a white cloth from head to foot, leaving no part of his person exposed.

The priest who has practised the four dhyánas aright, has the power to bring into existence a figure similar to himself, with like senses and members; but he knows that it is not himself, as a man who distinguishes one kind of grass from another, or a sword from its scabbard, or a serpent from its cast-off skin. This priest has the power of irdhi, which is thus exercised.

1. Being one, he multiplies himself, and becomes many; being many, he individualizes himself, and becomes one; and he makes himself visible or invisible at will. As one who goes into the water and comes up again, so does he descend into the earth, and again rise out of it; he walks on water as others walk on dry land; as a bird he can rise into the air, sitting cross-legged; he can feel, and touch, and grasp, the sun and moon; in any part of space, as high up as the brahma-lókas, he can do anything he likes with his body, like a potter who has the power to fashion as he likes the clay, or as a carver in ivory with his figures, or a goldsmith with his ornaments.

2. By the possession of divine ears, he can distinguish the sounds made by men and déwas, that are not audible to others, whether near or distant; and he can tell one sound from another, as a traveller, when he hears the sound of different drums and chanques, can distinguish the roll of the drum from the blast of the trumpet, and the blast of the trumpet from the roll of the drum.

3. By directing his mind to the thoughts of others, he can know the mind of all beings; if there be attachment to sensuous objects, he can perceive it, and he knows whether it is there or not; it is the same with all other

evils and ignorances; and he knows who are firm or fixed, and who are unstable. This knowledge extends both to the rúpa and arúpa worlds, the worlds in which there is body and in which there is not, and it obtains as to those who are about to enter nirwána, and are rahats. As a youth fond of pleasure, when he looks into a mirror, or still water, learns therefrom all about his face and appearance, so the priest can distinguish the thoughts of others of whatever kind.

4. By directing his mind to the remembrance of former births, he sees one, two, a hundred, a thousand, ten thousand, and many kalpas, of existences; and thinks—I have been there, in such a place; and my name, family, colour, food, and circumstances, were of such a kind; I went from this place, and was born in that place—tracing the manner of his existence from one birth to another, and from one locality to another. As a man who has business in another village goes there, and on his return remembers, I stood there, and I sat there; there I spoke, and there I was silent; in the same way a man remembers his former births, whether one thousand or ten thousand.

5. By directing his mind to the attainment of chakkhu-passaná-gnyána, or divine vision, he sees sentient beings as they pass from one state of existence to another, and the position in which they are born, whether they are mean or noble, ill favoured or good looking. He sees that others, on account of errors they have embraced, or propagated, are born in hell, and that others again, on account of their merit and truthfulness, are born in some heavenly world. As a man with good sight, from the upper story

of his house, sees the people in the street; some entering the dwelling and some coming out, and others riding in vehicles of different descriptions; so the priest sees the circumstances of other beings in all worlds.

6. By directing his mind to the four kinds of evil, viz., anger, a desire for existence, ignorance, and scepticism; he knows that this is sorrow, this the cause of sorrow, this the cessation of sorrow, and this the cause of the cessation of sorrow; and again, that this is evil, this the cause of evil, this the cessation of evil, and this the cause of the cessation of evil. His mind is free from the four kinds of evil. He knows, I have overcome the repetition of existence; I have completed my observance of the precepts; that which is proper to be done, I have done; there is nothing further to which I have to attend; my work is completed and ended. As a man who stands by the side of a lake, when the water is clear and still, sees under the surface different kinds of shells, stones, potsherds, and fishes, some in motion and some at rest, and thinks, Here are shells, here are stones, here are potsherds, and here are fishes; so the priest knows, I have overcome the repetition of existence; all that I have to do, is done.

The above paragraphs are taken from the Suttanta called Sámanya Phala, or the advantages of the priesthood. It is said of each observance, that it is good and profitable, but the last is declared to be the most excellent of all; it has nothing higher, no superior.

Here I pause; and I ask myself, in bitterness of soul, Is this all? With all his reputed wisdom, can Buddha lead his followers to "nothing higher, nothing superior?"

After a sentient being has existed more myriads of years than tongue can utter, and throughout the whole of this period, from the commencement of his existence until its last stage, been subject to "birth, decay, sorrow, weeping, grief, discontent, and vexation," according to the teaching of the patichcha samuppáda, has Buddhism nothing better to present to him than that which is seen in the extract I have made from the Sámanya Phala Suttanta? What is it? It is first, a rejoicing. But in what way? Is it from thoughts that fill the soul with their grandeur and magnificence, pouring within it, from a thousand origins, stream upon stream of the glorious imaginations that enable man to revel in the free exercise of intellectual power, as he seeks to grasp all present knowledge, or exults before the radiant visions of eternity? There is no soul about it at all, whether in reality or figure. It is just a sensation of the body; as when the nose smells the perfume, or the tongue tastes the pleasant flavour, or the skin is shampooed by the soft hand; and with far less of the great and grand about it than when the eye looks upon the beautiful vision, or the ear listens to harmonious sounds. There is an effort to take from man all that is noble in his heritage, and make him lower than the lowest creature that moves; with no more vitality about him than there is in the nidikumba sensitive plant, in the last moment of its drooping, when all its leaves are folded, and it lies in weakness, having life yet within it, but not apparent. What real benefit would there be in the power to multiply forms and appearances? Were it true that the priest, by the aid of irdhi, could listen to all sounds, and know all thoughts, and see all former births, and watch the course of all transmigrations, and learn the cause of all causes, what advantage is derived therefrom, if the acquirement of this power is to lead to results so insignificant? For what is the next stage in the supposed uprising of this privileged priest? He has done all that he has to do; the work of existence is completed; life's labour, in births innumerable, is over; the goal, the long anticipated reward, the final consummation of the whole series of births and deaths, is now attained. But what is it? NOTHINGNESS.

In the whole story of humanity; in all the confessions of heathen philosophy; in all that we learn from the misery produced by caste, slavery, and the foul deeds of war; in all the conclusions to which disappointed man has come, in his far wanderings from God; there is nothing more cheerless, more depressing, or more afflictive, than the revelations of the Suttanta in which Buddha tries to set forth the highest privilege of the highest order of sentient being. As we read it, we should be ready to rebuke, with all severity, the religious guide who thus takes from man all that is eminent in present attainment, and all that is bright in anticipation, did we not know that its representations arose from ignorance of the mercy and love of the one and only Lord of earth and heaven, and that they are another illustration of the apostle's words, "the whole creation groaneth and travaileth in pain together until now." But the angelic song has been heard, proclaiming "good tidings of great joy which shall be to all people," through Him who was then born "in the city of David, a Saviour, which is Christ, the Lord," and by whose atonement upon the cross there is now offered to every one who, through faith, will accept it, a "joy unspeakable, and full of glory," and "to them who by patient endurance in well doing seek for glory and honour and immortality, ETERNAL LIFE."

# CHAPTER IV.

## THE DEVELOPMENT OF BUDDHISM.

### 1. GOTAMA BUDDHA.

In the preceding pages, I have spoken of Buddha as a real personage; I have attributed to an individual words and acts, and have regarded the words and acts recorded in the Pitákas as said and done by that individual; but in this I have used the language of the Buddhist, and not that of my own conviction or belief. I will not say that I think no such person as Sákya Singha ever existed; but I affirm that we cannot know anything about him with certainty; and that, as it is not possible to separate the myth from the truth, we cannot rely implicitly on any one statement that is made in relation to him, either in the Text or Commentary. There is doubt as to his birth-place, his race, and the age in which he lived; and in a still greater degree, about almost every other event connected with his history. There are a few things said about him that we might believe, because they are such as are common to man; but even upon these we cannot look without suspicion, from the overcrowding of the page that records them with the most glaring untruths; and whether Gótama, prince and philosopher, ever existed or not, we are quite certain that the Gótama

Buddha of the Pitakas is an imaginary being, and never did exist.

## 2. THE LEGENDS OF BUDDHA AND MAHOMET COMPARED.

It will be said, "How do you account, then, for the production of these works, if the sage whose teachings they profess to contain, and whose miraculous power they set forth, never did teach these doctrines, and never did perform these supernatural deeds?" In answering this question, there may be an apparent difficulty; but it is not real. The fables invented by the Buddhists have had their counterpart in other ages, and among other people. There are the Purános and other works of the Brahmans, and the Zend Avesta of the Parsees, abounding with exaggerations almost equally extravagant. The Talmuds of the Jews are of a similar character. In classic history, without mentioning the innumerable myths about imaginary heroes and gods, we have Pythagoras of Samos, Apollonius of Tyana, Apuleius the African, and Melampus of Argos, who may have been real personages, but have become mythical through the miraculous endowments that are attributed to them, and the tales that have been invented about their knowledge and power. In fact, wherever the word of God is unknown, or it is regarded as a sealed book to be read only by the priest, all classes and races have formed for themselves, like the Buddhists, a mythology, with a host of imaginary beings, whom they have invested with prodigious strength, unbounded wisdom, or unearthly purity.

The manner in which these inventions arise, may be traced the most clearly in the history of Mahomet. Against the supposition that legends of this character would be invented about the impostor of Mecca, there is the existence of the Koran, collected soon after his death, and the fact that he laid no claim to the possession of miraculous powers. But about 200 years after the Hegira, the traditions respecting him had multiplied to such an extent, that it was thought necessary to collect them together, and separate the trustworthy from the fabulous. "Reliance upon oral traditions," says Dr. Weil, "at a time when they were transmitted by memory alone, and every day produced new divisions among the professors of Islam, opened up a wide field for fabrication and distortion. There was nothing easier, when required to defend any religious or political system, than to appeal to an oral tradition of the prophet. The nature of these so-called traditions, and the manner in which the name of Mahomet was abused to support all possible lies and absurdities, may be gathered most clearly from the fact that Bockhári, who travelled from land to land to gather from the learned the traditions they had received, came to the conclusion, after many years' sifting, that out of 600,000 traditions ascertained by him to be then current, only 4,000 were authentic." We may remark, that Mahomet began to contemplate his pretended mission about six centuries after Christ, and Gótama is represented as looking towards his exalted office the same number of years before Christ. Nor is this the only resemblance in the circumstances of the two men. As there was no pain to the mother of

Buddha before his birth, so the mother of Mahomet suffered no inconvenience from the treasure with which she was entrusted. As Buddha stepped upon the ground immediately after his birth, and proclaimed his dignity with a loud voice; so, at the instant Mahomet was born, he prostrated himself on the ground and recited the creed. As Brahma and Sekra were in attendance at the birth of Buddha, and to wash and refresh the mother and child "two streams of water were sent by the déwas;" so three angels, "brighter than the sun," appeared from heaven to welcome the prophet, and they afterwards washed him seven times. The whole sakwala was enlightened at the birth of the son of Máyá, and the streets and palaces of Boska, about sixty miles from the Jordan, were illuminated at the birth of the son of Amina. Each of the mothers had only one child. As the rishi Káladéwala examined the person of the young prince, to see whether the signs of Buddhaship were to be found, and when he saw them declared his future exaltation; so the monk Bahira examined the body of Mahomet to discover the seal of prophesy; and seeing it plainly impressed upon his back, he referred to the sacred books, and finding all the marks to correspond, declared the boy to be the expected apostle. As no one could measure the height of Buddha, because however extended the instrument by which they tried to measure him, he was higher still; so, when Mahomet was weighed by the angels against a thousand of his people, "he outweighed them all." As Buddha was protected from the storm by the extended hood of the nága Muchalinda; so Mahomet was shaded by the angels during the heat of the day, and at other times was screened from the sun by a cloud, "moving as he moved, and stopping as he stopped." As Buddha, at three steps, went to the heaven of Sekra; so Mahomet, mounted on the horse Borak, in the tenth part of a night, passed beyond the third heaven, and approached within two bow-shots of the eternal throne.* We thus learn, that tradition soon invests with impossible endowments those whom it delights to honour; and that in the legends that are connected with religious widely different from each other, there is sometimes a great similarity as to character and extravagance.

## 3. THE PITAKAS.

Nearly the whole of the Mohammedan legends I have enumerated, were the growth of about two hundred years; but more than twice that number of years elapsed between the death of Buddha and the period when the Pitakas are said to have been committed to writing. In this long interval there would be time for the invention of the wonderful tales that are contained in the sacred books. Of the rapid increase of these legends we have an instance on record, as, though only one hundred years elapsed between the visit of Fa Hian to India and that of Soung yun, "in the interval the absurd traditions respecting Sákya Muni's life and actions would appear to have been infinitely multiplied, enlarged, and distorted."† I have already expressed my doubts as to the truth of the statements

* Muir's Life of Mahomet, passim.

† Lieut.-Colonel Sykes: Notes on the Religious, Moral, and Political State of Ancient India.—Journal of the Royal Asiatic Society, No. xii. 280.

given by the historians of Ceylon, both in reference to the mode in which the Pitakas are said to have been written by the priest, and the time in which they were written. There were books in existence, regarded by the Buddhists as of authority, before B. C. 90. It was the opinion of Turnour that there were records in the island previous to the writing of the Pitakas at the Alu wihára, "and that the concealment of the record till the reign of the Ceylonese ruler, Wattagamini, between B. C. 101 and 76, was a part of the esoteric scheme of that (Buddhist) creed, had recourse to in order to keep up the impression as to the priesthood being endowed with the gift of inspiration."* By inspiration is meant rahatship. This power is not ascribed to the writers of the Pitakas in the Mahawanso, but we meet with it in the Sára Sangaha. "After the nirwána of Buddha, for the space of 450 years, the Text and Commentaries, and all the words of the Tathágato, were preserved and transmitted by wise priests, orally, mukha-pathéna. But having seen the evils attendant upon this mode of transmission, five hundred and fifty rahats, of great authority, in the cave called Alóka (Alu) in the province of Malaya, in Lanká, under the guardianship of the chief of that province, caused the (sacred) books to be written." The third convocation is said to have been held in the reign of Asóka, B. C. 307, and inscriptions are still found in many parts of India that were cut in his reign. Now we can scarcely think that if the art of writing was commonly practised in that age, and for Buddhist purposes, the same medium would not be used

* Journal of the Asiatic Society of Bengal, vol. vii. 722.

for the preservation and transmission of the sacred compilations. The Brahmans had a fanciful notion that it would be a desecration of the Vedas to commit them to writing, but the disciples of Buddha could have no such prejudice about the Dharmma, as the benefit of its doctrines was for all classes of men that would embrace its supposed truths, or obey the ordinances of its discipline.

There are other difficulties connected with the alleged manner of the introduction of the Pitakas into Ceylon. With the Commentaries, they are ten times the size of the Holy Scriptures. Allowing that Mahindo retained the whole in his own mind, exactly and perfectly, how could he teach them to others, without their being written? On the supposition that he repeated the whole once every two years that he spent in Ceylon, as he resided here forty-seven years, no priest could have heard the recitation more than twenty-four times; and how is it possible that any one could remember thirty million letters from hearing them only twenty-four times, and with an interval of a year between the repetition of each sentence or sermon? And if certain priests heard and remembered only a part, which part they taught to others, the difficulties are not lessened thereby, as the first instructors must have learnt all they did learn from the mouth of Mahindo. Nor must we forget that the priests of Ceylon were at that time ignorant of Pali, and would have to acquire a knowledge of this language before they could derive any advantage from the teachings of their royal preceptor; and if it be true that Mahindo translated the Commentaries into Singhalese, this would be a further call upon his time, of a formidable character. My Buddhist friends will say that I am entirely overlooking the fact that there were rahats in those days. But this I cannot believe, because the Greeks had then begun to hold intercourse with the very city whence Mahindo came; and if men with powers like those attributed to the rahats had existed, they would, doubtless, have made it known to their countrymen, along with the other wonders they told them about India. The recollective faculty was cultivated to its utmost perfection by the Arabian; but though the Koran is trifling in size when compared with the Pitakas, Kátib al Wackadi mentions only four or five persons who could repeat the whole at the time of Mahomet's death; and to make it credible that the whole had been retained in his own mind, it was fabled that the angel Gabriel had with him an annual recitation of the entire word.*

All analogy, all collateral facts that we can bring to bear upon the question, forbid the receiving of the statement that the Pitakas were first written in the reign of Wattagamini. We are told of "sacred books" being carried to China before this period. It may be said that this invalidates an argument I have presented above, that the number of the false traditions of Buddhism was multiplied because of the length of the interval between the death of the sage and the writing of the Dharmma. But this objection is set aside by another fact, that wherever we meet with books at an earlier period than the reign of Wattagamini, the era of Buddha is carried backward several hundred years beyond the date of his death, as

* Muir's Life of Mahomet, vol. i. p. 5.

given by the Singhalese records. The Tibetan version of the Pitakas is said to have been translated from works "compiled" at three different places, and we are told that the Sutras in general "were first written in the Sindhu language."* There are many evidences that the Commentaries were not written by Buddhaghóso in the exact form in which they are said to have come down to his age. He tells us that he omits certain portions; and in other instances refers us for further information to the Wisuddhi Margga. This is not the manner of a man who undertakes to translate a record, every sentence of which he regards as divine; as he would know that if some parts were omitted, and others added, such a course would prevent his work from being acknowledged as an authoritative rule of faith and conduct. He also refers to Milinda Panha, as explaining more fully certain subjects that he introduces. In the Commentary on the Dígha Nikáya he says, that "this Commentary, which is called Sumangalawilásini, is *made*, katá, by the venerable one who is named by his teachers, Buddhaghóso, whose knowledge of the Pitakas and the Commentaries is unlimited (without anything to obstruct it)." The author of the Sára Sangha says, that on one occasion he made a wrong statement, "from carelessness or want of thought." And if upon one occasion, what certainty have we that it was not the same in other instances?

The names of the principal books in Tibetan agree with those in Pali, but I can find no reference to any Commentary like that which is said to have been brought from

* Csoma de Korosi: Journal of the Bengal Asiatic Society, vol. vi. p. 687.

India by Mahindo. According to the opinion of the Buddhists of Ceylon, and upon the principles they assume, the Atuwáwas, as we have seen, must be of equal authority with the Text, and there is no possibility of evading this conclusion. The same men who wrote the Atuwáwas, in the reign of Wattagámini, wrote the Text. The same priest who brought the Text from India, brought also the Atuwáwas. Both the priests who wrote them, and the priest who brought them, are regarded as being rahats, and, therefore, as unerring in their knowlege of religious truth. They were not inspired in the Christian sense of the word, because there was no one to inspire them; but they had within themselves that which is equivalent to inspiration in other systems. The Buddhists of Ceylon have thus welded the Text and the Commentary so firmly together, that if one is proved to be in error, the other loses its authority; and as we have proved that the Commentary rests on no solid foundation, we are obliged to put the Text in the same position of uncertainty and mistrust. Independent of the absurdities and impossibilities contained in the Commentaries, the common rules of criticism would oblige us to declare this compilation to be of little value as a record of facts, and of no authority as an exponent of the system of Buddha as originally promulgated by the sage himself, when he instituted the religion known by his name.

There is this difference between a secular and sacred record. From the former we may cull what we suppose to be correct, and reject the rest, without denying the general authority of the author, as he presents himself before us as a man liable to be mistaken. But we cannot do the same with books that are regarded as sacred, without taking away their power entirely as a divine rescript. The supposition that they contain error is fatal to their claims as a religious authority. Therefore, as we have proved that the Pitakas contain that which is not true, that which is contrary to known fact, not in isolated instances only, but in connexion with their most essential principles, we must place them in the same category as the works of any other author, who is neither rahat nor rishi. It follows, as a necessary consequence, that he who puts his trust in their sarana, under the supposition that it is based upon divine truth, will find, to his utter undoing, that there is in it no power to save. But there are many who will read my work that cannot be brought to see or acknowledge this consequence. They say that nobody now believes the tales about Maha Méru; and about waves, trees, or fishes, many miles in size, and about lions as swift as sound; and, yet, with strange and reprehensible inconsistency, they still profess to believe that the books containing them are a divine and authoritative canon. They say these things are intended as allegories, figures, and hyperboles; but a moment's unprejudiced thought must convince them that this is impossible, as they rest upon the same foundation, and possess the same warrant, as the most important of Buddha's doctrines and revelations. The connexion between the one and the other is so indissoluble, that if Maha Méru, and the other things I have enumerated above, are proved to have no existence, or to be impossibilities, Buddhism cannot be a true religion, and must be rejected as a guide to salvation or to heaven.

## 4. THE SOURCE OF BUDDHA'S REVELATIONS.

Among the most singular of the claims put forth in behalf of Buddha, we may name the assertion, that though he taught the same doctrines that former Buddhas had done, all his revelations were the result of his own personal discovery, by means of intuition, entirely apart from experience, without any instruction from another, and without any aid from tradition, or from any other of the sources by which knowledge is generally communicated to man. In the interval between one Buddha and another, "not only does the religion of the preceding Buddhas become extinct, but the recollection and record of all preceding events are also lost."* In the first sermon preached by Buddha at Benares, he says, "Within me, priests, for the attainment of these *previously unknown* doctrines, the (divine) eye was developed, knowledge was developed, wisdom was developed, perception was developed, light was developed." But the claim to exclusive clearness of perception, and extent of knowledge, put forth by Buddha, is inconsistent with the power he attributed to the rishis. In the twelve kalpas previous to Gótama, twenty-four Buddhas appeared, and the doctrines of all former Buddhas are the same as those of Gótama, though not always developed to the same extent. Then, if Kaladéwála, and other rishis, could see backward forty kalpas, why were they not as able to tell the doctrines of former Buddhas

* Turnour, Manawanso, xxviii.

as Gótama himself? If the tirttaka unbelievers could see the past in the manner that Buddha affirms, how could any of them oppose him, when, from the power to see backward forty kalpas, they must have known that their predecessors were in error? And if these men, who could receive no aid from Buddha, because they were the promoters of another system, could see the past, and learn all about it, where was the necessity for Buddha, through numberless births, to seek the attainment of the Buddhaship, in order that he might teach men the way to nirwána, when others, according to his own principles, were able to learn all that was required to be known, in order to secure the same consummation? Buddha must be wrong, on one side or the other; either when he says that his doctrines were "previously unknown," or when he says that his opponents could see backward "forty kalpas."

There are other facts that lead us to question the truth of Buddha's statement, as to men's entire ignorance of the existence and doctrines of the former Buddhas. He tells us that the Vedas were given in the time of Kásyapa Buddha. When I ask how all knowledge of the former Buddhas was lost, if the Vedas then given were still in existence, though corrupted, I am told that the oblivion of the past extends only to matters connected with Buddhism; which reply is too unsatisfactory to be received. But there are other events that tend to shake our faith in this statement, unless the knowledge that so extensively prevailed of former Buddhas was the consequence of his own revelations, which it would be difficult to prove, as the Pitakas give no sanction to such a conjecture. Fa Hian tells us, in reference to the hill Kakutapéda: "It is here that the great Kia she (Késyapa Buddha) is actually present. He perforated the foot of the hill that he might enter it, and prevented any other from entering in the same way. At a considerable distance thence, there is a lateral opening, in which is the entire body of Kia she. The Tao kiao of all kingdoms and countries come here annually to adore Kia she." The Chinese have this formula: "Namo Buddháya. Namo Dhammáya. Namo Sangáya. Namo Kásyapaya. Om! Hara, hara, hara. Ho, he, he. Namo Kásyapaya. Arhate. Samyak-Sambuddháya." In the Journals of Fa Hian the references to Kasyapa are so frequent, as to lead to the conclusion that in the age in which he visited India, this Buddha was regarded with much and widely-extended reverence. In the temple at Sanchi, there is an inscription which records that a female devotee "caused money to be given for the lamps of the four Buddhas." It is, therefore, probable that much more was known of the former Buddhas in the time of Gótama than is acknowledged by the Pitakas of the Singhalese, who worship no Buddha but the last. That there were ever any beings in existence with endowments similar to those attributed to the Buddhas, I must again deny, from the arguments I have previously advanced; but there may have been religious teachers, sages, or philosophers, whose system was embraced and extended by the son of Máya. In some instances honours were paid to these former Buddhas that were denied to Gótama. Fa Hian says: "Thiao tha (Déwadatta) has sectaries who still subsist; these honour the three Foes (Buddhas) of the past time;

Shy kia wen foe (Sákya) they honour not." From this it appears that the religion founded by Déwadatta, the brother-in-law of Gótama, was yet in existence eight hundred years after his death. According to the Ceylonese records, Déwadatta, after endeavouring in vain to reach Buddha that he might ask and receive forgiveness for his evil deeds, went to the Awichi hell, having previously been abandoned by all his disciples. But how could his followers have been led to worship the former Buddhas, and refuse to worship Gótama, if all they knew about his predecessors was derived from his own revelations? And if all Déwadatta's disciples left him prior to his death, how is it that we find his system still followed after the lapse of so many centuries?

## 5. BUDDHISM IN INDIA.

The rapid spread of Buddhism on the Continent of India may be accounted for, in part, by the circumstances of the age in which Gótama is said to have lived. Whatever that age might be, it is evident that in it the Brahmans had begun to put forth their claims to superiority, which were opposed by all classes, and especially by all persons of royal lineage. Whoever, at such a crisis, presented himself as their opponent, would soon have followers in abundance; but in Gótama there was a prince, who, in addition to the influence he possessed from being a royal personage, was himself a subtle disputant, able to contend with any adversary whatever in the dialectics of the time. It was an age of controversy, one of those eras that occasionally occur, when men wake up from their usual apathy, and restless thinkers appear, sometimes for the world's weal and sometimes for its hurt, contending with each other in the arena of debate, with all the eagerness of the warrior on the field of battle, when the destiny of empires is at stake. But at such times the masses of the people are perplexed by the contests and contradictions of rival systems; and though interested for a time by the war of words, they are soon wearied, and long for repose. The boldest pretender has then the best chance of securing their regard; and when once their confidence has been gained, they follow their leader with enthusiasm, as the watch-words of a party save them from the trouble of searching after truth. The doctrines ascribed to Buddha were popular in their character, and well designed to secure the attention of all. They were just what men like to listen to; as they were invited thereby to take refuge in something that promised to be a protection, yet requiring little more than the repetition of a form to secure its privileges. The rules were definite, the keeping of them was not irksome, and the reward promised to the obedient was ample. It was enough to secure high recompence, if its votaries gave alms and rendered homage to Bhagawá during his lifetime, or to his representatives when he was dead; for though these things would not secure nirwána, they would ensure an admittance to the sensuous pleasures of a déwalóka, which to many minds would be much more desirable than the extinction of being.

Of the manner in which Buddhism gained its hold on countries away from India we know too little to be able to speak with certainty. Whatever might be its moral superiority when first brought in contact with other systems, that advantage was not retained. The character given by travellers of the priests in China is, that they are "low," "stupid and unintellectual," "wretched specimens of humanity," and that many of them are fugitives, outlaws, and bandits, who have been driven by want or fear to seek an asylum in the temples. Of the priests who wear the yellow robe in other countries a similar character is given—they are said to be idle, ignorant, untruthful and without respect.

In all countries, the honours claimed by the priesthood have won many to its ranks. In the course of time they were carried out to so great an extent, that the mendicant sramanas succeeded in placing the members of their Sangha in a higher position than even the Brahman himself seeks to secure. In the one instance there is pride of caste; in the other, pride of office; but the principle is the same in both instances. The priesthood (as we call the office, from the want of a better name), was at first open to nearly all, whether men or women. The man who had been a slave, if set free by his master, might receive admission; and when once the yellow robe was around him, he could claim the reverence of kings. Even higher honours than this were gained, when the use of the tun-sarana, the threefold protective formula, was established, as the poor misguided worshipper was led to say, "I take refuge in the priesthood." And when the discourse called Ratana was composed, now read as part of the Pirit, the priests proceeded to a still more daring usurpation, and made the ruler of the déwa-lóka Tawutisá say, "Ye demons who are here assembled, celestial or terrestial, we adore the associated priesthood, the Tathágato, worshipped by gods and men. May there be prosperity." They thus represent themselves, not only as being higher than the gods, but as being on an equality with the supreme Buddha, and as receiving an equality of worship. In the Khanda Pirit the following words are attributed to Buddha. "Infinite (in excellence) is Buddha; infinite his doctrines; infinite his priesthood." It was in consistency with these teachings, that when bishop Heber asked a priest, in Kandy, if he worshipped the gods, he replied, "No: the gods worship me."

From its commencement, notwithstanding the advantages it offered, and the gentleness of its professions, Buddhism met with numerous opponents. It is by no means certain that it was ever the religion of India generally, though at one time its monuments might be everywhere seen, and its formularies everywhere proclaimed. The worship of fire, the system of the earlier Védas, seems to have prevailed to a greater extent than any other faith in the time of Gótama. With this, the spirit of asceticism exercised an almost equal, and an increasing influence. Had Buddhism been left to work its own way, according to its own principles, it might have flourished among the Hindus at the present day, as one of their many forms of religion. But in the gathering together of the armies, and the fierce contentions of the kings, at the burning of Buddha's body, we have a key to much of its subsequent history. It was used as a political instrument. The kings allied themselves to Buddhism, to save their race from the degradation that threatened it from the Brahman. But its tacit condemnation of caste was remembered, by its royal partizans, when its denouncement of contention and war was unheeded. The struggle that ensued is, perhaps, one of the most sanguinary in the history of man, from the bitterness of the passions it called forth, the length of its duration, and the extent of the area in which it prevailed; but no red record tells us now of its alternations of conquest and defeat. Parasu Ráma, regarded as the champion of the Brahmans, is said to have cleared the earth seven times of the whole Kshatriya race. The names of various kings are known who perished in the strife.* Nágaséna refers to a battle between the brahman Bhadrasála, and Chandagutta, of the race of Sákya, in which a hundred kelas (1,000,000,000) of soldiers were slain; and though the number is an oriental exaggeration, the battle may be a fact. The adherents of Buddha were worsted in this prolonged struggle; and about the sixth century after Christ, the prince Sudhanvan gave orders to put all the Buddhists in India to death. Mádhava Acháraya says: "A-setor-á-tushádre Bauddhánám vriddhabálakán na hanti sa hantavyo bhrityán ityanwasát nripah. The king commanded his servants to put to death the old men and the children of the Bauddhas, from the bridge of Ráma to the snowy mountain: let him who slays not be slain."† The fusion of three castes out of the four, leaving the Brahmans paramount, and alone in integrity of race, is a proof of the severity of the strife. Among the millions of the Hindus,

* Monier Williams's Inaugural Lecture.

† Professor Wilson: Journal of the Royal Asiatic Society, vol. xvi. p. 258.

Buddha has not now a single worshipper. Even in the time of Fa Hian, Kapila-wattu was one vast solitude, without either king or people, and the roads were infested by elephants and lions. The minister of the powerful Akbar, in the sixteenth century, could find no one in the wide dominions of his master who could give him any explanation of the doctrines of Gótama.*

## 6. ANOMALIES.

It would be unfair to Buddhism, were I to allow the supposition to go forth, that I regard the present work as containing anything like a complete exposition of the system; though it so happens that nearly all its leading principles have come under our review, from the whole of them being founded in error. I am here a controversialist, and not an expositor: but I may express my conviction, that little more is to be learnt about its principia from the numerous works written by its disciples. Its leading facts and most important doctrines are now known; and when our expositions of the system are confirmed, there will be little to reward further research. But in the development of its character and tendency, its bearing upon the interests of mankind, and the place it holds among the agencies that have exerted an extensive influence in the east, there is a

* "Mádhava a writer of the fourteenth century, places the Buddhas nc nearer than in Cashmir, and Abufazl declares that he never had met with a follower of Buddha in Hindustan, and had only encountered some old men of that faith in his third visit to Cashmir. Later periods are out of the question, for in the present day I never heard of a person who had met with natives of India proper of this faith, and it does appear that an utter extirpation of the Buddha religion in India was effected between the twelfth and sixteenth centuries."—Professor Wilson.

vast field for cultivation, and a harvest of admonitory instruction for future generations. I have proved that Buddhism is not a revelation of truth, that its founder was an erring and imperfect teacher, and ignorant of many things that are now almost universally known; and that the claim to the exercise of omniscience made for him by his followers is an imposition and pretence. These conclusions I have founded upon statements taken from the sacred writings. Were it possible to form a true history of the rise and progress of Buddhism, it would be a record of great value. But this can never be, as the attempt to accomplish it, with the documents now in existence, would be like the search for a portion of the water of the Ganges in the southern extremity of the Indian ocean. We can now only regard Buddha as an impostor; whereas, if we could learn the truth, it might have changed our censure into respect. We might have seen the struggles of a mind honestly, though unsuccessfully, contending with evil, and have been led to invest his name with honours equal to those given to other sages and moralists. If the compilers of the Pitakas had had the magnanimity of the followers of Mahomet, and rejected from the canon all spurious traditions, it would have been a great boon to the real interests of Buddhism. The inconsistencies and mistakes with which it is now charged, and the most apparent of its defects, may be the result of misconception and misrepresentation on the part of the exponents of the original system, as propounded by Sákya Singha. It now presents various anomalies, a few of which I enumerate, that his own words might have explained. We can scarcely think that one who set himself so strongly against the pretensions of caste would render to it the greatest homage in his power, by declaring that the Buddhas are always born of the two highest castes, the Kshatriya or the Brahman. There are evidences throughout the records of Buddhism, of an awkward attempt to join together three opposite systems; that of the householder, the mendicant priest, and the hermit, or jungle-ascetic. The revels that take place in the déwa-lókas, with the imperfections, grossness, and bad passions of their inhabitants, do not agree with the renunciation of pleasure, or the freedom from evil, represented as necessary in those who seek the rewards of religion. All idea of atonement by sacrifice, or of salvation through the vicarious sufferings of another, is set at nought and rejected, and yet the "painful births" of Bódhisat are represented as being voluntarily endured to prepare him for the reception of the Buddhaship, by which he was enabled to guide men to "the city of peace," nirwána. Though Buddha is made to declare that there is no self, nothing like a soul, that goes from one state of existence to another, he says continually, speaking of existence in bygone ages, "I was that person;" as in the Sussondiya Játaka, when, in the gurulu (a fabulous bird) birth, he committed sin with the queen of Tambatáda, and declares expressly, after narrating the circumstances under which the deed was done, "I am he that was a gurulu at that time."

## 7. DEFECTS.

Other defects may have been inherent in the original system. The universal practice of two out of the five great precepts is an impossibility—the first and third—not to take life, and not to have sexual intercourse. The prohibition of things not wrong in themselves is absolute—not to drink intoxicating liquors, and not to receive money. We are taught, from a higher source, that it is not the use of these things, but the abuse, that is an evil. But as Buddhism can offer no hand of help, to enable man to be "temperate in all things," it can only confess its weakness, and forbid them altogether, as other systems have done that are not of God.

The principle of the third precept is most insulting to the woman, inasmuch as its infraction is not a wrong done to her, but to her possessor or guardian. It was my intention to have inserted an extract from the Sammadithi Sutra Wannaná, on the position of woman; but the licence given to her to do wrong is so great, and the preservation of her chastity regarded as so small a matter, that I fear to publish the quotation, lest it should lead any of those who may read it to regard themselves as under no restraint. There are twenty kinds of women who are not to be approached, among whom the wife is not mentioned, unless she comes under the class, "protected by some one;" though it is the consequence to another, and not the act itself, that is regarded as constituting the crime. There are some circumstances under which it is not sin to the woman, and others under which it is not sin to either party. The consent of the protector, whether relative or guardian, renders the act blameless that would otherwise be a sin. The woman who has personally no social or legal protector has no protection from any other source. She who is forlorn and friendless, and needs a shield the most, is deserted in her exposed position, and is accounted as having none of the rights of woman. About the plighting of the troth between one man and one woman, till death them do part, Buddhism knows nothing. The morality of the system has been praised; but for what reason? It is sometimes said that it has ten commandments, very little different from those of the Holy Scriptures. But is it so? In reality, there is no command at all. When a man or a woman chooses, they can go to the temple, and say before the priest, "I take the ordinance not to approach one of the other sex;" and if no time be stated, when it is taken, the obligation ceases, at the end of the póyá day. It is an absolute continence that is declared, and has little more relation to the seventh commandment of Sinai, than a vow to abstain from animal food for a day would have to the command, "Thou shalt do no murder."

The five precepts may be regarded as among the institutions of primitive Buddhism, ordained in the time of its founders; but I must confess that the more closely I look into the system, the less respect I feel for the character of its originators. That which at first sight appears to be the real glory of Buddhism, its moral code, loses all its distinction when minutely examined. Its seeming brightness is not that of the morning star, leading onward to intenser radiance, but that of the meteor; and not even that; for the meteor warns the traveller that the dangerous morass is near; but Buddhism makes a fool of man by promising to guide him to safety, whilst it leads him to the very verge of the fatal precipice. We need not wonder at the moral circumstances of the people who profess this system. In many instances the door of evil is thrown open by the record they take as their religious guide, whilst they know nothing of the solemn thought implied by the question, "How can I do this great wickedness and sin against God?"

The result of a sincere reception of Buddhism, as its purpose is presented in the Pitakas, is to reduce man to the smallest minimum of vitality. The wisdom of sentient existence is, to seek to become non-sentient and non-existent; and as man does not possess an immortal soul, it is possible for this to be effected. To prove the impossibility of the existence of a soul, many a long and weary conversation is recorded in the Abhidamma. All thought is regarded as a material result. The operation of the mind is no different in mode to that of the eye, or ear; vision is eye-touch, hearing is ear-touch, and thinking is heart-touch. The man, as we have repeatedly seen, is a mere mass, or cluster; a name, and nothing more. He who can reduce himself to a state most resembling a fish when it lies torpid in the mud, or an animal when it hibernates, is regarded as having attained to the most exalted state of existence. The world next to nirwána, in the order of privilege, is the fourth brahma-loka, where the brahmas live 80,000 maha kalpas, in a state neither conscious nor unconscious; like the infant that lies in its cradle in a dim uncertainty of thought and feeling, partly sensible, and partly senseless. Our own fair world, and all its scenes of beauty, with all the sweetnesses of social communion, are to be turned away from, and despised.

To act wisely in the highest degree, is to retire to the wilderness, and shut up all the senses, and get to be so near nothing that whilst yet living there shall be a universal paralysis of body and soul. The devotee has then only to commit the suicide of immortality, and secure non-existence, and he has reached the perfection of being, which is, not to be.

In such a system, there can be none of the activities of benevolence. Words of kindness are whispered gently by the lip, because this can be done without an effort to be practically kind, and such words are plentiful. In a discourse connected with the Pirit, the following sentences are repeated: "May every being experience happiness, peace, and mental enjoyment! Whatever sentient beings may exist, erratic or stationary; or of whatever kind, long, or tall, or middle-sized; or short, or stout; seen, or unseen; near, or remote; born, or otherwise existing—may every being be happy...As a mother protects her child, the child of her bosom; so let immeasurable benevolence, prevail among all beings! Let unbounded kindness and benevolence, prevail throughout the universe above, below, around, without partiality, anger, or enmity! Let these dispositions be established in all who are awake, whether standing, walking, sitting, or reclining; this place is thus constituted a holy residence!" Yet the priest who utters these words knows that if he were to make any movement whatever towards carrying the sentiments they express into effect, he would thereby expose himself to ecclesiastical censure. He blesses by words, and not by works. He is an overflowing fountain of mercy, but receives back within himself all the streams that proceed therefrom. He receives, and does not give. His is the kindness of the heart, and not of the hand. It is forbidden to him to prescribe in cases of sickness, or to prepare medicines, or to perform any surgical operation. One half of the human race is entirely shut out from his sympathy and regard, as he may not look upon a woman, and the sound of her voice is represented as a snare. To gain a livelihood by calculating eclipses, or studying the motions of the planets, or cultivating the ground, is called, as in the other instances just named, the seeking of an unworthy livelihood by an animal (tirachchána) science. We need not wonder at the vacant look of the robed mendicant. The worship of the people can afford little satisfaction to one excluded from the smile of woman, the gleam of the stars, and all opportunity of doing good.

The proper idea of sin cannot enter into the mind of the Buddhist. His system knows nothing of a supreme intelligent Ruler of the universe. The priest is to consider, "I am the result of karmma; this forms my inheritance, my state of birth, my relatives, my support: I shall be heir of all the actions I perform, whether they be good or evil." There is no law, because there is no lawgiver, no authority from which law can proceed. Buddha is superior in honour and wisdom to all other beings; but he claims no right to impose restrictions on other men. He points out the course to be taken, if merit is to be gained; but he who refuses to heed his words, does the Tathágato no wrong. Religion is a mere code of proprieties, a mental opiate, a plan for being free from discomfort, a system of personal profit, a traffic in merit, a venal process. In addressing itself to the individual man, apart from its honied words, it is a principle of selfishness; and yet, though this is its beginning, centre, and end, it seeks to hide its selfishness by denying that there is any self. As there is no infinite and all-worthy Being, to whose glory we are called upon to live, when we commit evil the wrong is done to ourselves, and not to another. There is no baseness about it; it is not an iniquity. Hence the impossibility of making the Buddhist feel that he is a sinner, when the attempt is made to bring the commandment home to his conscience. A native has been heard to say that he never committed sin since he was born, unless it were in catching fish; and some free themselves from the consequences of this transgression, by saying that they only take the fish out of the water, and they die of themselves. The vilest profligacy may be committed without offence, and may even become a virtue, as in the case of the courtezan Bindumati, if in its commission preference be avoided, and the mind remain unmoved.

The supposed absence of a holy and ever present Intelligence from the universe, throws light on many of the other institutions of Buddhism, and makes that possible which would otherwise be too manifest an absurdity for it ever to have been put in practice. 1. The priest can receive permission to put off his robe for a time, and break the precept of continence, and be again admitted into the Sangha, without the forfeiture of any privilege he previously possessed. 2. In former years, when the worshipper entered the temple, on taking upon himself the obligations, he said, "Ahan bhanté ajja ito pattháya yáwa pahómitáwa wisuń wisuń rakkhanattháya pańcha sikkhápadáni samádiyámi. To-day, my lord, I take the five precepts, to obey them, severally, as far as I am able, from this time forward." The strange clause, yáwa pahomitáwa, as far as, or as long as, I am able, has recently been omitted, not from its incongruity with the system, but from the evil consequences that followed from its recital. Its use, at any time, reveals the absence of all power or authority beyond the will of the devotee. 3. There can be no intelligent prayer in Buddhism, as there is no one to listen to its voice. The people repeat the tun-sarana before the image of Buddha.

| | |
|---|---|
| Buddhan' saranan' gachchámi | I take refuge in Buddha |
| Dhamman' saranan' gachchámi | I take refuge in the Truth |
| Sanghan' saranan' gachchámi | I take refuge in the Priesthood. |

Once, twice, thrice, this is repeated. But the refuge of Buddha can be of no avail, as he has ceased to be; and as well might men appeal to the light that once shone in the festive hall of his summer palace, or the rainbow that spanned his native city, in the hour of the passing storm. The Dharmma, the doctrines of Buddha, are equally without power. How can a sound, a law, a recitation, help any one, by the exercise of its own influence, when it is itself a mere abstraction, a name? And as to the Sangha, the associated Priesthood, I should like to ask any of my readers who repeat the formula as an act of worship, in what members of the Sangha it is that they seek refuge. Not in the dead priests; as some of them have become flies or fishes, and others have become nothing in nirwána.

It must be in some portion of the living priesthood. Then I ask, Which? Is it in those who are so frequently seen, as plaintiffs or defendants, in our courts of justice; or those who are breaking the precept by adding land to land, and by lending out money on usury; or those whose stolid countenances we see in the streets as they carry the alms-bowl; or those who utter words of blasphemy against their Maker and Judge, and revile the servants of Christ, forgetful of the advice of Buddha: "Priests, if others speak against me, or speak anything against my doctrines, or speak anything against the priesthood, that is no reason why you should be angry, discontented, and displeased with them, thereby bringing yourselves into danger?*

The want of reality in the system leads, as a necessary consequence, to moral imbecility. Buddha acknowledges that there are things excellent in other religions, and hence he did not persecute. He declares that even his opponents had a degree of wisdom, and exercised miraculous power. But this very indifference about error, as about every thing else; this apparent candour and catholicity; is attended by an influence too often fatal to the best interests of those by whom it is professed. There can be little difference in the mind of the Buddhist between truth and error, right and wrong; and from this source arises the apparent inability of many persons in this island to see the essential difference between Christianity and Buddhism, or to learn that to be a Christian a man must regard Buddha as a false teacher and his claim to supremacy as a sin against Almighty God. Not in any other part of the earth, to the same extent, are

* Brahma Jála Suttanta.

such saddening scenes presented as are here daily witnessed. To name one instance will be sufficient to establish the fact; and I choose this, because it comes under my own immediate notice: Not many miles to the south of Colombo, there is one holding office under government, who does all he can to support Buddhism, by sending for priests of name to live in his korla, by using his influence to establish Dharmma-sabháwas, the members of which are made to pledge themselves to avoid all countenance of Christianity, and to regard all as outcasts who act otherwise, into whose families they will not marry, and whose funerals they will not attend. Yet this same person, though he exhorts his dependents to act otherwise, swears as a Christian in a court of justice; unable, it would seem, to see the inconsistency, or to understand the iniquity, of professing to take an oath, and yet appealing to a God in whose existence he does not believe. Nor is he alone in his perilous course. Too many of his countrymen are Christians in the church and court, and heathens everywhere else. It is on this account that the present revival of Buddhism in some parts of this island is to be regarded with satisfaction. Its consequence will be, to separate from the professing church those who are in alliance with idolatry; and when once this has been accomplished, and not till then, the host of the Lord will go on from conquering to conquer, until the whole of the people have become truthful, and walk as the children of light.

The system of Buddha is humiliating, cheerless, man-marring, soul-crushing. It tells me that I am not a reality; I have no soul. It tells me that there is no unalloyed happiness, no plenitude of enjoyment, no perfect unbroken peace, in the possession of any being whatever, from the highest to the lowest, in any world. It tells me that I may live myriads of millions of ages, and that not in any of these ages, nor in any portion of an age, can I be free from apprehension as to the future, until I attain to a state of unconsciousness; and that in order to arrive at this consummation I must turn away from all that is pleasant, or lovely, or instructive, or elevating, or sublime. It tells me, by voices ever-repeated, like the ceaseless sound of the sea-wave on the shore, that I shall be subject to "sorrow, impermanence, and unreality," so long as I exist, and yet that I cannot now cease to exist, nor for countless ages to come, as I can only attain nirwána in the time of a supreme Buddha. In my distress, I ask for the sympathy and guidance of an all-wise and all-powerful Friend, who can be touched with the feeling of my infirmities, soothing me with words of solace, and permitting me to come to him in my darkness, and perplexity, and cast my care upon Him, as the troubled child casts its care upon a mother's love, and is then at sweet rest. But I am mocked, instead, by the semblance of relief; and am told to look to Buddha, who has ceased to exist; to the Dharmma, that never was an existence; and to the Sangha, the members of which are real existences, but like myself, partakers of sorrow and sin.

Of late years there have been evidences of a growing disposition to receive as truth only the words spoken by Buddha, and to reject all comments, glosses, and explanations, or to regard them as of less authority. But the

Buddhist has no other assurance that the words attributed to the Tathágato were actually spoken by him, besides that which he receives from the Pitakas. Why should these books, which profess to have been transmitted from unerring rahats, be less trustworthy when they speak about other matters than when they profess to give the words of Buddha, as their authors had in both instances the same opportunity of knowing the truth or untruth of the statements they record? The warrant for receiving the comment is just the same as that for receiving the word; and the common principles that guide us when placing our trust in evidence, oblige us to receive both word and comment with equal confidence, or to reject both with equal incredulity, when they come to us with the same authority, and when both profess to be revealed truth, whether that revelation be from an inner and personal light, or from the inspiration of some other being. The principles of the eclectic cannot be applied to an inspired record. The very moment we begin to choose one portion rather than another, we set aside its sovereign authority, and reduce it to the same level as any other work. When we ask the Buddhist why he believes certain words to have been spoken by Bhagawá, he says, Because the Pitakas declare it. We then reply, By rejecting other parts of the Pitakas as being unworthy of credence, and yet founding upon them, and upon them alone, your trust in the words they ascribe to Buddha, you do that which no wise worshipper would do, and what you have no liberty to do as a man guided by the requirements of reason.

I have thus endeavoured, fairly and faithfully, to set

forth the errors of Buddhism, as we learn them from its sacred books. The moral character of the system, as I have presented it, is almost uniformly reflected in the conduct of the inhabitants of the island who are guided by its precepts. Too commonly, among its adherents, a high sense of honour is wanting; there is no resolute up-standing for truth, no willingness to suffer rather than to sin. There may be exceptions, but I have not met with them, in my intercourse with persons of this creed. Few things surprise the newly-arrived European so much as to find so entire an absence of truthfulness in men who seem otherwise to be respectable. There is the appearance of all that is honest, and trustworthy; in conversation, the bated breath, and every token of respect for the person addressed; a complacent smile, never intermitted; a willing assent to every proposition; promises falling fast from the lip, like flowers of the araliya tree at early dawn; and at parting a ready re-iteration of all that has been promised, and a renewed and more positive declaration that every command shall be obeyed. But as to the fulfilment, weary will be the eye that watches for its coming, and long empty the hand that expects from this source to be filled. How can it be otherwise, if no higher motive for integrity than that which Buddhism presents is found within the heart? But in the circle where Christian influence extends, even though there may not be the profession of scriptural faith, I can mark a great improvement in honesty and truthfulness, since I first stepped upon these shores as a youth.

The belief in a soul is, perhaps, general among the Singhalese, though so contrary to the teaching of Buddha.

The divinity that stirs within all men speaks with too loud a voice for them not to know that the no-soul doctrine must be wrong; and the statement that Buddha told men there is no self, is regarded as a misrepresentation.

The atheism of the Dharmma prevails more generally, but it is not universal. There are some, especially among those who are more conversant with the truths of the Bible, who believe in the existence of one Almighty God; others confer upon the déwas the attributes of God; and others, like their so-called Bhagawá, are out-and-out atheists. The arguments against the possibility of the existence of a supreme intelligent Being are regarded as so conclusive, that any attempt to disprove them would be a mark of extreme folly. We find that their great difficulty, when they set themselves in sincerity to seek out the truth, is, to realise the great idea of the existence of God. We are frequently told that our religion would be an excellent one, if we could leave out of it all that is said about a Creator; for as holy men of old, in all that they reveal, proceed upon the certainty that God is, "and that he is a rewarder of them that diligently seek him," so all that Buddha teaches proceeds upon the supposition, dark and joyless, that THERE IS NO GOD.

---

Before I conclude my little book, I ask permission, as a minister of Christ fast hastening towards the sun-set hour of life, to address a few words of affectionate counsel to those whose instruction I have now more immediately in view, in the task I have undertaken, to expose the more prominent errors of Buddhism. At some personal inconvenience, at the cost of severance from children whom I love as my own soul, I have again visited this island, that I may give to the Society to which it is my privilege to belong, the benefit of my acquaintance with the principal race here resident, and of my matured experience as to its interests and wants. The friends of my youth, the brave men whose zeal I tried to imitate when I saw them strong in faith amidst the shouts of the battle-field—where are they? I know where. Not in a nirwána of nothingness; not amidst the uncertainties of a repetition of existence; but with God. I shall see them again; and we shall no longer have to toil together, but to triumph; through the one sacrifice made for all sinners. By the memory of these servants of Christ—for many loved them as well as myself—I ask of all those who shall read, and can understand, the sentences I now write, to give me their further attention, whilst I seek to express to them the yearnings of my soul, and to bare before them the throbbings of an anxious heart. I will no longer speak as to an impersonality, but suppose that I am standing before you, as an old acquaintance; and that under the shade of one of your own palm-groves, or by the perfume of your ná trees, we are talking over the story of days that to you, as well as myself, were days of high resolve and bright hope.

Then, my friends, I will not insult you by asking if you believe in the statements of Buddha and his disciples, the fallacy of which I have endeavoured to expose. I know that you do not; you cannot. But if this is your position, it involves consequences that are of an importance over which you will do well most seriously to ponder. There *is* truth among the children of men—absolute, saving, ennobling and divine. Have you embraced this truth? and has it brought to you all that it professes to impart, in the promises of the word of God? Is there that difference in your peace of mind, as to the present, and in your assurance of safety, as to the future, that gives a surer testimony of the divinity of the Gospel of Jesus Christ, than can be learnt from books, or taught by man? I lament, that as to many of you—though you are indebted for nearly all you know to the minister of God, and have listened to his prayers, as again and again he has poured out his heart before the throne of the heavenly grace in your behalf—you have been no more influenced by the saving power of Christianity, than if you had lived in some distant age, and had learnt your hódiya at the pansala of Mahindo, or fought in the wars of Prákrama Bahu.

Now, no placid smile, if you please, in commendation of Christianity, whilst in your inner soul you disavow all that you say or seem. There must be no trifling in the presence of the all-seeing God, around whose throne is the terrible thunder. If there be, indeed, a revelation from above, a Gospel, a Redeemer, a Holy Spirit, a Father in heaven, the danger that awaits you, if you wilfully neglect the truth, or deliberately reject it, must be more appalling than all the horrors that are told of Awichi, for it will be everlasting. If the mighty Lord of all could not, in consistence with his attribute of justice, save man without an atonement, neither will he save you, if you reject that atonement. I feel for you; I sympathise with you; I know something of the difficulties with which you have to contend. For many generations your forefathers have been taught to regard the sacrifice of blood with aversion, as a thing impure in itself, and as the root of all evil; and whilst these thoughts are cherished, or the remembrance of them retained, there can be no sincere trust in the expiation wrought out for man upon the cross; though it is by this alone that we can be saved from God's wrath and eternal perdition. When the flower and the fruit are thought to be an adequate offering, as an expression of religious thought and feeling, there can be no right appreciation of the vileness of sin, or of man's need of an all-worthy Substitution. We can only learn this from the saddest of all sights, the outpouring of the life's blood; but that which is the saddest of all sights in itself, is the most cheering of all in its character as a symbol, as it tells of the ransom-price, "not without blood," paid for us men and for our salvation; when Christ Jesus, "the everlasting Son of the Father," in the infinitude of his mercy, and of his own free will, became "the propitiation for our sins; and not for ours only, but also for the sins of the whole world." This one sentence is more cheering than all the revelations of Buddhism, whether uttered by Bhagawá or rahat.

There is another barrier to your reception of Christianity —the indifference of many of my own countrymen to the duties that are insisted on as essential to a meetness for heaven. But I wish to impress upon your minds, that no man is a Christian, in the sight of God, because of his birth, or name, or profession, or rank, or society, or church, or nation; or because of anything that he himself can do, or say, or give, or learn, or believe, whilst he continues in sin. Every Briton needs a personal and individual conversion, as much as any native of Ceylon. In the heart of every unconverted Briton there is naturally the same hatred to stern and uncompromising truth, that there is in the heart of the heathen and the idolator; and there is needed, for the removal of this enmity, the influence of the Holy Ghost, in the one case as much as the other. But the souls of men go out after the honours, riches, or pleasures, of this impermanent world; and they thus forget, through the influence of inner evil, and the temptations of Satan, that the grand duty of this life is to prepare for the life eternal. We are forewarned in the Scriptures, that the saved are few; the perishing many: an awful thought, but its truth is confirmed by all experience, if those only are to be saved, who in sincerity of heart obey and love God. It was thus in the days of Christ. "This is the condemnation, that light is come into the world, but men love darkness rather than light, lest their deeds should be reproved. For every one that doeth evil hateth the light, neither cometh he to the light, lest his deeds should be reproved." But all my countrymen are not careless of religious duty. There are some who have lived in the midst of you as the sincere servants of God; whose virtues you have seen, and from whom you have learnt the loveliness and beauty of true Christianity.

I want to bring before you the way of the government of God, as presented by ancient prophet and holy apostle. "No man liveth to himself." There are duties peculiar to your position, as men of influence in this island, that may

15

not be overlooked with impunity. The spread of Christianity, nationally, has been, in most instances, through the instrumentality of the higher classes, whilst its power and vitality have been best presented amongst the poor. To you light has come, whilst the masses around you are still involved in darkness and error. It is not enough that you yourselves embrace the truth. It is incumbent upon you, as a momentous and paramount obligation, to seek to bring this island, and all its people, into the only fold, under the one Shepherd. But how few there are, among you all, away from the paid agents of the church, that are seeking, with their whole souls, to save their countrymen from the wreck of eternal ruin. Whose are the names, among those who within the last fifty years have been making a profession of Christianity, that will go down to future ages as prominent in seeking to set aside the errors of Buddhism, and convert men's souls to God? There is a glorious work before you, if you will set about its accomplishment in sincerity and earnestness; but it will be a sad account you will have to give, if, in the day of judgment, Jesus Christ shall have to say to you, impersonating those whom he has redeemed, "I was ignorant, and ye taught me not." It is not enough that you be baptised, or have your name in some church registry, and occasionally attend the house of God. Religion must be made the work of your life; it must enter into everything; and it must be seen by your children, and servants, and neighbours, that your heart is not here, but in heaven. The power to do all this cannot be gained by your having learnt some catechism at school, or by your having read the Scriptures as a lesson when a youth. To teach you further, to aid you in your contest with evil, to save you from the pollution and power of sin, to bring you into happy communion with God, there must be a *constancy* of attention to "the means of grace;" and your religion must be a labour, a devotion, a sacrifice, never neglected and never intermitted.

The work of missions in this land has not been a failure; among the poor and the suffering there have been seen the sweetness, the power, and the joyousness of religion, as these were known in the primitive church; and now, among the seraphim in heaven, there are many with the dazzling diadem upon the brow, who learnt, in some humble school, or mud-walled chapel, or unpretending church, the word of reconciliation, and embraced the offer of mercy made to them in the name of Christ. But among those to whom we once looked forward, because of the superiority of the advantages they have possessed, as the heralds of the cross to their countrymen, as those who were to take Christianity into their households, and beseech the throne of God in earnest supplication, until their every relative and servant has been converted from the error of their way, there has been severe disappointment. In the exhibition of generous and elevated sentiment, in the successful pursuit of acquirements and accomplishments of a high order, there has been, of late years, a marked improvement. The names of some of you, among which we may specially mention that of the learned editor and translator of the Sidath Sangaráwa, are heard in the halls of science and literature along with those borne by men of world-wide reputation. The author of Wiswapriya, by his invaluable publications, has shewn that there are among you able and accomplished controversialists. There are others who, as extensive cultivators, as judges upon the bench, or as rulers of korlas, have exhibited an integrity and uprightness that were formerly unknown in the land. But the church wants to see more of the spirit that fired the soul of the apostle Paul, when he said, "God forbid that I should glory, save in the cross of our Lord Jesus Christ, by whom the world is crucified to me and I unto the world." There are many of you, especially among the more aged, who have had other adverse influences to contend with, that are now passing away. Your ayahs, your sisters, and your mothers, were all heathen; and home authority is the most powerful of all modes of mastery. It is hard to have to say that Buddha was a false teacher, and to have to reject his doctrines, when those whom you have loved most taught you to revere him as the best and greatest of beings. But there are now mothers, in the homes of the highest families in the land, who teach their children to bow their knees to Jesus, once an infant, "meek and mild." Even of those whose parents are yet unbelievers in Christianity, we may cherish hope. The reply of the Déwa Nilama, when our good bishop recently addressed an assembly of chiefs and priests at the pavilion in Kandy, is worthy of grateful record. "I have no doubt," he said, "that the next generation will be likely to embrace Christianity, seeing that my own son, who was educated in a Christian school. is now a Christian."

The cross must triumph, whenever it is upheld in its simplicity, by men who are willing to be nothing in its presence, that the name of the Redeemer may be high over all. Where are the old idols of Europe, Jupiter and Mars, Woden and Thor, and all the other lords many, and gods many, whom my own forefathers worshipped? Not one of them has now a single votary in the whole world. And thus it shall be with Buddha, and all the myriads of deities in the east. The time will come when the wihára will be deserted, the dágoba unhonoured, and the bana unread. I can suppose no lovelier spot in this wide world than Ceylon will be, when in every household there shall be an altar erected to the Lord God of heaven and earth. There is a winningness, a pleasantness, and a natural gentleness about its people, that when converted to Christianity will make them like angel-spirits; and to the high destiny of that coming race, whether those who form it shall reap the luxuriance of the rice-clad plain, or dwell amidst the plenty that shall then be put forth on the slopes of the cultivated mountain, we may look forward with shouts of exultation. Welcome, then, toil, and difficulty, and reproach, if a consummation so blessed as this is to be the reward of the servants of Christ. And thus it shall be; "for the mouth of the Lord hath spoken it." "There were great voices in heaven, saying, The kingdoms of this world are become the kingdoms of our Lord, and of his Christ; and he shall reign for ever and ever." Rev. xi. 15.

# APPENDIX.

Note A. Page 23. Pali the root of all languages.

Sá Mágadhi múla bhásá,
Nará yá yadikappiká,
Brahmáṇo chassutálápá,
Sambuddháchápi bhásaré.

Note B. Page 55. Buddha acknowledges the power of the Rishis.

Idang watwána Mátango,
Isi sachchaparakkamo,
Antalikkasmiń pakkámi,
Bráhmánáṇań udikkhatan.

*Játaka Wannaná.*

Note C. Page 80. The Sakwalas are in Sections of three.

Lókantarikáti tiṇṇań tiṇṇań chakkawálánań antaré ékéká lókantariká hóti; tiṇṇań sakaṭa chakkánań pattánań wá aṇṇyamaṇṇyánań áhachcha t'hapitánań majhhé ókásowiya.

*Mahápadána Suttawannaná.*

Note D. Page 80. The infinite Worlds known to Buddha.

Wisayakkhettańpana anantáparimánésuhi chakkawálésu yańyań Tathágato ákańkhati tańtań jánáti.

*Sára Sangaha. Wisuddhi Magga.*

Note E. Page 81. The siz of Maha Méru.

Sinéru bhikkhawé pabbatarájá chaturásíti yójanasahssáni ayáména chaturásíti yójanasahassáni witthárén̆a chaturásíti-yójanasahassáni mahásamuddé ajjhogálho chaturásítiyója-nasahassáni mahásamuddá achchuggato.

*Satta Suryuggamana Suttanta.*

---

Note F. Page 81. The colour of Maha Méru.

Tassapana Sinérunó páchínapassań rajatamayań tasmá tassá pabháya ajjohittaṭhań tassań disáyań smuddodakań khírań wiya paṇṇyáyati dakkhiṇapassańpana indaníla-manimayań tasmá dakkhiṇadisáya samuddódakań yébhuy-yéna nílawaṇṇańhutwá paṇṇyáyati taṭhá ákásań.

*Sára Sangaha. Wisuddhi Magga. Jinálankára.*

---

Note G. Page 82. The size of the Sakwala.

Ekań chakkawálań áyámató witthháratócha yójanánań dwádasasatasahassáni chatuttińsa satáni paṇṇyásaṇcha yójanani. Parikkhépato.

Sabbań sata sahassání,<br>
Chattińsa parimaṇḍalań,<br>
Dasachéwa sahassání,<br>
Aḍḍhuḍḍháni satánicha.

*Wisuddhi Magga.*

---

Note H. Page 82. The seven Circles of Ṛock.

Été satta mahá sélá<br>
Sinérussa samantató.

*Sára Sangaha. Wisuddhi Magga. Jinálankára.*

Note I. Page 84. The seven Seas.

Sinéru Yugandharádínań antaré sídanta samuddánáma honti.

*Sára Sangaha. Wisuddhi Magga. Jinálankára.*

---

Note J. Page 84. The rays pass from Maha Méru to the Sakwala rock.

Tatáhi pubbadakkhinapasséhi nikkihantá rajatamaṇirasmiyo ékatóhutwá samuddapiṭṭhéna gantwá chakkawálapabbatań ahachcha titthanti.

*Sára Sángaha Jinálankára.*

---

Note K. Page 85. The thickness of the Worlds of Stone, Earth, Water, and Wind.

Dwé satasahassáni,
Chattári nahutánicha,
Ettakań bahalatténa,
Sankhátáyań wasundhará.

Chattárisatasahassáni,
Attéwanahutánicha,
Ettakań bahalatténa,
Jalan' wâté patiṭṭhitan.

Nawasatasahassáni,
Máluto nabhamuggato,
Saṭṭhiṇchéwasahassáni,
Esá lókassa saṇṭṭhiti.

*Wisuddhi Magga.*

---

Note L. Page 85. The distance from Maha Méru to Jambudípa.

Sinérupabbatapassató paṭṭháya yáwa Jumbudípa majjhan' dwésaṭasahassáni ékuṇásítisahassáni aṭṭhasatáni saṭṭhiyójanáni,......Jambudípamajjható paṭṭháya yáwa chakkawálapabbatan' táwa lónaságaro dwésatasahassáni ékuṇásitisahassáni aṭṭhasatáni saṭṭhiyójanáni. *Jinálankára.*

Note M. Page 86. The causes of Earthquakes.

Ayan′ Ananda mahápaṭhawi udaké patiṭṭhitá udakan wáté patiṭṭhitan′ wáto ákásaṭṭohoti yókhó Ananda samayo yan′ maháwátá wáyantá udakan′ kampenti udakan′ kampitan′ pathawin kampéti.

*Maha Parinibbána Suttanta.*

---

Note N. Page 87. The Sun and Moon.

Tattha chandamaṇḍalan′ ujukan′ áyámató witthárató ubbédhato ékúnapaṇṇyásayójanan′ parimaṇḍalatopana tíhiyójanéhi únan′ diyaḍḍha satayójanan′...Suriyamaṇḍalan′-pana ujukan′ paṇṇyásayójanan′ parimaṇḍalatopana diyaḍḍha satayójanan′......Tésupana chanḍamaṇḍalan′ heṭṭhá suriyamaṇḍalan′ upari antaran′ nésan′ yójanan′ hóti...... Chandawimánan′ antomaṇimayan′ bahi rajaténa parikkittan′ antocha bahicha sítalaméwa hoti......Suriyawimánan′ anto kanakamayan′ báhiran′ phalika parikkhittan′ hóti antócha bahícha uṇha méwa.

*Sára Sangaha.*

---

Note O. Page 87. The Distance of the Moon from the Sun.

Suriyókálapakkhupósaté atikkhanté páṭipadadiwaséyójanánan′ satasahassan′ chandamaṇḍalan′ paháya gachchati.

*Jinálankára.*

---

Note P. Page 88. The three Paths.

Imésan′pana ajawíthi nágawíthi gówíthiti; tisso withiyó honti; tathá ajánan′ udakan′ paṭikkúlan′ hóti; hatthínan manápan′ gunnan′ sítuṇhasamatáya phásuhóti.

*Sára Sangaha.*

Note Q. Page 89. The Sun shines upon three Continents at once.

Ewan wicharant`icha Ekappahàréna tisu dwípésu álókan karonti.
*Sára Sangaha.*

---

Note R. Page 89. The size of Ráhu, and his seizure of the Sun and Moon.

Ewan mahiddhiké éwan mahánubháwé chandimasuriyé kin Ráhu gilatíti: éma gilati; Ráhussahi attabháwó maha. uchchanténa aṭṭhayójanasatádhikánichattáriyojanasahassáni.
*Sára Sangaha.*

---

Note S. Page 91. The waters of the Ocean and the size of the Waves.

Ewan saṇṭṭhitassa tassa heṭṭhá chattálísayójanasahassamatté ṭháné udakan′ machchéhi chalati upari táwatakeyéwa ṭhàné udakan′ wáténa chalati majjhé chatuyójanasahassamatté ṭhàné udakan′ nichchalan′ tiṭṭhati; tasminkhópanamahásamuddé mahindawíchináma saṭṭhiyójanáni uggachchati póránawíchináma chattálísayójáni uggachchati.
*Sára Sangaha.*

---

Note T. Page 91. The size of Ananda and other fishes.

Anando timindo ajjháróhó mahátimíti imé chattáro machchá yójanasahassiká.

*Sára Sangaha.*

---

Note U. Page 91. The size of Jambudípa.

Jambudípépana chatusahassayójanappamáṇó padésó tadupabhógíyasattánan′ puṇṇyakkhayá udakéna ajjóthaṭho samuddóti sankhangató; tisahassayójanappamáné manussá wasanti; tisahassayójanappamáné himawá patiṭṭhito.
*Sára Sangaha.*

Note V. Page 95. The swiftness of the lions in Himálawana.

Tatiyanpana síhanádan′ naditwá tónéwasaddhin′ tiyójanaṭṭháne panyyáyati tiyójanan′ gantwá niwattitwá ṭhito attanowa nádassa anunádan′ suṇáti; éwan′ síghéna jawéna pakkamati.

*Anguttara Nikáya Wannaná.*

---

Note W. Page 96. The size of the Jambu-tree.

Himawatiyéwa patiṭṭhitassa yassa ánubháwéna ayan′ Jambudípóti wucchati tan′ múlato yáwach aggá yójana satappamánan. *Sára Sangaha.*

---

Note X. Page 98. The extent to which Buddha's voice could be heard.

Akan′khamáno Ananda Tathagato tisahassí mahásahassí lókadhátun′ saréna wiṇṇyàpeyya yáwatáyápana ákan′kheyyáti. *Anguttara Nikáya.*

---

Note Y. Page 99. The extent of the Universe.

Gamanèn áhan′ lokassa antan′ papuṇissámíti. sókhó ahan′ Bhanté aṇṇyatréwa asíta píta kháyita sáyitá aṇṇyata uchchárapassáwakammá aṇṇyatra niddákilamatha paṭiwinódaná wassa satáyukó wassa satajíwi wassa satan′ gantwá appatwána lokassa antan′ antará kálakato..

*Anguttara Nikáya.*

---

Note Z. Page 163. The non-existence of the Soul.

In consequence of the importance of this subject, and the singularity of the teachings of Buddha respecting it, I insert an extract from the writings of the late Rev. D. J. Gogerly. The rare powers of mind possessed by my gifted predecessor and lamented friend, were never seen to greater advantage than when seeking to unravel the intricate web of Buddhist metaphysics. His discoveries took the priests by surprise; but there are none of authority who now dispute his conclusions. I take this opportunity of stating, that I am indebted to the same source for the quotations I have made from the Pirit. It is much to be lamented, that so far as my search has extended, I have not been able to find among the papers he has left, any that are so connected or perfect as to be available for publication.

"From Budha's description of the khandas, transmigration, in the ordinary sense of the word, is impossible. This may also be inferred from a passage in the comment on the Sanyutto discourses. The commentator mentions five opinions as belonging to the uchédadítthi, or school of philosophy which teaches that death is the termination of existence. The opinions are, (1) that rupa, material organization, constitutes the soul; (2) that wédaná, sensation, is the soul; (3) that sannyá, perception, is the soul; (4) that sankhárá, thought, is the soul; and (5) that winnyána, consciousness, is the soul. These five opinions could only have been attributed to the annihilation school on this principle, that Budha taught that each and all of the five enumerated khandas cease and determine at death.

"This further appears from his definition of death, which among other things he states to be antaradhánan′, a disappearance, and khandánan′ bhédo, breaking up of the khandas, a dissolution of the system; and even if bhédo should be translated separation, and not dissolution, the result would be the same, for we have seen the khandas to be so mutually dependent that their separation into individual khandas would be identical with the cessation of their existence, excepting the body, which speedily is dissolved after the other khandas are removed from it. It may be observed that although Budha has given definitions of death in many discourses, he has never intimated its being the departure of a soul from the body to exist in another form. Yet the doctrine was known, and among the heterodox opinions one is stated to be, the representing the soul upon death as 'flying happily away like a bird from its cage.' How could he state it to be the departure of the soul from the body, when he expressly states, as I will show, that there is *no soul?*

"In his definition of birth, among other things, he states it to be áyatanánan patílábho, the attainment of the áyatanas, which comprise the 10 bodily and 2 mental organs, and khandánan' pátubháwo, the springing up into existence of the khandas; for the verb pátubhawati signifies that beginning which had no previous existence, and therefore when a distinction is to be made between at present non-existences, the word used for that which never had a being, in opposition to that which once existed but has ceased to be, is apátubhútan', being the negative adjective from the verb pátubhawati. In another place also the khandas, áyatanans, etc. are said uppattikhané-pátubhawanti, to spring into being at the moment of conception (or of existence commencing in any way:) and as 10 of the áyatanas are decidedly material, and evidently commence their being at that moment, how can the remaining two áyatanas be regarded as having a previous existence, and only at that moment united to the others, when all are governed by the same verb, and the áyatanas are spoken of jointly and not severally.

"These subjects did not escape king Milinda's penetration: he therefore enquires if a living soul is received upon transmigration (that being the subject under discussion); and the priest replied, in the higher, or proper sense (parametthéna), there is not. The only question is, whether

I have correctly translated wédagu, by the words *living soul.* But the king had used the same word before, in a discussion on sensations and perceptions, and there the priest asks, What is this wédagu? The king replied, 'that inward life, jíwo, which sees figure by the eye, hears sound by the ear, smells odour by the nose, tastes flavour by the tongue, touches objects with the body, and knows circumstances by the mano, consciousness:' thus explaining what we mean by the word *soul,* a living conscious being, who acts through the medium of the organs of sense In further explanation he adds, 'even as I sit in this palace and view external objects through any window I please to look out of, so the wédagu looks through the window of the eye, of the nose, etc.' The priest denies the existence of such a wédagu or soul, and among other reasons states, that if what the king said were true, the wédagu, or inward soul, might hear with its nose and smell with its eyes. Whatever potency may be in the priest's reasoning, this is clear, by wédagu the king meant the soul, and that the priest denied that any such thing was received upon transmigration.

"The king enquires further, 'Is there any thing (or being, satto) which goes from this body to another body?' 'No, great king.' 'If, then, my Lord Nagasena, there be no departure from this body to another body, certainly there will be a deliverance from the consequence of sin.' This consequence the priest denies, explaining it by the Mango metaphor, and using the same words he had spoken before, viz. 'by this námarúpa actions are performed, good or bad, and by those actions another námarúpa commences existence.'

"But Budha denies the existence of a soul, or any thing concerning which a man may say, This is (1), myself; and (2) states that what by accommodation may be called the man is ever fluctuating, never at two given periods the same, although not properly different. Of this peculiar doctrine of identity I will endeavour to give a brief explanation. The following is a close translation of part of a discourse in the Sanyutto division. 'The soul, Priests, is variously considered by some recluses and Bramins, but they all regard it as united with the five khandas or with one of the five. What are the five? The sensual and unlearned man considers (1) body to be the soul, or (2) that the soul possesses corporiety, or (3) that body emanates from the soul, or (4) that the soul resides in the body.* Or they regard (5) sensation to be the soul, or (6) that the soul possesses sensation, or (7) that sensation emanates from the soul, or (8) that the soul resides in the sensations. Or they regard (9) perception to be the soul, etc. Or they regard (13) thought to be the soul, etc. Or they regard (17) consciousness to be the soul, etc., (making 20 opinions). In consequence of these considerations they come to the conclusion, 'I am' (asmí). Now, priests, *I am* is the state of having the soul. The five organs, (indriyáni) namely, the organ of the eye, of the ear, of the tongue, and of the body are conceived (in the womb or otherwise.) There is consciousness (mano); there is dhammá (the three khandas of sensation, perception, and thought); there is the base of wisdom (wijjá dhátu.) The unlearned and sensual man being affected by the sensations resulting from ignorance, thinks '*I am*' '*this is I.*'—But concerning these the learned

* Thus explained in the Comment: *he considers body to be the soul; i.e.* Is there any body? that is I, is there any I, that is body; body and soul are not divers (adwayang, not two.) *The soul possesses corporiety; i.e.* taking the soul to be immaterial, he regards it as being body-possessing, as a tree is shadow-possessing. *Body emanates from the soul; i.e.* regarding the soul to be immaterial he thinks that body emanates from it, as odour emanates from a flower. *That the soul resides in the body; i.e.* taking the soul to be immaterial he regards it as residing in the body, as a jewel resides in a casket. I need not add, all these views are declared to be heterodox.

disciple of Budha being separated from ignorance and obtaining wisdom, does not think 'I am, or this is I.'

"The following formula is used by him repeatedly in connection with each of the five khandas, and twelve áyatanas, which two classifications embrace everything that is an integral part of the man, or corporeal. I shall only quote it in connection with rúpa, but it is used verbatim respecting the others; rupan bhikkhawé anitchang, yadanitchang tang dukkhang, yang dukkhang tadanattá, yadanattá tang nétang mama, nésohamasmi, naméso attá. Body, priests, is impermanent; is anything impermanent, that is sorrow (substantially and naturally so); is anything sorrow that is not the soul (not attá, *the self*); is anything not the self, that (*i.e.* that rúpa, or wédaná, etc., etc.) is not mine, I am not it, it is not my soul. The same is declared not only of the 10 corporeal áyatanas but also of manó, consciousness, or the principle of consciousness, dhammá, the combined sensations, perceptions, and reasonings, whether regarded as acts or powers. Of each and all of them he teaches, I am not this, this is not my soul, or (namé éso attá) this is not to me a soul.

"In a discourse addressed to a person named Sóna he is, if possible, more definite: he says, If there be any organized form, sensation, perception, thought or consciousness, past, future, or present, internal or external, great or small, remote or proximate, of all it should be clearly and distinctly known, This is not mine, I am not it, it is not to me a Soul. The learned disciple of Budha understanding this, is weaned from attachment to body, sensation, perception, thought and consciousness."—*The Ceylon Friend*, vol. ii. No. 5.

# INDEX.